Gender, Writing,

MW01716633

This original study makes a valuable contribution to Italian feminist/women's history, spectatorship studies, and cultural history by examining women as protagonists, producers, and consumers of literature, theatre, opera, and film. Drawing on archival material – female correspondence, life-writings, and journalism – as well as an impressive range of canonical texts, it brings together detailed engagement with female performance and female spectators' material responses to "women's opera, theatre and film," placing these in the context of melodrama from the 1880s to the 1920s in Italy, France, the United States, and elsewhere. It is unique in its interdisciplinary approach and in its consideration of female relationships based on *admiration* among performers and writers – the embodiment of a vibrant, mobile, and successful Italian female culture industry during the first wave of feminism.

Katharine Mitchell is Senior Lecturer in Italian Culture and Gender at the University of Strathclyde, Glasgow. She is the author of *Italian Women Writers: Gender and Everyday Life in Fiction and Journalism, 1870–1910* (Toronto University Press, 2014), and among her co-edited volumes are *Women and Gender in Post-Unification Italy: Between Private and Public Spheres* (Peter Lang, 2013) and *Matilde Serao: International Profile, Reception, and Networks* (Classiques Garnier, 2022).

Figure 0.1 John Copley, *Interested Spectators* (1910).

The Nineteenth Century Series
Series editors: Joanne Shattock and Julian North

The series focuses primarily upon major authors and subjects within Romantic and Victorian literature. It also includes studies of other nineteenth-century British writers and issues, where these are matters of current debate: for example, biography and autobiography; journalism; periodical literature; travel writing; book production; gender; non-canonical writing.

Recent in this series:

Victorian Culture and the Origin of Disciplines
Edited by Bernard Lightman and Bennett Zon

Literary Experiments in Magazine Publishing
Beyond Serialization
Thomas Vranken

Women's Letters as Life Writing 1840–1885
Catherine Delafield

Reading Transatlantic Girlhood in the Long Nineteenth Century
Edited by Robin L. Cadwallader and LuElla D'Amico

Dickens and the Bible
'What Providence Meant'
Jennifer Gribble

Gender, Writing, Spectatorships
Evenings at the Theatre, Opera, and Silent Screen in Late Nineteenth-Century Italy and Beyond
Katharine Mitchell

For more information about this series, please visit: www.routledge.com/The-Nineteenth-Century-Series/book-series/ASHSER2017

Gender, Writing, Spectatorships

Evenings at the Theatre, Opera, and Silent Screen in Late Nineteenth-Century Italy and Beyond

Katharine Mitchell

Routledge
Taylor & Francis Group
NEW YORK AND LONDON

First published 2022
by Routledge
605 Third Avenue, New York, NY 10158

and by Routledge
2 Park Square, Milton Park, Abingdon, Oxon OX14 4RN

Routledge is an imprint of the Taylor & Francis Group, an informa business

Library of Congress Cataloging-in-Publication Data
Names: Mitchell, Katharine, author.
Title: Gender, writing, spectatorships: evenings at the theatre, opera, and silent screen in late nineteenth-century Italy and beyond / Katharine Mitchell.
Description: New York: Routledge, 2021. |
Series: The nineteenth century series |
Includes bibliographical references and index. |
Identifiers: LCCN 2021018009 |
Subjects: LCSH: Italian literature–19th century–History and criticism. | Italian literature–Women authors. | Italian literature–20th century–History and criticism. | Women in the performing arts–Italy–History–19th century. | Women in the performing arts–Italy–History–20th century. | Women and the arts–Italy–History–19th century. | Women and the arts–Italy–History–20th century. | Feminist theory.
Classification: LCC PQ4063 .M5824 2021 | DDC 853/.8099287–dc23
LC record available at https://lccn.loc.gov/2021018009

ISBN: 9780367265014 (hbk)
ISBN: 9781032109510 (pbk)
ISBN: 9780429293511 (ebk)

DOI: 10.4324/9780429293511

Typeset in Sabon
by Newgen Publishing UK

For Elizabeth, Christopher, Oliver, and Alfred

Contents

Acknowledgements

Little did I know at the time that the tragic roles I performed in amateur dramatic plays in my late teens and early twenties would culminate in the writing of this book. Its origins began life over 20 years ago as research for a Masters on Female Roles in Italian Tragic Opera at the University of Leeds, supervised by Richard Andrews. Inspired, later on, by the work of Susan Rutherford and Ann Hallamore Caesar (who I thank also for her and Mike Caesar's support and generosity), I began to research historical female spectatorships thanks to fully-funded postdoctoral projects from 2008 onwards (first from the Ministry of Education of the Italian government, then from Lucy Cavendish College, University of Cambridge). I subsequently benefitted from further research grants to continue archival work in Italy's theatre archives from the British Academy, the Royal Society of Edinburgh, the Carnegie Trust for the Universities of Scotland, as well as Visiting Fellowships at the University of Bologna, Seton Hall University, New Jersey, and California State University, Long Beach. I thank the University of Strathclyde for two semesters of research leave – the second of which I spent as a Visiting Fellow at St. Catherine's College (Hilary Term), and Harris Manchester College (Trinity Term) at the University of Oxford, where I began to draft this book. I warmly thank friends and colleagues at both colleges for engaging with my research and for their hospitality, generosity, and friendship. In particular, I am grateful to John Charles Smith (whose attentive reading of the final draft of this book has resulted in something I would never have been able to produce alone), Laura Tunbridge, Alex Teytelboym, Sam Wolfe, Olivia Tolley, Colin Thompson, Richard Parish, Peter Franklin (by whom I was taught Music at Leeds), Kirsten Shepherd-Barr, Sarah Ogilvie, Jane Shaw, and Eric Eve. I thank my students from 2008 to 2021 at Cambridge, Manchester, and Strathclyde, whose participation and discussion in my lectures and seminars on the topic of this book I always learned from. I also thank Patrizia Favero, an associate of the *Archivio Diaristico Nazionale*, for carefully and patiently transcribing over 100 semi-illegible letters. I am grateful to my friends and colleagues Danielle Hipkins and Catherine O'Rawe, who, along with Alan O'Leary, supported my teaching of Italian film studies from 2016 onwards and helped steer this book in new directions. I thank Karen Boyle, Janet Todd, Michael Higgins, David Goldie, and Simon Gilson for their input and support, and in particular Lisa Downing for her careful reading of an entire earlier draft, and for providing expert guidance. I also thank Mark Seymour for his constructive comments on the introduction and opening and closing sections of chapters. A small, all-female army of librarians, archivists, and friends mobilised in the final stages of the drafting of this book (made difficult due to the Covid-19 lockdown), and I was extremely touched by their generosity and willingness to help. They are: Isabelle McNeill, Faye Hammill, Aoife Bophry, and librarians Sarah Kevill (University of Strathclyde) and Francesca Maturo (National Central Library of Florence). I am grateful also to Laura Pritchard Mellor, Beth Buxton, Julie Gilson, Anne Holloway, Leanne Morgan, Kate Murray, Janine Watson, Raymond Reynolds, Tanya Barker, and Louise Mor for their love and support. Finally, I would like to thank my family for always being there for me, and, in particular, my father, who provided me with a room of my own during lockdown in which to complete this book, and who has cheered me on from the beginning.

Unless otherwise stated, all translations are my own.

Chronology of Significant Events

1854 – Pope Pius IX formally pronounces Mary's "immaculate conception," claiming she gave birth to Jesus Christ without having sexual intercourse.

1859 – The Casati Law introduces two years' compulsory elementary schooling for girls, though 50 per cent of children do not receive an education.

– The first girls' secondary school is founded.

1861–71 – Italian unification: Turin becomes the first capital of Italy in 1861. In 1865 the capital moves to Florence, where it remains until 1871. Rome is declared the capital in principle in 1861 but is not captured until 1870. Having been taken from the Pope, in 1871 Rome becomes the capital.

– The Florentine dialect is established as the national language. Around a third of Italians are literate and in many parts of the South, the figure is closer to 100 per cent. Female illiteracy is at 81 per cent (86 per cent in rural areas and 77 per cent in towns and cities).

– In 1870, 60 per cent of the entire population (27 million) is directly dependent on agriculture.

– Piedmontese statesman Camillo Cavour institutes a series of regulations to address the increase in venereal disease: the regulation requires prostitutes to register with the police and pay a tax to work in the brothels (*case chiuse*).

1863 – Milanese writer and philosopher Carlo Cattaneo publishes his essay "Sul romanzo delle donne contemporanee in Italia" (On novels written by women in contemporary Italy), in which he argues that women writers of the novel are "better able to offer an exquisite analysis of sentiment," a "delicate and highly refined knowledge of the human heart."

1864 – Milanese Emancipationist Anna Maria Mozzoni publishes *La donna e i suoi rapporti sociali* (Woman and Her Social Relationships).

– Charles Darwin's *On the Origin of Species* is translated into Italian.

1865 – Pisanelli's Civil Code, based on the Napoleonic Code, is introduced, sanctioning the *maritalis auctoritas* (husband's authority). Women are not permitted to have a bank account without their husband's permission and are required to seek their husband's authorisation in all economic transactions and legal matters, including inheritance. Divorce is illegal, yet courts regularly authorise personal separation where the wife has been sexually active and makes no concession if she has been raped. Wives are not permitted to have custody over their children in the absence of their father; adultery is considered a crime for women only, and unmarried women who work or have property are expected to pay taxes (despite earning a third of a man's salary for equal work) but are not able to vote. Women over the age of 21 are no longer forced into arranged marriages, yet culturally it is an integral part of Italian life. Single women can engage in commerce, make their own wills and own property. Girls and single women cannot leave the home without being accompanied by a parent or a guardian.

1868–92 – The emancipationist bimonthly journal *La donna* is founded by Gualberta Alaide Beccari (in Padua until 1871; in Venice until 1877; and in Bologna until 1892) including regular articles on the *grande attrice* Giacinta Pezzana and featuring readers' experiences of watching her performances in published letters.

1870–90 – The railway network expands from 1,250 to 8,060 miles. Naples is the most populous city with 449,000 inhabitants, nearly twice as many as Rome and Milan.

1872 – Protests against rising food prices result in demonstrations for better pay and shorter working hours throughout northern Italy.

1874 – The Coppino law grants women permission to enter the universities, though professions available to them remain limited.

1876 – Italy's largest industry is silk, and has around 382,000 factory labourers, half of whom are women and children. In the textile industries, four times as many women than men are employed.

– Positive criminologist Cesare Lombroso publishes *The Criminal Man*.

1877 – Thomas Edison invents the phonograph, enabling listeners to freely record and play back any sound.

1879 – Angelo De Gubernatis's *Dizionario biografico degli scrittori italiani* records 180 active women writers in Italy.

1881 – 34 per cent of the population lives in towns with over 10,000 inhabitants. Proprietors, industrialists, professionals, teachers, private and public employees, and shopkeepers number little over 1 million or 6.7 per cent of the total population (*cf.* France, 14 per cent).

– A bill presented to parliament calling for universal suffrage is defeated.

– Alexander Bell develops a wax-cylinder version of the phonograph – the graphophone, allowing for lengthier recordings and a superior play back powered (later) by electricity.

1881–1910 – Women publish 1,894 new titles of poetry, novels, essays, conference proceedings, conduct literature, translations, plays, and biographies.

1883 – Carlo Collodi's *Pinocchio* is published.
– The Ministry of Education grants girls and young women access to all levels of education, including *ginnasi-licei* (grammar schools) and *istituti tecnici* (technical colleges), yet the first woman awarded a Law degree (Lidia Poët) is denied the right to practise at the Bar.
1886 – Edmondo De Amicis' *Cuore* is published.
1888 – The Crispi law abolishes the registration of prostitutes and mandatory medical visits.
1891 – The Nicotera law restores the regulation of prostitution almost completely.
1893 – Cesare Lombroso and Guglielmo Ferrero publish *La donna delinquente: la prostituta e la donna normale* (The Female Offender: the Prostitute and the Normal Woman).
1894 – Emile Berliner invents the gramophone, enabling flat-shaped discs to be played.
1895 – Louis and Auguste Lumière invent the *Cinématographe*, a camera that can record, develop, and project film.
– Josef Breuer and Sigmund Freud publish *Studies on Hysteria* which includes Breuer's famous case of Anna O.
1896 – There are 1,896 libraries in Italy.
– Electricity has replaced gas lighting in the majority of Italian theatres.
1897 – Anna Vertua Gentile's best-selling conduct manual *Come devo comportarmi* (How I Should Behave) is published in which she disapproves of women spectators who are indifferent to, and disdainful of performances and screenings. 11 editions are issued up to 1923.
– Guglielmo Marconi sends the first-ever wireless telecommunication overseas.
1898 – People protest on the streets of Milan against an increase in the price of bread.
1899 – 19,864 women are enrolled on teacher training courses compared with 1,323 men.
1900 – Freud publishes *The Interpretation of Dreams*.
– 24,000 lawyers are employed in Italy; in the south, there are twice as many lawyers per head of the population as in the north. There are a similar number of doctors.
1901 – 55 per cent of Italian women are recorded as illiterate.
1905 – Filoteo Alberini films *La presa di Roma* (The Capture of Rome), the first Italian fiction film based on a historical subject.
1906 – Committees for female suffrage exist in all major cities as far south as Naples.
– Sibilla Aleramo publishes her feminist autobiographical novel *Una donna*.
1907 – The Italian suffrage movement collects only 600 signatures for a petition to the Italian parliament demanding female suffrage.

1909 – The first full-length feature film, *Inferno*, directed by Francesco Bertolini, Giuseppe De Liguoro and Adolfo Padovan, goes into production (Milano Films).

1910 – Arranged marriages are no longer *de rigueur*.

1911 – Italy declares war on Turkey for the conquest of Libya.

– 55 per cent of the population is still directly dependent on agriculture and 40 per cent of Italians can still neither read nor write.

– 42 per cent of the population lives in towns with over 10,000 inhabitants.

– Rome and Milan have more than half a million inhabitants by 1911, yet they are still smaller than Naples.

– A woman in Turin wears trousers in public for the first time.

1912 – Universal male suffrage is granted.

1914 – Less than 4 per cent of university students are women; they are still not entitled to work as doctors or lawyers.

– The Italian film industry reaches its height of popularity according to actor Emilio Ghione, writing in *L'Art cinématographique*. He cites 22 film companies as active until 1919. Italy is producing and exporting, on average, 562 films per year.

1919 – The *maritalis auctoritas* is abolished.

– The camera point-of-view shot and shot/reverse shot in cinema are introduced.

Introduction

This book develops the notion of a multipolar, gendered, mass, critical, and affective female spectatorship-in-the-making at the end of the nineteenth and the beginning of the twentieth century in Italy and beyond. Adopting a cross-disciplinary methodological approach, it takes account of the visibility in early post-unification Italy of performing women artists and writers as metaphors and metonyms of modernity, cosmopolitanism, and as exemplars of various spectating practices. It is not the plots of texts referred to that are its primary focus; rather, I am interested in the descriptions and scenes of theatre sociability as windows onto previously unremarked-upon woman-centred worlds. These are drawn on and referred to in order to historicise and contextualise a crucial and pivotal moment in Italy's gender history for women writers, performers, and spectators, during which a middle-class critical and visceral female gaze began to emerge *en masse*. Bram Dijkstra was famously the first to show that new technologies and inventions were fuelling misogynistic and patriarchal attitudes towards real and represented women in the cultural imaginary in his 1986 interdisciplinary study (he drew on a selection of European pseudoscientific tracts, novels, and paintings of eroticised and fetishised women which purportedly "warned" men against the supposed consequences of being "lured" by the "evils" of so-called feminine deception).[1] And yet, at no other time, neither before nor since, were page, stage, and screen so symbiotically connected with women at the helm – as celebrated producers and consumers (they were performers, writers, readers, spectators, translators, directors) – of a popular cultural moment in the collective melodramatic imagination.

The composer and pianist Franz Liszt (1811–86), writing about his tour of Italy in the 1830s, implied that women went to the theatre merely to "flirt with their lovers;"[2] and yet, following unification, professional middle-class women writers began to emerge on the Italian literary scene as never before.[3] They were writing not only as novelists, journalists, commentators, and translators, but also as *spectators* – of realist theatre and tragic opera performances, and later, of the silent diva film. As such, the beginnings of a modern-day middle-class female critical community, with its own lexicon of cultural criticism, began to establish itself

DOI: 10.4324/9780429293511-1

alongside the development of a national culture industry during Italy's emergence as a nation state. At this crucial juncture in Italy's nation-making process, and thanks to the rise in literacy levels following the opening up of schools to girls and young women at all levels during the 1880s (they typically left school between the ages of 12 and 16 years), women writers and performers as/and spectators became more engaged in the action taking place on stage and screen, and more discerning of performances than they had ever been previously. As if to prophesy the theory and practice of *affidamento* (meaning "entrustment") – a term coined by Italian feminist philosophers at the University of Verona in 1983, in which a more powerful and authoritative woman facilitates, through dialogue and friendship, a younger woman's access to a stronger sense of self and her social and symbolic value as a woman – women writers were intermediaries for female spectators, whose affect and admiration for women performers enabled the development of their spectators' sense of self-awareness and determination.[4]

In the following chapters, I analyse women spectators' reflections on, and engagement with female performers in letters, diary entries, narrative realist fiction, and reviews in women's magazines and newspaper columns in early post-unification Italy. By putting these materials into close dialogue with recent theoretical work on women's spectatorship from feminist film theory and literary, theatre, opera, and cultural studies, and by taking a broad new historicist approach, I uncover an array of textual evidence *as points of entry* into further understanding women spectators in the historical and cultural context in question. By identifying and analysing a gendered public sphere in Italy during the late nineteenth century, I argue that middle-class women, as professional writers and/or theatre, opera, and early film spectators, were operating as unprecedented critical cultural consumers and producers of the melodramatic mode on stage and screen.

Borrowing the term "woman's film" coined by feminist film scholar Christine Gledhill to describe narratives about women's personal dilemmas and sufferings (the "woman's film" has arguably evolved into the modern-day "chick flick"), I apply it to turn-of-the-twentieth-century bourgeois theatre, tragic opera, and the silent diva film (I exclude from my discussion non-Italian operas performed in Italy and Italian operas performed outside Italy. My focus is specifically on tragic opera, drama, and silent diva films produced and first performed during the 1850s until the 1920s).[5] My argument is that the pleasure derived from watching performances and screenings of women's film, theatre, and tragic opera, together with affective responses to, and critical reflections on them, opened up for women readers and spectators new ways of feeling and thinking about their sexual, social, and economic selves. At the same time, I contend that women began to assert their social selves in the public sphere as never before, and to forge friendships with like-minded women towards whom they practised solidarity and showed admiration. This was thanks not only to their access to education, which was granted at all levels during the period 1874–83 and the beginnings of the emancipationist movement in the 1890s, but also the increasing popularity, accessibility, and circulation among growing numbers of women writers and readers of serialised novels, short stories, and magazines that addressed a female readership-in-the-making. Thanks to industrialisation and early capitalism, for the first time in print culture in Italy, professional, celebrated middle-class women writers presented themselves as being in close connection with, and proximity to (through sincere and close bonds), celebrated women performers in ways which, heretofore, had not been articulated and in circulation to quite the same degree. Taking on board Miriam Hansen's idea that the emergence of cinema spectatorship is profoundly intertwined with the transformation of the public sphere, in particular "the gendered itineraries of everyday life and leisure," I apply this to women's theatre, opera, and early film female spectatorships to argue that women writers created a critical community with their own lexicon by, and for women readers as/and spectators.[6]

According to Susan Haywood, melodrama's intended audience with its themes of the domestic, the family, morality, and the social *is* the female spectator.[7] (Melodrama is not to be confused here with *melodramma*, which literally translates as "sung drama," a seventeenth-century Italian term for text to be set as an opera; rather, I am referring to melodrama as a "mode" (not a genre) of expression whose elements "make visible the ineffable and use gesture as an expression of meaning.")[8] Operatic melodrama, like theatre melodrama, like silent film melodrama at the turn of the twentieth century – what Angela Dalle Vacche refers to as the "Silent Diva Film" – since Verdi's *La traviata* (1853), revolved around the private lives – the longings, sufferings and losses within the family, or the domestic – of the female protagonist, who was typically a fascinating yet threatening so-called "Fallen Woman."[9] This "Magdalene" archetype dominated the Italian stage at the *fin de siècle*, and from the 1910s onwards found expression on screen in the figure of the silent diva, who, according to Stephen Gundle, "was essentially an adaptation of an invention of Scandinavian cinema."[10] Yet, as critics have recently shown, like the *femme fatale* archetype, the Fallen Woman cannot simply be reduced to a stereotypical product of the misogynistic imagination as the effect of apparent male fears about women's emancipation, for she was also the subject, for both women and men spectators, of feminine desire and pleasure.[11]

Louis Bayman's definition of what constitutes film melodrama in the Italian context as a narrative whose primary concern is affect, a careful attention to aesthetics, and the use of moral categories for illustrating the drama of everyday life,[12] can be applied to Italian tragic opera. Referred to throughout this book interchangeably as "women's opera" or "tragic opera," this genre emerged in the early-to-mid-nineteenth century with the first performance of Vincenzo Bellini's *Norma* (1831).

In *Norma*, the eponymous protagonist is portrayed musically with sympathy, yet suffers for the duration of the narrative and is punished for her transgressions at the *finale* in order that the *status quo* may be re-established. (Norma commits suicide to redeem herself in the eyes of her people.) Similarly, the genre of naturalist bourgeois theatre in Italy, or "women's theatre" – for example, Giovanni Verga's *Cavalleria rusticana* (1884), whose performers came from a very particular performance tradition (one that emphasised gesture, aesthetics, and affect) – displays the characteristics mentioned by Bayman. So, too, does the silent diva film (referred to here also as "women's film"). John Champagne has recently argued that melodrama was indeed invented in Italy (and not in France, as Peter Brooks has contended), locating the origins of the genre in the Counter-Reformation in the paintings of Caravaggio.[13] Giovanni Ragone has argued that "melodrama, newspapers, and novels" were at the heart of the cultural circuit in turn-of-the-twentieth-century Italy, amid rapid industrialisation, modernisation, and the rise of early capitalism, particularly in the north of the peninsula.[14] Writing in the cinema journal *L'Art cinématographique* in 1914, the actor Emilio Ghione (1879–1930) described that year as the one in which Italian cinema reached its height in popularity (the first diva film, Mario Caserini's *Ma l'amor mio non muore* (Everlasting Love), débuted in 1913).[15] The divas who played the Fallen Women central characters, as celebrated performers, were often seen as transcending the social constructs of class, race, and gender.

Originating in Mediterranean Catholic cultures, the contemporary Western diva offers consumers a secular alternative to female religious iconicity. Dalle Vacche draws an analogy between the silent film diva and the *mater dolorosa* in Catholic iconography, describing her as "a combination of the *femme fatale* and the modern woman," who is submissive, chaste, and introvert, yet she also exuded eroticism, being alluring and extrovert whilst she was by no means anti-religious.[16] And yet, the silent diva is more Magdalene figure than *mater dolorosa*. These masculine constructs differ insofar as the Fallen Woman/Magdalene metaphor bears a close association to Catholicism, prostitution, and ordinary women's lives, whereas the *femme fatale* is more removed from the everyday and rooted in male fantasy, carrying connotations of feminine deception, eroticisation, and power over men to "destroy" them. Fallen Women were typically blamed for their so-called transgressions and punished with their deaths at the end of the narrative's denouement, in which themes of forbidden or unrequited love, adultery, out-of-wedlock pregnancy, abandonment, shame, prostitution, and financial ruin dominated. Whereas Dalle Vacche argues they were redeemed by their beauty, which was "a positive value in a culture sensitive to an ancient aesthetic practice at odds with the glitches and rough spots of mechanical reproduction," they were first and foremost redeemed because they were appealing to audiences, who pitied them for their sufferings, which were societally imposed.[17] Yet, they were far from "undone," and French feminist philosopher Catherine Clément, who controversially proclaimed that opera was a misogynist genre and synonymous with the "undoing of women," may well have misjudged the effects of performance and the performer on the female spectator.[18] The diva/o harnesses the discourses of religion and propriety and uses them to her/his own ends; Madonna, Lady Gaga, Rihanna, Beyoncé, Ariana Grande – to name a few contemporary divas – are Latinate names originating in Romance languages and cultures.

During the nineteenth century in Italy, the term "diva" did not carry the same negative connotations as it does today to signify a woman or man who is regarded as temperamental or haughty. According to Niccolò Tommaséo and Bernardo Bellini in their *Dizionario della lingua italiana* (Dictionary of the Italian Language, 1879), then the term "diva" was still synonymous with that of "dea," meaning "female deity"; before Dante, there were lyric poets who used the term to refer to women as divinities.[19] For this reason, throughout this book I use the terms "diva" and "woman performer" interchangeably; the figure of the diva is intimately linked to modernity in Italy, from the stage actors and opera celebrities of the late nineteenth century to the rise of cinema divas, with stars such as Lyda Borelli (1884–1959), Francesca Bertini (1892–1985), and Pina Menichelli (1890–1984). According to Julie K. Allen, the Italian diva personified a "serious, melancholy character type,"[20] and the evolution of the diva in tune with gender, social, and technological contexts, offers rich ground for analysis. As this book demonstrates, divas created a marketing revolution as theatre and film artists whose ability to offer their spectators an illusory sense of shared intimacy and availability made them irresistible to their consumers. Moreover, whereas the American film industry relied on a strict division of labour between specialists (scriptwriters, wardrobe "mistresses," etc.)

> many European film companies allowed talented employees, regardless of gender, to involve themselves in a range of production activities [which] created a power dynamic that gave women unprecedented freedom to participate in the largely male-dominated film industry in many different capacities – not just in front of the camera but also behind the scenes, as producers, directors, editors, screenwriters, studio owners, costume designers and technicians, particularly in the years prior to World War One.[21]

Discussing the history of women photographers representing women in the nineteenth century, the literary and cultural theorist Elisabeth Bronfen argues that women photographers' critical engagement with the culturally prevalent fetishisation of femininity was a form of self-empowerment and subversion:

> [I]f, in the way she imagines and carries herself, woman is always accompanied by an image performed for the masculine gaze, this entails an uncanny doubling of the self. Oscillating between the gaze directed at her and her own engagement with this gaze, her self-perception thrives off a productive tension between her "true" self and the image she is meant to resemble.[22]

The reified, archetypal Fallen Woman figure was frequently in vogue as the central character on page and stage from the 1830s – and later, on screen – until the onset of fascism. These tragic, realist, or naturalist texts on stage and screen centred around women: they were *about* women – their emotional and romantic lives, their sufferings, their ideological dilemmas – they were *performed* by women, and they were *consumed* by women. From the Fallen Woman archetype in realist and naturalist fiction to her reappearance in bourgeois theatre, to her *re*-reappearance on screen in women's film, this crucial moment of female artistic expression and performance in Italy arguably marked the beginnings of a history of women's cultural production and consumption that emerged along with the first wave of feminism. This has been brought into sharp focus in recent times thanks to the dawn of social media and questions surrounding women's power (or lack thereof), visibility, and female representation in a #MeToo era.[23] Following World War I, this heightened moment of intense middle-class, woman-oriented production and consumption changed forever.

My definition of this female-gaze-in-the-making in this book is not the polar opposite of the "male gaze" famously coined and defined by feminist film scholar Laura Mulvey.[24] Nor do I wish to stake a claim for an allegedly "genuinely feminine" way of seeing in contradistinction to John Berger's masculine gaze in which "men act" and "women appear."[25] Similarly, I am not positing that only white, middle-class, heterosexual women are subject to an economy of the gaze which reifies, splits (into binary oppositions of female/male), and distorts its subjects; black and ethnic minority, and LGBTQI+ working-class humans are just as likely – if not more so – to be the subjects of multipolar, objectifying gazes. There are different contradictory perspectives, perceptions, and responses to spectating practices that can be renegotiated under different emotional circumstances.[26] My approach in this book is largely in harmony with Bronfen's historical analysis of women's photography from the nineteenth century in which she emphasises a difference between women's and men's artistic production on the basis of their particular relationships to historically rooted notions of genius. Bronfen argues

> [t]he history of women photographers representing women exhibits a genealogy differing significantly from the traditional poetics of genius. The patriarchal tradition, identified by Harold Bloom as the anxiety of influence, governs the relationship between male artists and their predecessors.[27]

Though women were by necessity bound up with this patriarchal tradition, their relationship to it differed largely because of their legal, social, and cultural status as second-class citizens, a topic that I will explore in more depth in Chapter 2. It is precisely in treating the texts – regardless of their form, and this includes photography – as more or less equal entries or insights in/onto the forms of popular culture under analysis (opera, serialised fiction, columns in newspapers, and women's magazines that reference the performing arts and silent cinema), and as narrative historical evidence, that I wish to put forward a case for this new mode of reading "lost" female spectatorships as multipolar and cross-disciplinary. While this summary may indeed imply the presence of the female spectator, reader, and (more crucially) writer, it does not explicitly acknowledge her, and the gendered nature of diverse audiences in late nineteenth-century Italy should not be overlooked. Not unlike the study of women writers, lost women spectators' contributions to the culture – their desires and pleasures – should also be acknowledged and interrogated with reference to the specificity of their individual experiences.

Political Context

The era with which this book is concerned was shot through with contradiction and ambivalence: culturally feminised and to some extent feminist on the one hand, it was also scathingly misogynist, patriarchal, racist and sexist, despite the gradual entrance of women into public spaces, the professions, and all levels of education. It is not by accident that this moment coincided with the emergence of the first wave of feminism in Italy. However short-lived and unsuccessful – by 1907, only 600 signatures had been collected in a petition to the Italian government demanding universal suffrage[28] – the emancipationist movement in Italy nevertheless took steps to pave the way for more and more women to challenge the masculine public sphere as defined by Jürgen Habermas, and blur the lines demarcated by the doctrine of the gendered separate spheres.[29] As writers of serialised novels, columns on theatre-going in weekly journals for women (I use the terms "journal" and "magazine" interchangeably), and later in cinema journals, as well as in epistolary culture, more and more women were expressing alternative forms of power for the first time in the written word – the new language of standard Italian, which was based on mediaeval Florentine. Indeed, for this very reason women were (and are) more likely to use standard linguistic forms than men.

Critics and scholars generally agree that culturally, the 1880s heralded a new era for Italy – a first phase of modernisation.[30] Despite just under 60 per cent of the population (nearly 27 million at the time of unification) being dependent on agriculture (the figure was still around 55 per cent in 1911[31]), growing numbers of educated middle-class women and men, particularly in the north, were becoming the consumers and producers *en masse* of a national (and, as we have seen in opera, international) culture industry made up of, among others, newspapers, magazines, serialised novels, etiquette books, books on hygiene and health, operas, ballets, plays and musical hall entertainment, as well as later on, the silent screen. In this era of nation-making and "making Italians" – as politician Massimo D'Azeglio (1798–1866) famously asserted – technological innovations, the development of a national transport network, internal migration to cities as well as abroad, and rhetoric in the printed media and conduct manuals sought to promote "Italianness."[32] National associations such as the Dante Alighieri societies were established at home and abroad from 1889 onwards to "defend the Italian language and culture wherever conflicts of nationality threaten them,"[33] while a modern and vibrant print industry with its centre in Milan and the "industrial triangle" made up of Milan, Turin, and Genoa, were all contributing to an unprecedented industrial boom (the first Italian car, manufactured by Ceriano and taken over by F.I.A.T. – the Welleyes/F.I.A.T. HP – was made in Turin in 1899).

And yet, Italy was struggling to affirm itself as a modern nation. This was in part due to low literacy rates (the Italian census measured literacy as the ability to sign, and took the marriage registers as its source, thereby excluding the unmarried as well as those who could read only). At least two-thirds of the entire population was illiterate in 1861, and in many parts of the south the figure was closer to 100 per cent.[34] (In France and Britain respectively in 1860, the literacy rate stood at 63 per cent and 69 per cent.)[35] Among women, only 19 per cent could read.[36] There were, of course, regional and gender differences in literacy levels: in Lombardy the figure was much lower, with 48 per cent of men and 59 per cent of women registered as illiterate. In Emilia Romagna, it was 72 per cent of the population as against 83 per cent of the female population.[37] Sixty-two per cent of Italian women were still illiterate in 1901, and ten years later 40 per cent of Italians could neither read nor write.[38] The gradual rise in literacy rates took place in part thanks to the opening up of schools to girls during the 1870s and 1880s and the government's efforts to widen access to education. Despite a boom in the early 1880s, Italian industry was predominantly rural and confined to the regions of Piedmont, Liguria, and Lombardy,[39] and only in the latter two regions was the professional class (made up of roughly one million) interested in newer forms of wealth, such as shares, bonds, and cash deposits.[40] Italy was mainly struggling with large-scale unemployment, mass-migration to both northern and southern cities, mass workers' demonstrations in the north, poverty, prostitution, and overly populated and neglected cities, especially in the south, as well as an absence of a national public of readers and a fully established tradition of Italian novels.[41]

During the mid-nineteenth century, intellectuals including Giacomo Leopardi (1798–1837) had written on the "deficiency" of Italy's art and culture since the mid-sixteenth century, and Cesare Balbo (1789–1853), Vincenzo Gioberti (1801–52), and D'Azeglio were among intellectuals who published their musings on the reasons for it.[42] As Alexandra Wilson explains,

> [M]oral regeneration was therefore as much an aim of the Risorgimento as political unification. The new nation had to be restored to its former greatness and rediscover what was widely referred to as its lost sense of *virtù*. Unification had given Italy a chance to reassert its prominence, and yet the moment had been lost. After an initial post-unitary period of optimism, Italy's perception of its own shortcomings was not lessened but aggravated, with commentators including Carducci, D'Annunzio, Capuana and Verga returning obsessively to the old theme of Italy's lost greatness as the twentieth century approached.[43]

Divisions widened among industrial and rural workers on the one hand, and the middle classes on the other (represented by proprietors, industrialists, professionals, teachers, private and public employees, and shopkeepers). By 1883, responding to a surge in political activism on the part of socialists, Catholics, radicals, and republicans – of whom the writer and poet Sibilla Aleramo (pseudonym for Rina Faccio, 1876–1960) was one – right-wing politician Giovanni Luzzi (1834–1910) wrote of the "profoundly pathological state of society, the government, parliaments, of everyone."[44] Until the late 1880s, there was a widespread belief that industrialisation would bring immorality and social disorder.

The Casati law of 1859 introduced in Piedmont – which was extended to all Italy by 1861 and introduced two years of compulsory schooling to girls as well as boys – aimed to educate and mould "good citizens," yet a number of enquires prior to World War I showed that around 50 per cent of children never set foot inside a classroom at all.[45] Christopher Duggan points to a commonly drawn distinction among the middle classes between "istruzione" (instruction, aimed at the middle classes) and "educazione" (education, aimed at the poor).[46] National loyalty and the ethic of work were the two main themes of "popular" education, yet the ethical aims of primary education reflected the concerns of the Italian ruling classes more than the needs of the poor, "and [so] it was hardly surprising that many peasants looked upon it as an irrelevance."[47] This division between the popular and ruling classes was also to be found in the culture industry, where hierarchies between "official," high-brow theatre culture including women's theatre, opera and later, silent film, began to establish themselves alongside low-brow, commercial and popular forms of entertainment, such as variety and magic shows, circus acts and musical halls, as well as *operetta*.[48]

Another important contributing factor to Italy's first phase of modernisation was the growing prestige of scientific and intellectual thought following Italian unification, which in turn weakened the traditional hegemony of Catholicism. A new branch of science – that of positivism – was established by Auguste Comte between 1830 and 1842, which held that reasoning based on empirical evidence was superior to the deductive method of philosophy and at odds with the Catholic. Moreover, Darwin's earth-shattering *On the Origin of Species* (1859), which argued that humans evolved from animals, was received by traditionalists as an outright attack on religion. Translated into Italian in 1864, it offered the new state a discourse compatible with its aspirations to liberalism and secularism, and signalled a transition, together with the French Revolution, to modernity. Upper-middle-class men in particular (doctors, lawyers) began applying positivism to social theory and the humanities in a bid to solve Italy's social problems, and in 1876 physician, psychiatrist and founder of criminal anthropology Cesare Lombroso (1835–1909) published *L'uomo delinquente* (Criminal Man, 1880), in which he presented his theory of the atavistic offender, or "born criminal." Controversial for negating free will and excusing criminals as irresponsible beings driven by defective biology rather than by choice or environment, it appeared at a time in which both literature and science were obsessed with observation, empirical analysis and studying pathological "dangerous" classes who threatened to impede the emergence of the new nation made up of respectable citizens. By the 1890s there had emerged many positivist studies around Europe which argued that women were inferior to men, including Lombroso's and Guglielmo Ferrero's *La donna delinquente: la prostituta e la donna normale* (The Criminal Woman: the Prostitute, and the Normal Woman, 1893).

First-Wave Feminism in Italy

The movement for female emancipation in Italy only emerged after 1880; before then, there were individual feminist thinkers, but they did not constitute a movement.[49] In the eighteenth century, the social and cultural life of the literary salons had provided bourgeois and aristocratic women with a degree of political awareness comparable to that of their male counterparts, and exceptional women had entered the public sphere. For instance, in 1727, the child prodigy, and later, mathematician, Maria Gaetana Agnesi (1718–99) from Milan delivered an oration in favour of women's education, and the period also saw a flourishing of female-authored journals.[50] Mary Wollstonecraft (1759–97) published *A Vindication of the Rights of Woman* in 1792, and it was translated anonymously into French in the same year.[51] Around the same time, the Milanese journalist Carolina Lattanzi (1771–1818) – who may indeed have read, and been inspired by, Wollstonecraft's text – published her lecture, "La schiavitù delle donne" (The Slavery of Women, 1797), which she had delivered at the Accademia della Pubblica Istruzione in Milan. This work represents one of the first writings in Italian by a woman on the condition of women under the *Ancien régime* and is an important precursor of essays by women that emerged further on in the nineteenth century.[52]

Later, in 1821, Cecilia Folliero De Luna from Naples published *La breve dissertazione sull'istruzione donnesca ed esortazione alle mie concittadine a sperarla* (A Brief Essay on Women's Education and an Exhortation to My Compatriots to Desire It), in which she argued in favour of making education available to women as a means of widening their occupational perspectives. This radical contribution differed from later programmes for education for women put forward by Catholic thinkers, such as the conservative Caterina Franceschi Ferrucci (1803–87), who held that middle-class women as the "Angels of the Hearth" should be educated only enough to be able to teach their sons exclusively from within the home.[53]

The early years of the Risorgimento – the period from the end of the Napoleonic wars to the Unification of Italy in 1861–70 – saw the birth of a number of journals on women and education, such as *Studi per le donne italiane* (Studies for Italian Women) in Milan in 1837, which advocated basic literacy for women who were assigned the role of educating their children to be "good citizens," rather than conceiving of education as a means of widening occupational perspectives to women. In addition, the emergence of patriotic journals founded by women between 1848 and 1861 – such as Rome's *La donna italiana* in 1848 and *Il circolo delle donne italiane* (Italian Women's Circular) from the same year in Venice – invited reflection on women's role in the political context.[54] Writing in *Il circolo delle donne italiane* on 26 September 1848, Adele Cortesi called for equal rights for women and men.[55] During this period, working-class women in the cities were directly involved in building barricades, in street fighting which required them to dress in men's clothes, and in collecting and distributing ammunition and delivering messages, whilst middle- and upper-class women campaigned for civil and religious rights, and began publishing articles in liberal newspapers and journals.[56] Between 1855 and 1858, the politically moderate journal *La donna* (not to be confused with Gualberta Alaide Beccari's emancipationist periodical), published in Genoa and directed by men sympathetic to the woman question, discussed the condition of women, their legal rights, and access to education for the first time. Women's journals tended to be financed and directed by men, presumably for economic reasons, although there were cases where women were founders and directors – for example, Neera (pseudonym for Anna Radius Zuccari, 1846–1918) founded and directed *Vita intima* (1890–91), which was financed by Guido Marcati.

The French Enlightenment, the utopian socialism of Charles Fourier (1772–1837) and Henri de Saint Simon (1760–1825), and the egalitarianism of John Stuart Mill (1806–73) all influenced to varying degrees debates on the emancipation of women in Italy, which, at the time meant educating oneself, being financially independent, marrying for love and not economic reasons, and freely choosing singlehood.[57] The support of aristocrat Cristina di Belgiojoso (1808–71) and the backing of Giuseppe Mazzini (1805–72) also contributed to the popularity of the movement in its initial stages. Although Mazzini supported the emancipationist movement, he maintained a conservative view in relation to what he saw as women's "natural" function, which, according to him, was as wife and mother. Belgiojoso invested her wealth in political causes, financing Mazzini's expedition to Savoy, and she founded journals hostile to the Austrian regime. In 1866, she published "Della presente condizione delle donne e del loro avenire" (On the Present Condition of Women and their Future) in *Nuova antologia*, where she argued that women should be educated because they are "naturally" intelligent.[58] The Liberal politician Salvatore Morelli (1824–80) published a book entitled *La donna e la scienza* (Woman and Science) in 1861, which followed the ideals of Mazzini and other radical thinkers of the time.[59] Morelli called for the abolition of religious teaching and of Latin and Greek in schools, as well as for the ending of university taxes, and he was the first Italian politician to speak out against the laws on prostitution, to ask for divorce laws and equal rights between married couples, as well as the vote for women in general elections. Morelli represents something of a last gasp for these ideals, for the emancipationist movement which was to arise in the 1880s had a much more conservative, as opposed to idealistic, timbre.

Morelli's views on the "woman question" provided ammunition for Mozzoni's 1864 pamphlet, in which she considered women's legal and social position in relation to religion, the family, society, and education. Mozzoni observed the anachronistic nature of the legislators' ideal role of women (especially from the lower classes), given that they had been working both inside and outside the home during most of the Risorgimento, and that they received unequal pay for equivalent work. A year later, Mozzoni criticised the failure of Pisanelli's Civil Code to measure up to the standards set by developments in women's rights in countries as diverse as England, Prussia, Austria, and the United States.[60] She translated John Stuart Mill's *The Subjection of Women* (1869) into Italian in 1870, the same year in which the first official national organisation for the emancipation of women, the "Società italiana per l'emancipazione della donna" (Italian Society for the Emancipation of Woman) was established, and she pioneered the fight against the regulation of prostitution and for the abolition of prostitution laws in Europe. In the introduction to her translation of Mill's work, Mozzoni argued that it was from the condition of its women that the degree of civility of any nation could best be judged.[61] In 1881, Mozzoni established the "Lega promotrice degli interessi femminili" (League Promoting Women's Interests), an association that aimed to extend to women of all social classes an awareness of their rights and duties in society.[62] In the same year, Mozzoni organised a famous committee meeting in Rome on the question of women's suffrage, and the Left presented a bill to parliament calling for universal suffrage, which was defeated.[63]

The year 1903 marked the foundation of the National Council for Italian Women, and by 1906, committees for female suffrage existed in all major cities as far south as Naples. The year 1908 saw the First Congress of Italian Women, and in 1910 the National Committee for Women's Suffrage was established.[64] Despite being a Mazzinian, and with the foundation of the Italian Socialist Party in 1892, a radical socialist, Mozzoni did not identify with one political party: it was her ambition to unite women from all political parties and classes on the basis that institutions oppressed women from all classes. Mozzoni campaigned constantly for an improvement in legislation for women. Along with her supporters, she fought to dissolve the bourgeois ideology of gendered separate spheres. Another well-known supporter of the movement was the aforementioned Russian-born Anna Kuliscioff (1857–1925).[65] As a socialist and supporter of Mikhail Bakunin (1814–76), Kuliscioff sought exile in Italy after conspiring against the tsarist government. In her essay "Il sentimentalismo nella questione femminile" (Sentimentalism in the Woman Question), published in the journal *Critica sociale* on 1 May 1892, she highlighted the new class of young women from the impoverished middle- and lower-middle classes who had neither a dowry nor a title, and who, if they did not enter a convent, were forced to go out to work to earn a living.

The movement for women's emancipation in Italy failed in its attempts to gain women the right to vote in national elections, which was finally granted only in 1946. Post-unification Italy was generally hostile to women's issues, and there was parliamentary opposition to female suffrage. Suffrage was extremely restricted at the time of unification: only two per cent of the population, or 600,000 males, had the right to vote. By 1882, this had risen to seven per cent of the population (slightly more than two million adult males), and in 1912, a new law gave the vote to all males over 30 who had served in the forces. Support for women's suffrage in Italy had its roots in bourgeois charitable organisations, and as a goal it became increasingly prominent towards the end of the nineteenth century. Though a law was passed in 1925 granting suffrage in local elections to bereaved mothers and war widows as long as they did not marry, this was nullified by Mussolini's decision to end local elections for good in 1926.

Many women were ignorant of, or indifferent to politics, and both the Right and Left were afraid of granting the vote to women; the Right held that women were ignorant of political and civil responsibilities, and the Left was fearful that women were politically conservative and overwhelmingly Catholic and, therefore, supportive of the Church. It is widely believed that with the onset of World War I the movement for emancipation in Italy died away, but as Simonetta Ortaggi Cammarosano has shown, after the war "Fascism was unable to stop the process of women's emancipation which was inexorably connected to economic development and to the needs of the labour market."[66]

Methodology

My methodological approach in this book shifts attention away from interpreting an aesthetic object (e.g., the text of a given opera, play and early film in the melodramatic mode) to focus on the cognitive and affective responses of actual women, whether these responses are imagined (in fiction, for example), or written about in women's journals, columns in newspapers addressed to female readers, letters, diary entries, or autobiographies by women who were performers and/or spectators. My premise is that melodrama in women's film, theatre, and opera in this period functioned as an instrument of dominant ideology, but not monolithically so. In terms of identification, for example, I seek to avoid making literal assumptions about "epistemophilia" (indicating an excessive love for knowledge) *only* occurring as a simple one-way process to her or his like: middle-class women in Turin were as likely to pity the "Fallen" Sicilian *contadina* Santuzza in Verga's adaptation of his short-story version of "Cavalleria rusticana" (1880) as they were Ibsen's bourgeois Nora in *A Doll's House* (1879) (Emilia Aliprandi Pieri (1856–1901) played the lead role in the first Italian production at the Teatro Gerbino in Turin on 15 February 1889).[67]

Due to new technologies influencing print and performance cultures, middle-class women in the north watched the same films, operas, and plays, and read the same serialised popular novels as (the fewer literate) middle-class women in the south. By the same token, while the stage and screen narratives depicted overwhelmingly heterosexual romantic relationships, in reclaiming "lost" women spectators in this book, many of their gazes at female and male performers reveal fascination, admiration, identification, erotic desire, and pleasure. Actors, writers, artists, spectators, and readers were also LGBTQI+. For example, we know that the great tragic actor Eleonore Duse (1858–1924) and the feminist writer and poet Aleramo had sexual relationships with women and men. Regrettably, and due to an absence of reliable primary and secondary sources, I have been unable to uncover evidence of spectatorships among people of colour and minority ethnic groups in Italy at this time. Indeed, the absence and silence surrounding discourses of same-sex pleasure and spectatorships among black and ethnic minority communities of women in late nineteenth-century modern Italian culture are in and of itself intriguing and an area of urgent future enquiry.[68]

In terms of my stance *vis-à-vis* feminist psychoanalytic film theory and female spectatorships in this book, I build on recent studies discussed in Chapter 1 while also attending to what has become known since the early 2000s as "the affective turn" as a way of understanding what falls outside the dominant paradigm of representation in rhetoric and semiotics. As Melissa Gregg and Gregory J. Seigworth argue, unlike emotion, affect

> arises in the midst of *in-betweenness*: in the capacities to act and be acted upon. [...] Affect, at its most anthropomorphic, is the name we give to those forces – visceral forces beneath, alongside, or generally *other than* conscious knowing, vital forces insisting beyond emotion – that can serve to drive us toward movement, toward thought and extension, that can likewise suspend us (as if in neutral) across a barely registering accretion of force-relations, or that can even leave us overwhelmed by the world's apparent intractability.[69]

In discussing the popular cultural significance of rock and roll, Lawrence Grossberg argues that in the spaces that develop between music and fans, an "affective alliance" develops which derives from the "production of a network of empowerment."[70] For Grossberg, affect is "ideologically, economically, and libidinally neutral except as it is articulated into these systems under specific historical conditions."[71] In thinking about the *fin de siècle* melodramatic mode in which the "visual power [and] disruptive energy [...] of the women who are their subjects and the women who are their interpreters cannot be contained,"[72] attention to the weight of feeling expressed by middle-class women spectators towards women performers can reveal much about what mattered to spectators.

The period in question was a fertile one for ideas that were emerging as Darwin put forward his views on the origin of species. Later, Sigmund Freud (1856–1939) declared we are not in control of our emotions, while Friedrich Nietzsche (1844–1900) pronounced the death of God. To a large extent, and as Silvana Patriarca has argued, the creation of a new national political framework in Italy, which saw a quiet but effective challenge of world-views to the Church, gave some women hope for progress and was a motivating factor in the transformations discussed in this book.[73] As previously stated, Milanese emancipationist Mozzoni published her feminist pamphlet in 1864, and the Italian emancipationist movement began to campaign for better working rights and access to education for women. Yet in law, working- and middle-class women were second-class citizens. Women actors and singers, from Duse to opera singer Adelina Patti (1843–1919), to the screen diva Bertini, were transforming overwhelmingly male-authored texts, creating their own physical enactments and realising their (written, textual) characters in their own particular ways. Watching and experiencing the emboldened diva play a Fallen Woman in the role of the central protagonist in women's film, theatre and opera during this era, performing time and again over a period of 40 years on stage, and then on screen (roughly from the 1870s to the 1910s) constituted an important means of self-discovery and identification for female spectators, regardless of any parasocial relationships that may, or may not, have existed. And if male roles figured more prominently in Verdi's operas,[74] a generation later in Puccini's tragic realist operas set in the here and now or, indeed, further back in time, women took centre stage. There, they enacted their desires, sufferings, conflicts, and defeats for the majority of the duration of the narrative over an emotional spectrum ranging from absolute despair to sheer *jouissance*.

My analyses in this book are indebted to the visionary cultural work of Alberto Mario Banti on the *figure profonde* of nation-making; the "deep images" of emotionally strong, sacrificing, suffering heroines – the Fallen (and virtuous) Women – in Italian tragic women's opera from the period in question, and in the affect in letters written by women writers to female performing artists.[75] I draw on these, as well as diary entries, reviews in women's and theatre journals, as well as narrative realist fiction, and apply contemporary feminist film theory to offer a cross-disciplinary contribution to the field of nineteenth- and early twentieth-century European cultural and spectatorship studies.

Writing on Italy's theatre audiences at this time, Laura Mariani has suggested that:

> [T]he formation of a class of professional women writers, and the expansion of cultural consumption for educated women and women workers – both manual and intellectual – evidently influenced the composition of theatre audiences, which, in this particular historical moment was made up largely of the middle-classes.[76]

Like the many skilled professional women singers performing Italian opera before them, women writers remained suspect for flouting their (expected) financial dependence on men and were careful not to identify with the growing movement for female emancipation for fear that their work would not be taken seriously.[77] Like the *grande attrici* and silent divas (some of whom were also directors), several of them also had international profiles.[78]

This book, therefore, treats the disciplines of theatre studies, opera studies, film studies, art history, and literary studies *on a par*, as conduits for examining women spectators' personal experiences of watching melodramatic plots, either as live performance or on-screen. I posit that the period in question saw the beginnings of a mass, national and international, nascent female spectatorship in-the-making, one that was characterised by an "epistemophilic" gaze, and which emerged in the aftermath of the arrival on the literary scene in Italy of the first wave of professional women writers. This gaze involved erotic curiosity, vicarious participation, identification with, and desire for the central female character and performer on behalf of her female spectators. It was *active* and revealed a sustained engagement by women as discerning, early capitalist consumers of the theatre, opera, and early film performances and screenings they attended and the films they watched. It was part of the development of a national, feminised culture industry during Italy's emergence as a nation state until the onset of fascism. And not only that, as I contend in Chapter 6, Italy was a case study of a more widespread phenomenon which also affected the Italian diaspora during the first period of mass migration, for example, to Britain, Australia, New Zealand, Canada, and North America. There, first-night performances of new Puccini operas were staged, novels by popular novelist Carolina Invernizio (1851–1916), "la gallina di Voghera" ("the mother-hen from Voghera", as Antonio Gramsci famously called her) were consumed by thousands of female readers, and spectators nostalgic for their homeland enjoyed the silent diva films featuring Bertini, Lyda Borelli, and Pina Menichelli, in which, as Francesco Pitassio has argued, "no male actors could compete [...] in terms of narrative and performative significance."[79]

Outline

Chapter 1 examines key directions in spectatorship studies since the 1960s in order to contextualise the present study and locate my own contribution to the field. Chapter 2, on women's access to culture, provides an overview of how Italian opera compared with opera in the rest of Europe, exploring the changing role of Italian theatres and *politeama* which hosted the silent screen from 1897 onwards until after World War I. Chapter 3 shifts from the public stage to the private realm of diaries and letters belonging to middle-class women in which they record their impressions of certain performances, as well as those of female performing artists; I suggest that these extended from performer and writer to reader to spectator and back to the performer, thereby constructing a continuous positive feedback loop. Chapter 4 examines reflections on theatre and cinema-going by women writers and readers in women's magazines and newspaper columns. It reveals how women were looking increasingly inwards, thus becoming self-questioning, self-aware, and self-determined, with a more developed sense of self. Chapter 5 examines a similar phenomenon in realist fiction to argue that representations of spectators were gendered and polarised at this specific juncture in Italy's cultural history. Finally, Chapter 6 looks beyond Italy to uncover a selection of affective and discerning responses among women spectators from Naples, to Paris, to Boston that signalled a Mediterranean, southern European "exportable" spectatorship-in-the-making; one whose origins were nevertheless rooted in the specificity of the relationship based on solidarity between Italy's female performers and their spectators. The book lays bare a plethora of rich textual writings to uncover a wave of gendered spectatorships based on *admiration*: these were the foundations of an active, self-conscious, and vibrant female culture industry at the turn of the twentieth century in Italy and beyond. Due to the onset of fascism, they were all too readily forgotten. Until now.

Notes

1 See: Bram Dijkstra, *Idols of Perversity: Fantasies of Feminine Evil in fin-de-siècle Culture* (Oxford: Oxford University Press, 1986).

2 Franz Liszt, "Lettres d'un bachelier ès musique," in Jean Chantavoine, *Franz Liszt: Pages Romantiques* (Paris: F. Alcan, 1912), pp. 147–240 (p. 178).

3 See: Katharine Mitchell, *Italian Women Writers: Gender and Everyday Life in Fiction and Journalism, 1870–1910* (Toronto: University of Toronto Press, 2014).

4 This feminist collective, which is still active today, takes its name from the Greek prophetess and philosopher Diotima, whose ideas founded the concept of Platonic love. Feminist philosophers Luisa Muraro (1940–) and Adrianna Cavarero (1947–) are among its proponents. They conceptualised the idea of "Il pensiero della differenza" (difference of thought), which they based on the thinking of Luce Irigaray's essentialist theory of sexual difference and the necessity to overcome the monism of male logic. This branch of feminism does not take into consideration ideas of gender and gender equality in Anglo-American feminism.

5 See: Christine Gledhill, *Home is Where the Heart Is: Studies in Melodrama and the Woman's Film* (London: British Film Institute, 1987). Feminist film scholar Mary Ann Doane published a book on the "woman's film" in the same year. See: *The Desire to Desire: The Woman's Film of the 1940s* (Bloomington: Indiana University Press, 1987).

6 Miriam Hansen, *Babel and Babylon: Spectatorship in American Silent Film* (Cambridge, MA and London: Harvard University Press, 1991), p. 2.

7 Susan Hayward, *Cinema Studies: The Key Concepts*, 3rd edn. (London and New York: Routledge, 2006), p. 236. Italics my emphasis.

8 Linda Williams, "Melodrama Revised," in *Emotions: A Cultural Studies Reader*, ed. by Shari Daya (London and New York: Routledge, 2002), pp. 336–50.

9 See: Angela Dalle Vacche, *Diva: Defiance and Passion in Early Italian Cinema* (Austin: University of Texas Press, 2008).

10 Stephen Gundle, "The Five Faces of the Femme Fatale," in *Italian Cinema from the Silent Screen to the Digital Image*, ed. by Joseph Luzzi (London: Bloomsbury, 2020), pp. 123–40 (p. 124).

11 See: Mary Ann Doane, *Femmes Fatales: Feminism, Film Theory, Psychoanalysis* (London: Routledge, 1991), pp. 2–3; Elisabeth Bronfen, "*Femme Fatale*: Negotiations of Tragic Desire," *New Literary History* 35:1 (2004), 103–16 (115); and, more recently, *The Femme Fatale: Images, Histories, Contexts*, ed. by Helen Hanson and Catherine O'Rawe (Baisingstoke, New York: Palgrave Macmillan, 2010), pp. 1–8.

12 Louis Bayman, *The Operatic and the Everyday in Post-War Italian Film Melodrama* (Edinburgh: Edinburgh University Press, 2014), p. 3.

13 John Champagne, *Italian Masculinity as Queer Melodrama: Caravaggio, Puccini, Contemporary Cinema* (Basingstoke: Palgrave Macmillan, 2015). See, also, Peter Brooks, "Melodrama, Body, Revolution," in *Melodrama: Stage, Picture, Screen*, ed. by Jacky Bratton and others (London: BFI, 1994), pp. 11–24, and Rebecca H. Bauman, "Melodrama and Italian Culture," *Italian Studies* 70:3 (2015), 416–20.

14 Giovanni Ragone, *Un secolo di libri. Storia dell'editoria in Italia dall'Unità al postmoderno* (Turin: Einaudi, 1999), p. 46.

15 Paul Fryer, "Duse Recorded," in *Eleonora Duse and* Cenere (Ashes), ed. by Maria Pia Pagani and Paul Fryer (Jefferson, North Carolina: McFarland, 2017), pp. 72–89 (p. 79).

16 Dalle Vacche, *Diva*, pp. 254–5.
17 *Ibid.*, p. 19.
18 See: Catherine Clément, *L'Opéra, ou la défaite des femmes* (Paris: Éditions Grasset & Fasquelle, 1979).
19 Niccolò Tommasèo and Bernardo Bellini, *Dizionario della lingua italiana* (Turin: UTET, 1879), p. 338.
20 Julie K. Allen, "Divas Down Under: The Circulation of Asta Nielsen's and Francesca Bertini's films in Australasian Cinemas in the 1910s," *Studies in Australasian Cinema* 11:2 (2017), 59–76 (70).
21 *Ibid.*, 63–4.
22 See: Elisabeth Bronfen, "Women Seeing Women Seeing Women," in *Women Seeing Women: A Pictorial History of Women's Photography from Julia Margaret Cameron to Annie Leibovitz*, ed. by Lothar Schirmer (London: Haus, 2002), pp. 9–34 (p. 13).
23 The Rome-based feminist collective "Se non ora, quando?" (*If not now, when?*) emerged in 2010, when thousands of women took to the streets to fight against female objectification in the media following the revelation that former Prime Minister Silvio Berlusconi paid for sex with an underage sex worker. More recently, Italy responded to denunciations of sexual harassment and misconduct in the film industry, including rape, on Twitter, with #quellavoltache, meaning "the time that" in the wake of the #MeToo phenomenon.
24 See: Laura Mulvey, "Visual Pleasure and Narrative Cinema," *Screen* 16:3 (October 1975), 6–18. Mulvey emphasised the prevalence of the masculine viewpoint in cinema to argue that the pleasure gained in looking is a male pleasure and that the "look" in cinema is controlled by the male and directed at the female.
25 See: John Berger, *Ways of Seeing* (London: Harmondsworth, 1972). Berger suggests that the surveyor of women in herself is male: the surveyed female.
26 One such example is "Stendhal's syndrome," whereby the spectator experiences dizzy spells, palpitations, hallucinations, disorientation, loss of identity, and physical exhaustion. Dubbed by psychiatrist Graziella Magherini in 1989 who had treated 106 visitors to Florence as emergencies in her department, she named the syndrome after Stendhal who experienced similar symptoms on his visit to the Basilica of Santa Croce in 1817. See: Graziella Magherini, *La sindrome di Stendhal* (Florence: Ponte alle Grazie, 1989).
27 Bronfen, "Women Seeing Women Seeing Women," pp. 9–34 (p. 10).
28 Richard Evans, *The Feminists: Women's Emancipation Movements in Europe, America and Australasia 1840–1920* (London: Barnes and Noble, 1977), p. 136.
29 On Jürgen Habermas's notion of the "public sphere" and feminist criticisms of his social theory as gender-blind and, in many respects, androcentric, see: *Feminists Read Habermas: Gendering the Subject of Discourse*, ed. by Johanna Meehan (New York and London: Routledge, 1995). On the doctrine of the separate spheres in women's history, see, for instance, Linda K. Kerber, "Female Worlds, Woman's Place: The Rhetoric of Women's History," *The Journal of American History* 75:1 (1988), 9–39.
30 Fausto Colombo identifies the publication of Collodi's *Le avventure di Pinocchio* (1883) as the event that inaugurated the opening of Italy's modern cultural industry. See: Fausto Colombo, *La cultura sottile: media e industria*

culturale in Italia dall'Ottocento agli anni Novanta (Milan: Bompiani, 1999), p. 39. See, also, *The Printed Media in Fin-de-siècle Italy: Publishers, Writers, and Readers*, ed. by Ann Hallamore Caesar and others (Oxford: Legenda, 2011), p. 2.

31 Christopher Duggan, *A Concise History of Italy* (2nd edn.) (Cambridge: Cambridge University Press, 2014), p. 147.

32 See: Silvana Patriarca, *Italian Vices: Nation and Character from the Risorgimento to the Republic* (Cambridge: CUP, 2010), pp. 2–3. The idea of *Italianità* or "Italianness" developed during the nineteenth century in discourses about the nation and involve claims to cultural uniqueness and national superiority.

33 Luigi Rava, "Il saluto di Ravenna," speech given at the eleventh Dante Conference, 27 September 1900, cited in Luigi Rava, *Per la "Dante Alighieri" (trenta anni di propaganda): discorsi e ricordi, 1900–1931* (Rome: Società Nazionale Dante Alighieri, 1932), p. 2.

34 Duggan, *A Concise History of Italy*, p. 155.

35 Gabriel Tortella, "Patterns of Economic Retardation and Recovery in South-Western Europe in the Nineteenth and Twentieth Centuries," *Economic History Review* 47:1 (1994), 1–21 (11).

36 Giuseppe Farinelli, *Storia del giornalismo italiano: dalle origini ai nostri giorni* (Turin: UTET, 1997), p. 212.

37 See: Daniele Marchesini, "L'analfabetismo femminile nell'Italia dell'Ottocento: caratteristiche e dinamiche," in *L'educazione delle donne: scuole e modelli di vita femminile nell'Italia dell'Ottocento*, ed. Simonetta Soldani (Milan: Franco Angeli, 1991, 2nd edn.), pp. 37–56 (p. 37).

38 Farinelli, *Storia del giornalismo*, p. 212.

39 Duggan, *A Concise History of Italy*, p. 153.

40 *Ibid.*, p. 158.

41 *The Printed Media in Fin-de-siècle Italy*, p. 4.

42 On the discourse of "Italian deficiency," see Patriarca, *Italian Vices*, p. 25.

43 Alexandra Wilson, *The Puccini Problem: Opera, Nationalism and Modernity* (Cambridge: Cambridge University Press, 2007), p. 15.

44 Francesca Socrate, "Commedia borghese e crisi di fine secolo," in *Scene di fine Ottocento: L'Italia fin de siècle a teatro*, ed. by Carlotta Sorba (Carocci, 2004), pp. 21–59 (p. 21).

45 Duggan, *A Concise History of Italy*, p. 155.

46 *Ibid.*, p. 156.

47 *Ibid.*

48 Carlotta Sorba, "Introduzione: Percorsi di ricerca fra teatro, cultura e società," in *Scene di fine Ottocento: L'Italia fin de siècle a teatro*, ed. by Carlotta Sorba (Rome: Carocci, 2004), pp. 9–20 (pp. 14–15).

49 Anna Buttafuoco, *Questioni di cittadinanza: donne e diritti sociali dell'Italia Liberale* (Siena: Protagon Editori Toscani, 1995), p. 26. The following section draws on material already published in "'Sorelle in arte (e politica)': The 'Woman Question' and Female Solidarity at the Fin de Siècle" in *Women and Gender in Post-Unification Italy: Between Private and Public Spheres,* ed. by Katharine Mitchell and Helena Sanson (Oxford: Peter Lang, 2013), pp. 197–223 (pp. 205–11).

50 Luisa Ricaldone, "Eighteenth-Century Literature," in *A History of Women's Writing in Italy*, ed. by Letizzia Panizza and Sharon Wood (Cambridge: Cambridge University Press, 2000), pp. 95–106 (p. 97).

51 The text was published with the title translated as *Défense des droits de la femme*. It is likely that educated Italian women would have read the text, assuming they had access to it. The earliest Italian translation of Wollstonecraft's treatise was edited and translated by Franca Ruggieri and published in 1977 with the title *I diritti delle donne* (Rome: Editori Riuniti).
52 Verina Jones, "Journalism, 1750–1850," in *A History of Women's Writing in Italy*, pp. 120–34 (p. 126).
53 The citation is taken from Coventry Patmore's 1854 classification in his poem modelled on the impossible religious icon of the Virgin Mary ("impossible" because in the late nineteenth century, no mother could have a biological child without having intercourse with a man). See: Coventry Patmore, *The Angel in the House*, 2nd edn. (London: John W. Parker and Son, West Strand, 1858).
54 See: Laura Pisano, "Introduzione," in *Le donne del giornalismo: da Eleonora Fonseca a Ilaria Alpi. Dizionario storico bio-bibliografico, secoli XVIII-XX*, ed. by Laura Pisano (Milan: Franco Angeli, 2004), pp. 18–20.
55 *Ibid.*, p. 19.
56 See: Derek Beales and Eugenio F. Biagini, *The Risorgimento and the Unification of Italy* (Harlow: Longman, 2002), pp. 134–49.
57 Beatrice Pisa, *Venticinque anni di emancipazionismo femminile in Italia: Gualberta Alaide Beccari e la rivista «La Donna» (1868–1890)* (Rome: Elengraf, 1982), p. 68.
58 Cristina di Belgiojoso, "Della presente condizione delle donne e del loro avvenire," *Nuova Antologia* 1 (1866), 96–113 (96).
59 See: Salvatore Morelli, *La donna e la scienza, o la soluzione dell'umano problema* (Naples: Stab. tip. dell'Ancora, 1861).
60 Pisanelli's Civil Code of 1865 is discussed in depth in Chapter 2.
61 See: John Stuart Mill, *La servitù delle donne* (Milan: F. Legros, 1870).
62 Pisa, *Venticinque anni*, p. 5. The league was particularly effective in the 1890s in campaigning for legislation in favour of women across the peninsula.
63 Lucienne Kroha, *The Woman Writer in Late-Nineteenth-Century Italy: Gender and the Formation of Literary Identity* (Lewiston, New York: E. Mellen Press, 1992), p. 8.
64 Sharon Wood, *Italian Women's Writing: 1860–1994* (London: Athlone Press, 1995), p. 10.
65 On Kuliscioff, see: Rosalia Colombo Ascari, "Feminism and Socialism in Anna Kuliscioff's Writings," in *Mothers of Invention: Women, Italian Fascism, and Culture*, ed. by Robin Pickering-Iazzi (Minneapolis, MN and London: University of Minnesota Press, 1995), pp. 1–25.
66 Simona Ortaggi Cammarosano, "Italian Women during the Great War," in *Evidence, History and the Great War: Historians and the Impact of 1914–18*, ed. G. Braybon (Oxford: Berghahn, 2003), pp. 216–38 (p. 235).
67 The term "epistemophilia" was first coined as a type of "gaze" by Laura Mulvey in her book *Fetishism and Curiosity* (Bloomington: Indiana University Press, 1996), p. 59.
68 On same-sex desire in late nineteenth-century Italian culture, see: Charlotte Ross, *Eccentricity and Sameness. Discourses on Lesbianism and Desire Between Women in Italy, 1860s–1930s* (Oxford and New York: Peter Lang, 2015). On African American performers in Paris in the early twentieth century, see: Olivette Otele, *African Europeans: An Untold History* (London: C. Hurst & Co., 2020), p. 143.

69 Melissa Gregg and Gregory J. Seigworth, "An Inventory of Shimmers," in *The Affect Theory Reader*, ed. by Melissa Gregg and Gregory J. Seigworth (Durham and London: Duke University Press, 2010), pp. 1–25 (pp. 1–2).
70 Lawrence Grossberg, "Another Boring Day in Paradise: Rock and Roll and the Empowerment of Everyday Life (1984)," in *Dancing In Spite of Myself: Essays on Popular Culture* (Durham: Duke University Press, 1997), pp. 29–63 (p. 44).
71 Grossberg, "Postmodernity and Affect: All Dressed Up with No Place to Go (1988)", pp. 145–65 (p. 161), op. cit.
72 Gundle, "The Five Faces of the Femme Fatale," p. 123.
73 Patriarca, *Italian Vices*, p. 8.
74 Susan Rutherford, *Verdi, Opera, Women* (Cambridge: Cambridge University Press, 2013), p. 8.
75 Alberto Mario Banti and Paul Ginsborg, "Introduzione," in *Storia d'Italia. Annali 22. Il Risorgimento*, ed. by Alberto Mario Banti and Paul Ginsborg (Turin: Einaudi, 2007), pp. xxiii–iv (p. xxiii).
76 Laura Mariani, "Introduzione: Scene e scrittura, politica e amicizia: una vita «da gigante»," in *L'attrice del cuore: storia di Giacinta Pezzana attraverso le lettere*, ed. by Laura Mariani (Florence: Le lettere, 2005), pp. 9–57 (p. 16).
77 The writers Matilde Serao (1856–1927) and Neera, for example, publicly proclaimed their supposed anti-feminist stances.
78 On female singers of Italian opera, see Chapter 3 of John Rosselli, *Singers of Italian Opera: A History of a Profession* (Cambridge: CUP, 1992).
79 Francesco Pitassio, "Famous Actors, Famous Actresses: Notes on Acting Style in Italian Silent Films," in *Italian Silent Cinema: A Reader*, ed. by Giorgio Bertellini (New Barnet, UK: John Libbey Publishing, 2013), pp. 255–62 (p. 258).

1 Towards Cross-Disciplinary Female Spectatorships

In what follows, I introduce the various female spectatorships which will figure in the subsequent chapters. The framework is a discussion of the very particular evolution of key movements and shifts in spectatorship theories in the various disciplines in order to situate them historically up to, and including, the present. Since the 1960s, first in art history then in literary studies followed by film studies and theatre studies, scholars have sought to theorise the role of spectators. Ongoing discussions and theorisations continue to draw on a wide range of approaches in the sciences and social sciences, including psychoanalysis, semiotics, cognitive science, cognitive psychology, sociology, linguistics, and ethnography. Indeed, so rich and complex is the theorisation of (mostly film) spectators that there is no space here to provide a comprehensive overview of studies in the various disciplines. These emerged from an awareness that texts (as plays, operas, works of art, novels) are meaningless without what in 1960 Ernst Gombrich described as the "beholder's share," embodied in the spectator, viewer, and reader respectively.[1] The differences and possible frictions that may arise when considering a collective approach to spectatorships combining theatre, opera, and film must at this point be acknowledged, and in what follows I summarise the various studies to have emerged in order to locate my position within ongoing debates. As we shall see, on the one hand, studies on spectators of theatre and opera have tended to define the spectator as either an individualised, actual recipient of a play, or an ideal or hypothetical one whose response is subdivided into cognitive and affective fields. On the other hand, scholarship on spectators of film since the 1970s has drawn on psychoanalysis to theorise a (mostly masculine) subject (as opposed to a spectator), while since the 1980s film theory has drawn on literary studies, cultural studies, and ethnography to conceptualise forms of address.

Women Film Spectators

Since cinema's inception in 1897, directors, producers, and film-makers have sought to control the spectator's gaze through camera editing, sound accompaniment, and the *mise en scène*. Prior to the advent of classical

DOI: 10.4324/9780429293511-2

narrative cinema following World War I, in which the range of feminine spectatorial positions was limited by women's supposed definition in relation to masculinity, silent cinema offered

> ways of redefining and reformulating the relationship between the spectator and film as customarily understood by feminist film theory, and offer[ed] the prospect of getting closer to an understanding of how women have experienced cinema and the meanings they create[d] out of that experience.[2]

We need only look to the silent divas in Italy who were also directors of the films in which they starred – Bertini and Duse, for example – to recognise the different viewing positions open to early cinema spectators compared with those of classical narrative cinema. Giorgio Bertellini has described the period from 1908 to 1914 as early Italian cinema's "brief and glorious season."[3] Whereas in 1915, Italy produced 562 films, many of which it exported to other European countries as well as to North America and Australia, by 1930 that number had dropped to 12.[4] The first film entrepreneurs held screenings in theatres, taverns, and hotels according to a practice that lasted well into the 1910s, and up until 1915, earlier forms of entertainment co-existed with cinema: popular entertainment venues such as the *politeama*. These venues eliminated the system in traditional theatres of separating spectators according to social class, favouring instead an amphitheatre-like *galleria*. They also staged different kinds of amusements, including ballets, plays, puppet shows, parties, circus-type entertainments, and sporting events.[5] By the late 1890s, the Italian theatre auditorium was darkened, and electricity had replaced the gas lighting in most *politeame*; they would soon be used – along with *caffè-concerti* and the summer arenas – as the first cinemas. Spectators would experience a combination of skating races, dancing nights, theatrical shows, ballets, and film screenings over different evenings.[6] Though there are obvious differences in watching a performer on stage in a theatre auditorium compared with watching them on screen in a darkened room, the common features theatre-going shared with what Sergio Raffaelli has dubbed the "oral cinema period" (1896–1905) should not be overlooked: early cinema, with its static camera to capture the *mise en scène*, was accompanied by live music. Plots were usually familiar, and typically, professional actors would perform the drama in front of the screen while someone in the audience would read aloud the intertitles for those who were illiterate.[7] Thus, cinema spectators in the period prior to World War I were self-conscious and cognisant of one another and the evening's entertainment as a *construct* in the same way as they were when attending a play or an opera. This made the experience a more sociable and less transcendent one akin to theatre-going. From World War I onwards, what was to become the practice of sitting in a darkened room with the screen finally overtook

Italy's "brief and glorious season" as the popularity of Hollywood's classical narrative cinema expanded.

Debates in Classical Narrative Cinema Spectatorship

Following the post-structuralist shift and Roland Barthes's declaration of the "death of the author" in the 1960s, reader-response theory paved the way for theories of film spectatorship to emerge.[8] Film theory of the 1970s presented a monolithic, ahistorical, and deterministic account of the "apparatus" of cinema as a "technological system with psychic ramifications, concerning fantasies of regression and affirmations of the imaginary order,"[9] in a way that theatre and opera are not. Spectators of live performances, including opera and theatre, have a heightened awareness of other spectators in the auditorium and the actors performing on stage. Theorists including Jean-Louis Baudry, Christian Metz, and Laura Mulvey were pivotal in discussions of the psychoanalytic workings of how classical cinema addresses an ideal male spectator by "[satisfy]ing a primordial wish for pleasurable looking."[10] For Baudry, sitting in the cinema in a darkened room created a regressive "womb like" sensation, and Metz introduced the idea that the regressive state encourages the possibilities of reactivating the Lacanian "imaginary signifier" associated with the development of subjectivity: voyeurism and the "primal scene."[11]

Cinema theorists who have contended with the issue of female spectatorship have all striven to negotiate and re-theorise the role of the feminine in an institutional mode of representation inscribed by the masculine. Drawing on Freudian psychoanalytic theory, Mulvey argued that the cinematic spectator's pleasure in looking ("scopophilia") is split between binaries of active/male and passive/female, and that these pleasures are based on fetishistic and voyeuristic forms of looking which construct woman as spectacle; the (male) spectator identifies with the male protagonist in the narrative, and thus with his objectification of the female figure via the "male gaze." For Mulvey, the feminine gaze is either aligned with the objectified portrayal of femininity, or with the active male protagonist as the locus of power. Later, feminist film scholar Mary Ann Doane agreed that the feminine gaze is indeed impossible because women's closeness to the female body means that she "overidentifies" with the image of the woman on screen.[12] In an attempt to theorise a feminine spectatorial position that cannot simply be reduced to a masculine (masochistic) heterosexual equivalent, a proliferation of publications during the 1980s responded to Mulvey's and Doane's polemics. Jackie Stacey drew on two narrative Hollywood films that develop around one woman's obsession with another woman to critique psychoanalytic film theory's "rigid distinction between *either* [male] desire *or* [female] identification" and its failure to "address the construction of desires which involve a specific interplay of both processes."[13] She called for a nuanced spectrum with which to explore feminine spectatorships, arguing that there is a "homoerotic component" in films about women with intimate friendships, even if there is no explicit lesbianism or bisexuality. Tania Modleski published a study on popular pleasure and feminine subjectivity in relation to the romance, the Gothic novel, and soap operas for female spectators and readers, in which she challenged those who dismissed these pleasures as "frivolous" escapism. Taking issue with the Frankfurt School's rejection of popular culture as merely reproductive of the *status quo* and the typical dismissal of popular women's texts as insignificant, trivial, and unworthy of critical analysis, she drew on psychoanalytic theories and the work of Fredric Jameson to shed light on the *pleasure* they gave to women.[14] In addition, through a study of Hitchcock films, Modleski also showed how the ways in which women are oppressed by patriarchy "allow the female spectator to feel anger that is very different from the masochistic response."[15]

Literary and cultural studies scholar Janice Radway's ethnographic study *Reading the Romance* (1984) signalled a new direction within feminist readings of popular culture to determine the specificity of a particular readership response. Radway analysed reading romantic novels as a practice within the social context of a particular group of women's lives, to argue that reading was a way for housewives to assert their autonomy within households in which they were there for others, despite the content of the romantic novel which defines women as dependent on men.[16] Modleski objected to Radway's comparison of women's reading of romances to "folk performances" which "contest the hegemonic imposition of bourgeois culture on [...] subordinate groups," calling instead for a more feminist critical view of mass cultural production and mass cultural artefacts.[17] Influenced by Richard Dyer's seminal work on stardom from the 1970s which introduced the idea of the "star text," and drawing on Radway's ethnographic work, in 1994 Jackie Stacey published *Star Gazing*, which challenged the universalism of the psychoanalytic approach.[18] Stacey argued that "[t]he uniformity of the trajectories of feminine subjectivity, based on the universal feminine psyche, leave little room for a diversity of positions of readership/viewership. [...] The conclusions [...] cannot tell us anything about how these texts are read differently by specific groups of women."[19] By carrying out oral history interviews with female cinema spectators of Hollywood films in the 1940s and '50s, Stacey instead focused on the consumption and escapism of, and identification with the film star to give a new direction to questions of popular culture, cinematic pleasures, and feminine desire.

Gaylyn Studlar also rejected Mulvey's and Doane's idea of women's masochistic identification with the passive female subject.[20] Drawing on the neo-Freudian idea presented by Julia Kristeva on the pre-Oedipal stage of psychoanalysis, in which the unresolved mother-daughter relationship is established and which the patriarchy attempts to repress and deny, Studlar argued that the male spectator finds it necessary to repress certain "feminine" aspects of himself.[21] Moreover, she argued that men are forced to project these almost exclusively onto the woman who *does the suffering for him*. Thus, the male spectator both identifies with, and dreads, the woman on screen because she potentially represents a threat to the patriarchy. At the same time, she articulates his (repressed) "feminine" aspects. It is this viewing position that I find most compelling and applicable to the thesis of this book.

In Italian film studies in Italy, Monica Dall'Asta has spearheaded important work on "lost" female film pioneers, and Silvio Alovisio and Cristina Jandelli have both written on female spectatorship and stars.[22] In the Anglophone context, Stephen Gundle was the first to examine the "star text" in Italian cinema; later, Catherine O'Rawe drew attention to an absence of work on feminine spectatorships in Italian culture.[23] Influenced by Stacey's ethnographic approach, O'Rawe and her co-authors recently published a monograph exploring elderly peoples' affective memories and experiences of cinema-going in post-war Italy.[24] Drawing on video interviews, questionnaires, archival material on distribution, exhibition and programming, box-office figures as well as film journals and popular magazines, they examine this rich data in the context of the booming film industry of the period. In literary and cultural studies in the British context, Lisa Stead recently explored cinema's place in the fiction and critical writings of major literary female figures who presented their reflections on cinema-going in their writings.[25]

Women Theatre Spectators

A crucial difference between classical narrative cinema and theatre spectators is that

> [E]ven more than cinema, [theatre] requires the active participation of many people [...]. The spectator is never alone; as his or her eye takes in what is presented on stage, it also takes in other spectators, just as indeed they observe him or her.[26]

While approaches to spectatorship in film studies have tended to draw on either psychoanalytic theories or ethnography, work on theatre audiences has largely taken a historical materialist approach.[27] Moreover, since the 1960s there has been a clear shift in thinking from the study of dramatic texts as literature *per se* to a multi-directional understanding of theatre as an "event" involving audiences, production teams (comprising directors, costume, and lighting designers), agents, publicists, and critics. Later, the disciplines of literary and dramatic criticism, as well as musicology, began drawing on social and historical anthropology in their analyses of audiences, as well as on semiotics and semantics in the 1980s and 1990s.[28] Taking a materialist approach, Jill Dolan published *The Feminist Spectator as Critic* (1988), which emphasised differences in spectators' viewing positions in the theatre according to gender.[29] Echoing

Mulvey's lament *vis-à-vis* the apparent absence of a feminine gaze, Dolan argued that

> [p]erformance usually addresses the male spectator as an active subject and encourages him to identify with the male hero in the narrative. The same representations tend to objectify women performers and female spectators as passive, invisible, unspoken subjects.[30]

Concomitantly, and thanks in no small measure to the emergence of the field of cultural studies pioneered by Stuart Hall, feminist scholars in studies of film, opera, literature, theatre, and art history began to apply new approaches to their respective disciplines. In particular, Griselda Pollock argued in *Vision and Difference* (1988) that American artist Mary Cassatt's painting, in which a woman spectator is represented looking through her eyeglasses leaning over her balcony to watch a performance intently, "actively looking [...], prevents her from being objectified and she figures as the subject of her own look."[31]

In 1989, Marvin Carlson published *Theatre Audiences and the Reading of Performance*, in which he called for theatre studies to apply reader-response theory to theatre audiences.[32] Susan Bennett's second edition of *Theatre Audiences: A Theory of Production and Reception* (first published in 1990) responded to the call by examining "the audience" (in the singular) as a cultural phenomenon and the practice of marginalised and non-traditional audiences of the 1960s.[33] More recently, Bruce McConachie's *Engaging Audiences* (2008) drew on cognitive science – specifically, our use of visuomotor representations: a process of simulation whereby mirror neurons within the brain enact the very action that is witnessed.[34] According to McConachie, simulation provides the theatre spectator with "the ability to 'read the minds' of actor/characters, to intuit their beliefs, intentions and emotions by watching their motor actions." As such, McConachie argues, the theatre spectator becomes a co-maker in the theatrical event.[35]

Work in Italy in theatre studies thus far has also been confined to a materialist approach. Bruno Sanguanini's 1989 *Il pubblico all'italiana: formazione del pubblico e politiche culturali tra stato e teatro* (Italian Audiences: The Formation of the Audience and Cultural Politics Between the State and Theatre) opened up discussions, but these did not include women spectators. It was Claudio Medolesi's and Ferdinando Taviani's 1991 *Teatro e spettacolo nel primo Ottocento* (Theatre and Spectacle in the Early Nineteenth Century) that first discussed a particularly exceptional, upper-class woman spectator: Madame De Staël.[36] Remarking on her 1810 essay *De l'Allemagne* in a five-page discussion, the authors considered Staël's cerebral musings on the romantic poet August Schlegel (1767–1845) performing Werner's *Der neunundzwanzigste Februar (Twenty-ninth of February).*[37] Similarly, Mirella Schino's 1992 book *Il teatro di Eleonora Duse* (The Theatre of Eleonora Duse) makes a passing

Figure 1.1 Mary Cassatt, *In the lodge* (1878).

reference to Duse and the *grande attrice* Adelaide Ristori (1822–1906) as spectators while referring to Silvio d'Amico's encounter with Duse in 1921, when he interviewed her.[38] In 2001 Carlotta Sorba included a chapter on spectators in her book *Teatri: L'Italia del melodramma nell'età del Risorgimento* (Theatres: Melodrama in Italy in the Age of the Risorgimento), though differences in spectating practices and positions according to gender go largely unremarked.[39] In addition, the recent publication by Matilde Tortora and Laura Mariani of late nineteenth-century Italian women writers' letters addressed to women performers have revealed their mutual solidarity and admiration.[40] In *L'attrice del cuore* (Actress of Hearts, 2005), for example, Mariani drew attention not only to the actor Giacinta Pezzana (1841–1919) as a *spectator* in her correspondence with the feminist writer and poet Sibilla Aleramo, but also women spectators in general, who, in the late nineteenth century, "became more visible and numerous" and "demand[ed] a repertoire that addresse[d] contemporary social and cultural change."[41] This paved the way for the 2013 publication *Nuove frontiere per la storia di genere* (New Frontiers in Gender History) which included an introduction and three essays on women theatre and opera spectators from the eighteenth century to the present day.[42] Though these Italian studies are important insofar as they are the first to theorise and examine a cultural history of feminine spectatorships by drawing on archival materials, studies in Italy have so far generally resisted dialogue with the feminist psychoanalytic work done in Anglophone film studies, oral history, and cultural studies.

Women Opera Spectators

Work in opera studies on the "female gaze" has followed a similar trajectory to theatre studies, insofar as it has tended not to incorporate work carried out in feminist psychoanalytic film theory. Susan McClary was the first to draw operatic music into feminist interpretation in 1991.[43] In seeking to uncover music's social meanings, she focused on how musical representations of gender can tell us much about a particular composer's attitude towards a given character, as well as how the characters will be read in a given geo-social and historical context. Taking performance as much into account as opera's plots, and contesting Mulvey's "male gaze," in the same year, Carolyn Abbate asserted that

> Listening to the female singing voice is a more complicated phenomenon [than watching her]. Visually, the character singing is the passive object of our gaze. But, aurally, she is resonant; her musical speech drowns out everything in range, and we sit as passive objects, battered by that voice. As a voice she slips into the "male/active/subject" position in other ways as well, since a singer, more than any other musical performer, enters into that Jacobin uprising inherent in the phenomenology of live performance and stands before us having wrested the composing voice away from the librettist and composer who wrote the score.

Abbate thus opened up a space for discussion of the "*physical* force of music" and the contribution of the performer over "the monological authority of 'the Composer'."[44] She viewed opera as the locus of women's victory: a realm beyond narrative plot in which women exist as sonority and sheer physical volume, asserting themselves outside spectacle and escaping murderous fates. Continuing with a celebratory notion of the female singing voice and focusing on women's roles in opera in the nineteenth century, in 1992, Susan Rutherford published an essay in which she described opera as "a positive symbol of liberation and artistic fulfilment, which was quintessentially the voice of freedom,"[45] after which, in 1993, Abbate coined the term "envoicing" – literally meaning *in* voice.[46] Through a reading of Patrick Conrad's film *Mascara* (1978), she suggested that

> opera, far from being a revenge tragedy that Catherine Clément calls the "undoing of women," is a genre that so displaces the authorial musical voice onto female characters and female singers that it largely reverses a conventional opposition of male (speaking) subject and female (observed) object.[47]

Adapting Abbate's ideas to the physical prowess of the dancer, Sally Banes in *Dancing Women: Female Bodies on Stage* (1998) argued that in performance, dancers' "stress on nuances of gesture or posture [...] seem to undermine or render ironic the narrative flow," thus usurping the male/active/subject position of the author of the narrative.[48] Later, feminist philosopher Adriana Cavarero in the Italian context argued that at the heart of opera lies the triumph of the female voice, of the vocal over the semantic, the feminine over the masculine (the *logos*).[49] Though women have had important roles in opera since Monteverdi, Simonetta Chiappini has recently argued in relation to women in opera during the Risorgimento

> women's voice arrived (and arrives) at the heart of the spectator with a potency that the rigid system of nineteenth-century patriarchal legitimacy believed unimaginable. Perhaps the responsibility lies with music, or rather, song [...].[50]

Thus, the potency of song, or voice, arguably functioned as a liberating force for women performers and their listeners. Any contradiction that the suffering heroine/Fallen Woman in Italian tragic opera signified in performance, through simultaneously embodying the desire for sex and virtue – regardless of any prowess her performer's acting and singing ability displayed – was surpassed by the sheer sonority of her voice due to her wider *tessitura* (her vocal range) and her ability to "out-sing" her male counterpart.

Work focusing on the experience of the spectator rather than the performer has only recently begun to emerge in opera studies. Alessandra Campana's *Opera and Modern Spectatorship in Late Nineteenth-Century Italy* (2013) drew on Kaja Silverman's notion of suture to show through a reading of detailed stage manuals how opera aspired to constitute its audiences as a reproducible commodity by regulating them.[51] In her final chapter Campana argues that film "sought to transform itself into art" by director Nino Oxilia's use of a film score composed by Pietro Mascagni for Oxilia's film *Rapsodia satanica* (1917).[52] Rutherford's *Verdi, Opera, Women* (also published in 2013) argued that Verdi's operas "provided a multi-faceted image of 'woman' that more closely responded to the lived experience of his spectators than that of any other previous Italian composer."[53] Drawing on historical sources (letters and realist fiction), and secondary sources to demonstrate that "Verdi's operas raised very real questions about some of the most fundamental matters concerning Ottocento society – women's relationship to state, to family, and to herself," Rutherford is concerned with the mediated relationship between Verdi's operas and the life-world of the female audience, asking: "[W]hat might the Italian female spectator have seen in Verdi's operas that connected her to her own lived experience? What was missing? Where did her life and that of the female character mesh, and where did it diverge?"[54] Rutherford drew on McConachie's cognitive approach, emphasising the commonalities of spectators rather than focusing on individual subjectivities; yet her study does not account for individual experiences of affect and the unconscious, or what Helen Freshwater calls the "cultural reference points, political beliefs, sexual preferences, personal histories, and immediate preoccupations" each individual audience member brings to their interpretation of a performance or screening.[55] Moreover, Rutherford cautions against drawing conclusions about women spectators on the basis that during the Risorgimento

> information [...] is tantalising but also fragmented, circumscribed and simply rather thin on the ground. In the absence of consistent material about substantial numbers of female spectators, we have to rely heavily on just a few – who may or may not be representative.[56]

In fact, and as will become clear in this book, the opposite is true of Italy at the *fin de siècle*. By extending what we know so far, I reveal here how the late nineteenth century contains an abundant archive of reviews, reflections and experiences of theatre, opera, and cinema-going among ordinary and extraordinary middle-class women (be they writers, actors, singers, translators, directors or journalists). For the first time, their fascination and identification with, and pleasure in watching the female performer on stage and screen is presented as representative of substantial and increasing numbers of discerning female spectators.

Women Spectators Across the Disciplines

What can a cross-disciplinary approach to women spectators add to these studies of spectatorships? Since spectators were often watching a combination of the performing arts and silent film in post-unification

Italy up to the end of World War I in any given evening – particularly if they were attending one of the many *politeame* (non-lavishly decorated egalitarian theatres, not unlike the British music halls that housed up to around 3,000 spectators, and were built throughout the peninsula from the 1870s onwards) – our understanding of their "gazes" becomes more complex and nuanced at this historical juncture, in which the symbiotic connections between the different arts were competing side by side for audiences' pleasure and engagement as never before. Male artists and writers in France had grown obsessed with studying the female subject following the French Revolution, which, as Peter Brooks has argued, required the body of the individual to become accountable and to converge with a later psychoanalytical emphasis on that body as a female victim.[57] This had found expression in French fictional works that bore the title of the name of the female protagonist, for example, Alexandre Soumet's *Norma, ou L'infanticide* (1831), Alexandre Dumas *fils*'s *La Dame aux camélias* (1852) adapted from his novel (1848), Gustave Flaubert's *Madame Bovary* (1956), and later, Émile Zola's *Thérèse Raquin* (1868), are just some examples among many that were adapted for the Italian page, stage, and screen. As Enza De Francisci observes

> [M]any of these roles later inspired [European] operatic composers to concentrate their operas on the *demi-monde*. Such operatic works include Giuseppe Verdi's *La traviata* (1853), based on Violetta in Dumas' *La dame aux caméllias* who was one of the first courtesans to emerge on the operatic stage; George Bizet's gypsy woman *Carmen* (1875) adapted from Prosper Mérimée's eponymous novella (1845); Giacomo Puccini's renowned singer *Tosca* (1900) based on Sardou's homonymous play (1887); and Richard Strauss's seductive *Salomé* (1905) taken from Oscar Wilde's eponymous play which he originally wrote in French (1894).[58]

Italians had a particular fascination with this melodramatic, hystericised embodiment of the Magdalene archetype. Of Giacomo Puccini's 13 operas, eight bear the name of the female lead, some of which are drawn from previously successful French novels and plays, for example: *Manon Lescaut* (first performed in 1893) from Antoine François Prévost's novel published in 1731; *La Bohème* (whose première was in 1896) is based on Henri Murger's *Scènes de la vie de bohème* (1851); and *Tosca* (1900) is drawn from Victorien Sardou's play first performed in 1887. Other titles are drawn from short stories, novels, and plays further afield: *Madama Butterfly* (which premièred in 1904) is from American John Luther Long's short story "Madame Butterfly" (1898); *La fanciulla del West* (first performed in 1910) comes from American theatrical producer David Belasco's *The Girl of the Golden West* (1905); *La Rondine* (1917) is based on a *libretto* by Alfred Maria Willner and Heinz Reichert. Still others are from national sources: *Suor Angelica* (1918) is based on a *libretto* by Giovacchino Forzano, while *Turandot* (1926) derives from Carlo Gozzi's 1762 play from the twelfth-century Persian epic *Haft Peykar* by Nizami.

Among Italy's silent diva films, there is Francesca Bertini's *Assunta Spina* (1915) based on Salvatore Di Giacomo's novel and play of the same name, and Alfredo De Antoni's *Tosca* (1918), to name but two. In these, the trope of the "realist" suffering heroine/Fallen Woman, neither before nor since, had ever been so visually prevalent in live performance and on-screen over a concentrated period. She is relatable to, and familiar to her audiences even while the opera in which she exists may be set a century prior. As a metaphor and repository for universal suffering and society's ills (e.g., widespread poverty, unemployment, venereal disease, sexual exploitation), the diva – the female performer – was as much an idealised projection of desire as she was a scapegoat for every (hu)man, following Studlar's notion of spectatorship. In her performance and the printed media, the diva had a celebrity following and was idolised by (mostly) women while othered as the "dark continent" by entrenched patriarchal societal structures and misogyny. And yet, she offered a possibility of hope and solidarity, and inspired admiration, while symbolising angst and transformation in an era of modernity and rapid industrialisation. Typically entangled in a conflict involving love, loss, betrayal, and desire, the woman performer was a catalyst for her female spectators' epistemophilia, engagement, pleasure, and imaginary desires and longings.

In his *Deceit, Desire and the Novel* (1961), the French philosopher René Girard put forward the idea of desire being triangular and mimetic: humans desire the idolised other because (s)he is desired by another. Referring to the protagonist of Flaubert's *Madame Bovary*, Girard argues that "Emma Bovary desires through the romantic heroines who fill her imagination"[59]; an idea that may well be applied more broadly to women spectators beyond the realm of fiction. For it was in the moment of live performance and, albeit curated, screened spectacle, with live musical accompaniment prior to the introduction of the point-of-view shot and the shot/reverse-shot (first used in Italian cinema in 1919), that middle-class spectators were invited to participate vicariously with the realist suffering heroine/Fallen Woman and/or to identify with her. Yet, simultaneously, they perceived her as a "threat" to the stability of the *status quo* and the new nation. In the same way as middle-class women readers of domestic realist fiction were invited to participate in the female protagonist's exploration of her personhood – as happens, for example, in Neera's *Teresa* (1886)[60] – at a time when literacy levels remained relatively low among women, the theatre and screen auditoria invited the forgetting of one's social self through the illusory barrier of the fourth wall.[61] Consequently, spectators were invited to explore their boundless imaginary inner lives; yet, beyond these, growing numbers of middle-class women were, in law, at least, strictly policed and circumscribed.

Pisanelli's Civil Code of 25 June 1865, which was based on the Napoleonic Code imposed in Italy during French rule, excluded women from all areas of political activity, reinforcing the gender stereotype of the domestic interior as female and private. The lead female performer of women's film, theatre, and opera thus provided an overarching, unifying bridge across stage and screen in her embodiment as the male-constructed Fallen Woman, signalling paradoxically at once hope for Italy's progress and transformation, and a threat symbolising Italy's moral decline, an "ineffable spirituality, [...] ritualistic otherness, and an intuitive aura about invisible things."[62]

Conclusion

Technology was advancing at a pace that was unprecedented: the American Thomas Edison (1847–1931) invented the phonograph in 1877, and Scottish-born Alexander Bell (1847–1922) developed a wax-cylinder version of it in the early 1880s known as the graphophone, allowing for lengthier recordings and a superior playback powered (later) by electricity. The gramophone, invented in 1894 by German-American Emile Berliner (1851–1921), was recording performances that were once believed to have been ineffable and ephemeral, while Guglielmo Marconi (1874–1937) had developed long-distance communication and founded his telecommunications company in 1897. The magic lantern had evolved into the silent screen, and mass production of the image and sound was starting to create a market; thanks to foreign exports, the entertainment industry in Italy had never been so lucrative. Young women were generally frowned upon by priests, parents, and right-wing politicians for reading novels for their association with themes including female desire, eroticism, and sexuality (thought to induce symptoms of so-called "hysteria"). Yet we know from first-person accounts, articles in periodicals, essays, and conduct literature, as well as paintings, that (young) women read fiction, and in increasing numbers towards the turn of the century, following the growth in the number of female pupils attending secondary schools from the 1880s onwards.[63] Similarly, though traditionalists felt that opera and theatre-going carried risks for women because of their associations with sexuality, we know from theatre and opera-going depictions in realist fiction from Flaubert's *Madame Bovary* onwards, as well as columns in newspapers and journals for women from the 1870s, that probably around half of the spectators were female.

In Chapter 2 we turn to Italy to look more closely at where women sat in the theatres and how they were expected to behave, and examine middle-class women's access to culture during the second half of the nineteenth century – a period in which Italians' fascination and obsession with suffering heroines/Fallen Women on stage and screen was at its height.

Notes

1 Ernst Gombrich, *Art and Illusion: A Study in the Psychology of Pictorial Representation* (New York: Pantheon Books, 1960), pp. 182–3; p. 222.
2 Silvia Diaz, "The Attractions of the 'Cinema Attractions' to Female Spectatorship," (unpublished doctoral thesis, Lehigh University, 2004), p. 2.
3 Giorgio Bertellini, "Introduction: Traveling Lightness," in *Italian Silent Cinema: A Reader*, ed. by Giorgio Bertellini (New Barnet: John Libbey Publishing Ltd., 2013), p. 3.
4 Christopher Wagstaff, "Cinema," in *Italian Cultural Studies: An Introduction*, ed. by David Forgacs and Robert Lumley (Oxford: Oxford University Press, 1996), pp. 216–32 (p. 219).
5 Carlotta Sorba, *Teatri: L'Italia del melodramma nell'età del Risorgimento* (Bologna: Il Mulino, 2001), p. 251.
6 Paolo Caneppele, "Research on Local Moviegoing: Trends and Future Perspectives," in *Italian Silent Cinema*, pp. 305–14 (p. 308).
7 Sergio Raffaelli, "On the Language in Silent Films in Italy," in *Italian Silent Cinema*, pp. 247–53 (p. 247).
8 Reader-response theory's main theorists include Stanley Fish and Wolfgang Iser. It focuses on reader or audience reaction to a text, perhaps more than the text itself, emphasising the role of the reader in actively constructing texts rather than passively consuming them.
9 Judith Mayne, *Cinema and Spectatorship* (London: New York: Routledge, 1993), p. 44.
10 Laura Mulvey, "Visual Pleasure and Narrative Cinema," *Screen* 16:3 (Autumn 1975), 6–18, (9).
11 Mayne, *Cinema and Spectatorship*, p. 44. In Freudian psychoanalysis, the "primal scene" refers to the (male) child's fantasy (or actual observation) of their parents engaging in sexual intercourse. Interpreted as an act of violence on the part of the father, it is thought to induce "castration anxiety" and lays the foundations for the Oedipus Complex (the male child's unconscious sexual desire for his mother). Lacan's imaginary "mirror stage" marks the beginning of the formation of the ego and occurs anywhere from age 6–18 months when the child identifies (his) own (literal or symbolic) image in the mirror. Metz relates the concept of Lacan's imaginary to the cinematic signifier where the screen is the mirror inducing identifications related to those of the mirror phase.
12 Mary Ann Doane, "Film and the Masquerade: Theorizing the Female Spectator," *Screen* 23:3–4 (1982), 78–87 (80).
13 Jackie Stacey, "Desperately Seeking Difference," *Screen* 28:1 (1987), 48–61, (61).
14 See: Tania Modleski, *Loving With a Vengeance: Mass-Produced Fantasies for Women* (London: Methuen, 1982). See, also: Fredric Jameson, "Reification and Utopia in Mass Culture," *Social Text* 1 (1979), 130–48.
15 Tania Modleski, "Hitchcock, Feminism and the Patriarchal Unconscious," in *Issues in Feminist Film Criticism*, ed. by Patricia Erens (Bloomington, IN: Indiana University Press, 1990), pp. 41–57. https://publish.iupress.indiana.edu/read/issues-in-feminist-film-criticism/section/f89f23a1-740a-4b81-bde5-92356d0a98c8 [accessed 20 May 2019].

16 See: Janice Radway, *Reading the Romance: Women, Patriarchy and Popular Literature* (London, Chapel Hill: University of North Carolina Press, 1984).
17 Tania Modleski, "Introduction," in *Studies in Entertainment: Critical Approaches to Mass Culture*, ed. by Tania Modleski (Bloomington and Indianapolis: Indiana University Press, 1986), pp. ix–xviii (p. xii).
18 See: Richard Dyer, *Stars* (London: British Film Institute, 1979). The "star text" refers to the production and construction of the star persona across a range of media and cultural practices, including promotional material and publicity. See, also: Jackie Stacey, *Star Gazing: Hollywood Cinema and Female Spectatorship* (London and New York: Routledge, 1994).
19 Stacey, *Star Gazing*, p. 44.
20 Gaylyn Studlar, *In the Realm of Pleasure: Von Sternberg, Dietrich, and the Masochistic Aesthetic* (New York: Columbia University Press, 1992), p. 2.
21 The pre-Oedipal stage in psychoanalytic theory refers to the time from birth to around three years in a female and male child's psychosexual development. During this stage, the mother is the child's exclusive love object and the father is not yet considered a rival.
22 See: Monica Dall'Asta, "L'altra metà del cinema muto italiano," in *Non solo dive: pioniere del cinema italiano*, ed. by Monica Dall'Asta (Bologna: Cineteca di Bologna, 2008), pp. 9–16; Silvio Alovisio, "La spettatrice muta: Il pubblico cinematografico femminile nell'Italia del primo Novecento," in *Non solo dive*, pp. 269–88; Cristina Jandelli, *Le dive italiane del cinema muto* (Palermo: L'Epos, 2006); Cristina Jandelli "La Marion di Vivanti e Bertini, dalla pagina allo schermo e ritorno," in *Cinema e scritture femminili: letterate italiane fra la pagina e lo schermo*, ed. by Lucia Cardone and Sara Filippelli (Rome: Trerefusi, 2011), pp. 19–30.
23 See: Stephen Gundle, "Stars and Stardom in the Study of Italian Cinema," *Italian Studies* 63:2 (2008), 261–66; Stephen Gundle, *Fame Amid the Ruins: Italian Film Stardom in the Age of Neorealism* (New York: Berghahn Books, 2019); Catherine O'Rawe, "The Italian Spectator and Her Critics," *The Italianist* 30 (2010), 272–89.
24 See: Daniela Treveri Gennari, Catherine O'Rawe, Danielle Hipkins, Silvia Dibeltulo, and Sarah Culhane, *Italian Cinema Audiences: Histories and Memories of Cinema-going in Post-war Italy* (London: Bloomsbury, 2020).
25 See: Lisa Stead, *Off to the Pictures: Cinemagoing, Women's Writing and Movie Culture in Interwar Britain* (Edinburgh: Edinburgh University Press, 2016).
26 Anne Ubersfeld, *Reading Theatre*, trans. by Frank Collins (Toronto: Toronto University Press, 2014), pp. 3–4.
27 First articulated by Karl Marx, this approach argues that history is the result of material conditions rather than ideals; that a society's material mode of production fundamentally determines society's organisation and development.
28 See, for example, Christopher Small, "Performance as Ritual: Sketch for an Inquiry into the True Nature of a Symphonic Concert," in *Lost in Music: Culture, Style and the Musical Event*, ed. by Avron Levine White (London: Routledge & Kegan Paul, 1987), pp. 6–32.
29 See: Jill Dolan, *The Feminist Spectator as Critic* (Ann Arbor: UMI Research Press, 1988).
30 Dolan, *The Feminist Spectator as Critic*, 2nd edition (Michigan: University of Michigan Press, 2012 [1988]), p. 2.

31 Griselda Pollock, *Vision and Difference: Femininity, Feminism and Histories of Art* (London: Routledge, 1988), p. 76.
32 See: Marvin Carlson, "Theatre Audiences and the Reading of Performance," in *Interpreting the Theatrical Past: Essays in the Historiography of Performance* ed. by Thomas Postlewait and Bruce A. McConachie (Iowa City: University of Iowa Press, 1989), pp. 82–98.
33 See: Susan Bennett, *Theatre Audiences: A Theory of Production and Reception* (London: Routledge, 1997).
34 Bruce McConachie, *Engaging Audiences: A Cognitive Approach to Spectating in the Theatre* (Basingstoke: Palgrave Macmillan, 2008), p. 65.
35 *Ibid.*
36 See: Bruno Sanguanini, *Il pubblico all'italiana: formazione del pubblico e politiche culturali tra stato e teatro* (Rome: Franco Angeli, 1989) and Claudio Medolesi and Ferdinando Taviani, *Teatro e spettacolo nel Primo Ottocento* (Rome: Laterza, 1991), pp. 144–9.
37 Medolesi and Taviani, *Teatro e spettacolo nel primo Ottocento*, p. 145.
38 Mirella Schino, *Il teatro di Eleonora Duse* (Bologna: Il Mulino, 1992), p. 247.
39 Sorba, *Teatri*, pp. 93–153. See, also: Carlotta Sorba, "To Please the Public: Composers and Audiences in Nineteenth-Century Italy," *Journal of Interdisciplinary History* 36:4 (Spring 2006), 595–614.
40 See: *Matilde Serao a Eleonora Duse: lettere*, ed. by Matilde Tortora (Naples: Graus, 2004) and *L'attrice del cuore: Storia di Giacinta Pezzana attraverso le lettere*, ed. by Laura Mariani (Florence: Le lettere, 2005).
41 Laura Mariani, "Scene e scrittura, politica e amicizia: una vita «da gigante»," in *L'attrice del cuore*, pp. 9–57 (p. 16); see, also: p. 16, ftn. 26.
42 See the section edited by Annamaria Cecconi, "Il genere del pubblico: questioni per una storia della ricezione femminile nelle arti della scena" in *Nuove frontiere per la storia di genere*, ed. by Laura Guidi and Maria Rosaria Pelizzari (Salerno: University of Salerno Press, 2013), pp. 181–213.
43 See: Susan McClary, *Feminine Endings: Music, Gender, & Sexuality* (Minneapolis: University of Minnesota Press, 1991).
44 Carolyn Abbate, *Unsung Voices: Opera and Musical Narrative in the Nineteenth Century* (Princeton, NJ.: Princeton University Press, 1991), p. x.
45 Susan Rutherford, "The Voice of Freedom: Images of the Prima Donna," in *The New Woman and Her Sisters: Feminism and the Theater, 1850–1914*, ed. by Viv Gardner and Susan Rutherford (London: Harvester Wheatsheaf, 1992), pp. 95–113 (p. 95).
46 See: Carolyn Abbate, "Opera, or the Envoicing of Women," in *Musicology and Difference: Gender and Sexuality in Music Scholarship*, ed. by Ruth A. Solie (Berkeley, 1993), pp. 225–58.
47 *Ibid.*, pp. 228–9. See, also: Catherine Clément, *Opera, Or, The Undoing of Women*, trans. by Betsy Wing, first published 1988 (London: Tauris, 1997).
48 Sally Banes, *Dancing Women: Female Bodies on Stage* (London: Routledge, 1998), p. 10.
49 Adriana Cavarero, *A più voci. Filosofia dell'espressione vocale* (Milan: Feltrinelli, 2003), p. 145.
50 Simonetta Chiappini, "La voce della martire. Dagli «evirati cantori» all'eroina romantica," in *Storia d'Italia*, Annali 22: Il Risorgimento, ed. by Alberto

Mario Banti and Paul Ginsborg (Turin: Einaudi, 2007), pp. 289–328 (p. 314). See, also: Annamaria Cecconi, "Le emozioni della spettatrice d'opera," *Nuova Civiltà delle Macchine*, 1–2 (1998), 164–71.

51 "Suture" is the idea that the construction of film as a physical object creates a kind of anxiety for the viewer due to it being bound on all sides by the periphery of the camera; thus, the viewer's point of view is limited, reduced, and fixed.

52 Alessandra Campana, *Opera and Modern Spectatorship in Late Nineteenth-Century Italy* (Cambridge: Cambridge University Press, 2013), p. xiii.

53 Susan Rutherford, *Verdi, Women, Opera* (Cambridge: Cambridge University Press, 2013), p. 211.

54 *Ibid.*, pp. 21–2.

55 Helen Freshwater, *Theatre & Audience* (Basingstoke: Palgrave MacMillan, 2009), p. 6.

56 *Ibid.*, p. 22.

57 See: Peter Brooks, "Melodrama, Body, Revolution," in *Melodrama: Stage, Picture, Screen*, ed. by Jacky Bratton, Jim Cook, and Christine Gledhill (London: British Film Institute, 1994), pp. 11–24. Her heavily-surveilled spectre has arguably re-emerged in British culture in recent times in footage of the public emotional outpouring at the death of Diana, Princess of Wales (1961–97), and the rise in popularity of reality TV with deceased celebrities, including Jade Goody (1981–2009) and, more recently, Caroline Flack (1979–2020).

58 Enza De Francisci, *A 'New' Woman in Verga and Pirandello: From Page to Stage* (Oxford: Legenda, 2018), p. 36.

59 René Girard, *Deceit, Desire and the Novel: Self and Other in Literary Structure*, trans. by Yvonne Freccero (Baltimore, Maryland: Johns Hopkins Press, 1965), p. 5. Girard's triangles are generally those in which two active males are rivals for an unspecified and apparently passive female. In her book *Between Men: English Literature and Male Homosocial Desire* (New York: Columbia University Press, 1985), Eve Kosofsky Sedgwick opposes the notion of symmetrical sexual relations, arguing that a dialectic of power ignoring the male/female dichotomy fails to represent the asymmetrical power relations that fuel triangular desire.

60 Katharine Mitchell, *Italian Women Writers: Gender and Everyday Life in Fiction and Journalism, 1870–1910* (Toronto: University of Toronto Press, 2014), p. 117.

61 This was unashamedly broken down by Luigi Pirandello's *Sei personaggi in cerca d'autore* (Six Characters in Search of an Author, 1921) and with the onset of modernism.

62 Dalle Vacche, *Diva*, p. 1.

63 Writing in his column "L'arte di vivere," (The Art of Living) in 1890, the pseudonymous Il dottor Gigi attributes the reading of naturalistic or *verist* novels as "pornographic or pessimistic" and as "creat[ing] *nervousness* in so many young women," *Vita intima*, 17 June 1890, p. 21. On the woman reader in Italy, see: Lucia Re, "Passion and Sexual Difference: The Risorgimento and the Gendering of Writing in Nineteenth-Century Italian Culture," in *Making and Remaking Italy: The Cultivation of National Identity around*

the Risorgimento ed. by Albert Russell Ascoli and Krystyna von Henneberg (Oxford: Berg, 2001), pp. 155–200, and Ann Hallamore Caesar, "Women Readers and the Novel in Nineteenth-Century Italy," *Italian Studies* 56:1 (2001), 80–97.

2 Spectators, *Traviate*, and Women's Access to Culture

This chapter discusses the role of nineteenth-century Italian tragic opera performed in Italy's theatres, and explores the changing natures of theatres and *politeame* which hosted the silent screen from around 1897 until the early 1920s. It also investigates the emergence of the frequent recurring figure of the suffering and penitent Fallen Woman archetype on Italy's stage and screen, as well as women's access to education and the professions. My main assertion in what follows is that the emergence of increasing numbers of women writers and readers went hand in hand with a shift in expectations on female spectators of stage and screen: no longer were they expected to mingle and converse; instead, audiences were required to forget their social selves at curtain-up and pay attention to the plot, the characters (their voices and acting style), the setting, and lighting. I argue that this shift in social expectations and behaviours contributed to the formation of a female critical community among writers, readers, and performers as women spectators became more affected, engaged, and more critical of performances and screenings.

Today, Italy's film and theatre industries are relatively localised,[1] yet Italian opera enjoys an unrivalled international profile. According to statistics from 2019 compiled by Operabase, of the top five most performed composers in the world, four are Italian (Verdi, Puccini, Rossini, Donizetti). Among the top 10 most performed operas in the world, 6 are by Italian composers.[2] More Italian opera is produced and performed in Italy by its 51 opera companies than any other national opera in the world.[3] The well-known early-1990s Wall's ice-cream advertisement featuring Pavarotti in Puccini's *Tosca* breaking into the Neapolitan song "O sole mio" mid-aria to steal a *cornetto* from a woman spectator, not only captured and reinforced a caricature of so-called *italianità* but also conveyed the unusual extent to which opera, and, specifically, melodrama, is central to the Italian national psyche, so embedded is it in Italy's cultural imagination.

Opera was "Made in Italy" by an elite group of composers, intellectuals, humanists, and dramatists belonging to the Camerata de' Bardi in late sixteenth-century Florence. Indeed, the proto-opera music dramas of Jacopo Pieri and Giulio Caccini formed the basis of Claudio

DOI: 10.4324/9780429293511-3

Monteverdi's operas during the seventeenth century. It has henceforth been an integral part of the country's national, cultural, and performance heritage, including visual cultures such as film and television. It is still today cherished and celebrated as an Italian invention and does not carry the same elitist connotations as its Northern European counterparts.[4] During the sixteenth and seventeenth centuries, the operatic genre had been solely the entertainment of the elite, enjoyed by representatives of the aristocracy and ruling classes; but from around the end of the eighteenth century onwards, the urban masses, including *artigiani*, could enjoy opera. In the nineteenth century – in which Italy moved from being an occupied and divided territory by region and state to political, economic, and linguistic unification (in print cultures, at least[5]) – Italian Grand Opera was a unifying force of patriotism and the primary entertainment of the masses, including students, shopkeepers, manual workers, and prostitutes. As Antonio Gramsci reminds us, in the nineteenth century, opera was the only national popular form of entertainment for the masses,[6] stating that "the only literature [the popular classes] know are the *libretti* of nineteenth-century opera [...] [and consequently] members of the popular classes behave "operatically."[7]

Theatre-going was a common pastime in Italy for the urban middle and upper classes following the democratisation of opera in the early nineteenth century. At least until the 1848 revolutions, theatres were the central part of civic life and Italian opera was in its heyday. Its popularity began to flourish as never before, and the increase in the number of newly constructed theatres was brought about by three factors: the Napoleonic government in the north between 1797 and 1815 whose administration approved the construction of a significant number of new theatres;[8] the onset of urbanisation; and the birth and growth of the bourgeoisie, particularly in Milan. Carlotta Sorba calculates that between 1815 and 1868, 613 theatres were built in towns and cities throughout the peninsula, among which the majority were located in the north (400), 357 were in the centre, and only 169 were to be found in the south; by 1871, there were 940 theatres in 699 towns.[9] The growth in the number of theatres took place predominantly in the more wealthy north, and it created a demand for new repertoire: in the early 1800s, the public wanted novelty – either a new work, or one that had recently been favourably received elsewhere, particularly when high-profile singers were performing.[10]

Women typically occupied the front rows of boxes, and therefore could not help but engage with the action taking place on stage (middle-class young women were "on display" in the marriage market from age 13 onwards).[11] In some theatres in Turin, women could sit in the stalls.[12] Writing under her pseudonym "Gibus" (meaning "opera hat" in French) in her conduct book *Saper vivere* (Knowing How to Live, 1900), Matilde Serao advises young girls aged 13 to 15 to go only "rarely" to the theatre or to a concert, but by age 16 – despite not yet having made their entrance in the world, she urges them to go to *many* concerts, plays, and operas (age 15 was the legal age at which young women could marry).[13] Similarly, in the second edition of her conduct manual *Come devo comportarmi?* (How should I behave?, 1896), the writer Anna Vertua Gentile (1846–1926) pronounces on "the real woman spectator" who "watches attentively" and "behaves respectfully towards other spectators and performing artists, whose aim it is to entertain and to move their public, and who very often deserve encouragement, applause and approval."[14] Vertua Gentile disapproves of women who go to the theatre and show indifference to, or disdain for the performance, preferring to converse and receive guests in their boxes. Instead, she urges women to "listen attentively, watch, and show respect and encouragement towards artists."[15] It was assumed that by age 18, women were frequently spending their evenings out at the theatre, opera, or silent screen, where they were advised to

> always sit in between two ladies, never to use the binoculars (or hardly ever, and only ever to look at the stage, not in the auditorium), to *listen to the music attentively*, not to talk, not to make noise, and when someone visits [their] box, not to turn around or change seats.[16]

After 1815 and prior to unification, the audience also comprised wealthy patrons, the nobility, Austrian military men in the front row of the stalls, young middle-class men, professionals, entrepreneurs, as well as prostitutes, and, in the gallery, servants, students, shopkeepers, and artisans could be found.[17] With the exception of theatres in Milan and Venice, where audiences had a choice of venues showing a particular genre of live entertainment (e.g., plays, opera, *vaudeville*), as elsewhere in Europe and the United States, in Italy, theatres were typically the central hub of sociability for all social classes, with the exception of labourers, *contadini*, and beggars. Venues also hosted dances, special events, exhibitions, circus acts, and puppet shows in between the main performance in the many *politeame* from unification onwards. The price of tickets varied according to different theatres and different seating areas in the auditorium, but until unification they were especially cheap in all of the Italian states, and demand was high. The gallery at La Scala in Milan cost roughly as much as "a builder's labourer could earn in a day," and the price of a ticket in the stalls or a box was between 1 or 2.50 francs or lire.[18] The leading theatres in pre-unification Italy (*primari teatri d'Italia*) included Turin, Milan, Genoa, Venice, Florence, Rome (two theatres), Naples, and Palermo.[19] If theatres staged operas, these were mostly performed by Italian singers and the majority were composed and produced by Italian composers, librettists, and impresarios, particularly before the 1880s (until the 1850s, operas were expected to be new).[20] Invariably, though, operas were performed with short interludes of ballet between the acts during a theatre's main opera season, which tended to begin in December and continue until June, with plays offering the principal form of entertainment from September.[21] The frequency of the staging of women's operas deriving from French plays, and that bore the name of the suffering heroine/Fallen Woman, whose yearning, loss and grief played out for the majority of the performance in contrast to the hero's (despite the period being the so-called "moment" of the tenor), is striking. During 1889 to 1909 at La Fenice theatre in Venice, suffering heroines/Fallen Women performed to packed audiences on average seven times a year, appearing in at least five different operas: Puccini's *La Bohème* and *Tosca*, Mascagni's *Iris* and *Amica*, and Verdi's *La traviata*.[22]

Live representations of human suffering may offer momentary catharsis for spectators, who may identify with, and project onto the performer their own personal sufferings so as to release pent-up emotions and tap into private, deeply buried trauma. Since the performer can be metres away from the first row of spectators, and is performing in real time, her performance may feel more immediate, intimate, and even more intrusive to the spectator than an equivalent spectacle on the silent screen. (Indeed, scientists at University College London have recently shown how watching a live performance has a deeper emotional impact on the spectator than watching a screening.[23]) As well as differences in the transmission of performances of human suffering according to genre, there are also variations according to gender. More often than not, near to curtain-down the suffering opera heroine was punished for transgressing social norms according to *bourgeois* mores and prescriptions of behaviour imposed on well-to-do women. As we saw in the introduction, her adaptation for the Italian stage has its origins in French *bourgeois* literature and theatre, and France's (and Italy's) preoccupation with and anxiety about the Fallen Woman trope following the French Revolution.

Of "Fallen" Women and *femmes fatales*

The so-called Fallen Woman's active sexuality is implicit in her archetype's nomenclature, and the construct is based on Christianity's Mary Magdalene, who, as Jesus' disciple (and, some have claimed, lover), is arguably the secular alternative to the Virgin Mary and the icon who is most relatable to, and most resembles, humankind.[24] As Lucy Bolton argues, "Mary Magdalene is a character of perennial cultural fascination, as the epitome of the classic dichotomy of virgin and whore in Western Judeo-Christian culture."[25] Her popularisation as a "dangerously sexual but utterly penitent woman" emerged as a construct at a time of unprecedented transformation in Italy's social, cultural, and economic history in which middle-class women were entering the public sphere as never before, as writers, artists, performers, and campaigners for the vote and access to education.[26] With the advent of the diva film, she found expression in the characters played by divas including Francesca Bertini and Pina Menichelli. If she can be used to "justify" the sacrifice of women to the state, she can also be used, sometimes within the very same text, to generate a more profound understanding of the position of women socially, politically, and economically within the structures of Italian society. Typically, she finds expression in a melodramatic, hystericised body like that described by Peter Brooks, "a victimised woman's body, on which desire has inscribed an impossible history, a story of desire in an impasse."[27] As Danielle Hipkins and I have argued elsewhere

> Italian eighteenth and nineteenth century borrowings from French culture met with earlier Italian literary associations dating as far back as Dante and gave rise to a particularly intense symbolic entanglement of the female prostitute body with the state in the new Italy and the notion of the body politic.[28]

We saw in the introduction that tragic women's opera in the Italian masculine tradition, from Verdi's *La traviata* to Puccini's *Turandot*, is about women – their affective and romantic lives, their sufferings and ideological dilemmas, and performed by women – insofar as the suffering heroine is the "othered" yet sympathetic central character in the opera and has an immense capacity for love. The narratives in which she featured were typically based on "dangerous" (in the eyes of the conservative elite) novels and plays imported from France, whose recurring themes included female sexuality, adultery, matricide, prostitution, and rape. To name a few, Amilcare Ponchielli's *La Gioconda* (1876) is based on Victor Hugo's *Angelo, Tyan de Padoue* (1835); Puccini's *La Bohème* (1896) is drawn from Henri Murger's *Scènes de la vie de bohème* (1851), while Francesco Cilea's *Adriana Lecouvreur* (1902) is drawn from Eugène Scribe and Ernest Legouvé's play from 1849. Her name typically served as the opera's, play's, or film's title, and the plots spoke directly to women spectators' emotional lives. It is not coincidental that the construct emerges as a staple of Italian tragic women's opera with the erotic and sexually self-aware Violetta on the Italian stage in Verdi's *La traviata* – whose meaning is the Fallen Woman – first performed in 1853 at the Teatro La Fenice.[29] With the arrival of film as a mass medium and the first silent diva film (Mario Caserini's *Ma l'amor mio non muore!* (Everlasting Love), 1913), she was transposed to the silver screen through Lyda Borelli's performance in the role of Elsa. Verdi's heroine Violetta Valery from *La traviata*, a high-class courtesan, represents the first in a long line of young and "beautiful," sexually desirous and assertive, yet sympathetic (because they are suffering), tragic opera heroines whose feelings of sexual desire for the hero threaten to usurp the dominant hegemony (she reappears in later Italian tragic realist operas; for example, in Mascagni's *Cavalleria rusticana* (1890) in the figure of Santuzza, and in Puccini's eponymous *Tosca* (1900), and has her origins in the *bel canto* tragic operas of Bellini and Donizetti, for example *Norma* (1831) and *Lucia di Lammermoor*,

1835). The Italian-styled Violetta (drawn from Dumas *fils*'s *La Dame aux camélias*, 1848) represents the first central character in a long line of sympathetic *traviate* in the popular imaginary, whose display of active sexuality, financial independence, as well as illness (Violetta is dying of tuberculosis) threatens to usurp the social order. And unlike the *femme fatale* (she never consciously sets out to "ensnare a man" in the manner of Merimée/Bizet's protagonist Carmen, or Gozzi/Puccini's Turandot in the operas who bear their names), Italy's Fallen Women on the sung stage and silent screen suffer at length in the dramaturgy while being exalted in the music: like Verdi's Violetta, Tosca is portrayed *sympathetically* in Puccini's musico-dramatic representations during moments when she is shown to be suffering. His spine-tingling musical numbers such as "Vissi d'arte" are intended to invite spectators' pity and *far piangere il mondo* (make the world weep).[30] Moreover, the suffering heroine's big musical moments invariably demonstrate the soprano's wider *tessitura* compared with her male counterpart – hence (arguably), her ability to outsing, as well as to outperform him. In spite of the loss of the majority of silent film musical scores, from the fragments that do remain the sympathy with which the Fallen Woman is depicted on screen in her musical accompaniment is apparent; for example, the piano musical accompaniment for *Cenere* first performed by Antonio Coppola at the Pordenone Silent Film Festival in 1992 and composed by Bruno Moretti, who based his score on the traces of the original held at the George Eastman House film archive in Rochester, New York, is suitably slow, funereal, chromatic, and composed in a minor key signature to convey Rosalia's suffering. When her abandoned son is on his way to see his mother for the first time in adulthood, the music switches to a major key, and is lighter and more optimistic to convey his hopeful mood. An operatic heightening of the emotions occurs when Rosalia finally receives news from her son that his betrothed does not accept her, and she expresses despair in emphatic, over-reactive gestures – also a feature of her son (Febo Mari)'s acting style during fraught moments.

Women's opera, theatre, and film were typically met with critical acclaim – if not on the first night of the performance or screening, then shortly after; Verdi's *La traviata* and Puccini's women's operas have stood the test of time. Their suffering heroines/Fallen Women were usually caught up in a forbidden love, and thus the theatre auditorium was a safety valve also for *bourgeois* young, naïve women spectators' vicarious participation. Violetta dies of tuberculosis; Tosca leaps to her death from the Castel Sant'Angelo; Rosalia commits suicide; Assunta is imprisoned for life. As she typically repents her "sins" (as Catholicism teaches), without exception the musical lyricism that represents the Fallen Woman on the sung stage and silent screen – on which she is frequently left alone to lament – takes up the majority of musical time in the orchestral score: Verdi's *La traviata* lasts for approximately 2 hours and 20 minutes, of which Violetta is held up as suffering on stage in grief or anxiety for roughly an hour. Violetta's suffering begins the moment Germont, her lover's father, asks her to sacrifice her love for his son in Act II (around the 44th minute), to when his son joins her on her death bed in Act III, at roughly 1 hour and 56 minutes into the opera. In Puccini's *Madama Butterfly*, the heroine sings and enacts *her* grief upon learning that her husband intends to take away her son, and subsequently commits suicide, in a scene that lasts more or less 12 minutes. These vignettes notwithstanding, if the dramaturgy of these operas and films undermines the suffering heroine for having "fallen from grace," the music and libretto or screenplay exalts and celebrates her; thus, there was an ambivalent fascination, desire, and distancing felt with regard to these lower-class suffering heroines and the performers who enacted their roles – the middle classes of turn-of-the-century Italy (and, indeed, Europe) still regarded a performing woman with suspicion for her overt performance of sexuality.[31] This analysis would support the controversial claim made by feminist philosopher Catherine Clément in 1979 that opera is a misogynist genre that demands the submission or death of women for the sake of narrative closure, even while it can surely be contested if one looks at the many comic operas in which women survive.[32] And yet, if we bear in mind the aforementioned tragic women's stage and screenplays, Clément's argument does hold true. Sympathy for the Fallen Woman/suffering heroine is thus compounded when filtered through the lens of Italian tragic realist women's opera, theatre, and the silent diva film. These were particular brands of Italian operatic, theatrical, and filmic melodrama that provided spectators with both a vicarious outlet for their emotions (or a deflection of them, as in the case of Flaubert's Emma Bovary, as we shall see in Chapter 5) and a necessary escapism or distraction from the increasingly complex vicissitudes of everyday modern life.

Male artists' and composers' eschewal of the Italian-styled *femme fatale* in the performance culture at this time may have stemmed from the same desire for, and a feeling of moral superiority from watching a "beautiful" and sympathetic (because penitent), sexually expressive and emotionally expansive, marked (because stigmatised and marginalised) naïve-in-love woman get her "comeuppance." Puccini once considered staging Verga's *La lupa* (1880), whose heroine, Mara, who is consumed by a savage passion for her daughter's husband, is murdered by him during a Good Friday procession. However, Puccini decided against it because he found her too unappealing.[33] As Rebecca Stott has shown, in Western literature and art the *femme fatale* "is only formulated as a clear and recognizable 'type' in the nineteenth century."[34] While she is curiously absent from Italian opera, she nevertheless features prominently in literary culture in the masculine tradition (which some women writers, including Serao, also adopt). Signalling an apparent degeneracy in the new Italy, for example, in Tarchetti's *Fosca* (1869) and in Verga's *La lupa*, where she functioned as an apparent warning sign of women's supposedly threatening and all-engulfing sexuality and agency, as with the figure of the Fallen Woman, the *femme fatale* in her modern incarnation in literary culture emerged in 1845 in France with Prosper Merimée's *novella* "Carmen," the story of a Spanish cigarette factory worker who "ensnares" a French officer to fall in lust with her and who is eventually killed by him. Typically, she was othered and a metaphor (and repository) for *bourgeois* society's ills at a time of colonialist fascination with, and vilification of the other.[35] A different, more reified, "dangerous" class of woman epitomised in the trope of the Fallen Woman and thought typically to be found on the streets in everyday life was the figure of the prostitute.

The rise in prostitution even as far back as 1855 had been remarked upon by the then prime minister of Piedmont-Sardinia, Camillo Cavour (1810–61), who had instituted a series of regulations to address the growing number of cases of venereal disease in the army and to safeguard the health of the moralising and increasing middle classes. This legislation was formally adopted by the new Kingdom of Italy in 1861 and was Cavour's first act as prime minister. The 1855 decree was introduced in the wake of the première of Verdi's *Rigoletto* (La Fenice, Venice, 1851), which features a mezzo-soprano minor character, tellingly named Maddalena (Magdalen(e)), who is a prostitute for the Duke (her name in Victor Hugo's original play on which the opera is based – *Le Roi s'amuse* – is Maguelonne). In the opera in Act III, Maddalena asserts that she loves the duke, and he tells her he loves her back. Thus, Verdi and his librettist, Francesco Piave, attribute sentiment to Maddalena, undercutting the motive of commercial gain that might otherwise lie behind her relationship with the handsome nobleman.[36] Paradoxically, one year prior to the regulations on prostitution, in December 1854, Pope Pius IX had formally pronounced Mary's "immaculate conception," whence the "cult of the Madonna," and an increased emphasis on women's purity and chastity at a time when the family and the state were taking on greater importance as the foundations of the new nation in the lead-up to unification.[37] Cavour's regulation of prostitution, which required prostitutes to register with the police, undergo intrusive medical examinations and pay a tax to work in the *case chiuse* (the state-owned brothels), was challenged by the Abolitionists (so-called because they viewed prostitution as white slavery). Under the Crispi law in 1888, the registration of prostitutes and the mandatory medical visits were abolished (though lists of *case chiuse* and of prostitutes continued to exist, even though they were now kept secret). The Nicotera law, passed in 1891, restored the regulation of prostitution almost completely. Though police were now required to help women to abandon their life as prostitutes, in reality, police never developed a strategy to assist prostitutes.[38] In the previous year, another "Magdalene" figure had captured the hearts and minds of the Italian theatre-going public in Pietro Mascagni's operatic rendition of Verga's Sicilian *novella*, "Cavalleria rusticana" (1880), which he turned into a play for a national audience in 1884. Santa (as she is known in the short story) becomes the "Fallen" and disrespected "Santuzza" in the play. In the operatic version, Mascagni and his librettists depict Santuzza similarly as dishonoured and disrespected, but she is more sympathetic than in the play (though less so than in the *novella*) – Turiddù, when saying goodbye to his mother before fighting a duel, having been involved in a sexual relationship with the married Lola, asks his mother to take care of Santuzza and to treat her as her own daughter, and Santuzza is portrayed sympathetically in the music; she is also "envoiced" to use Abbate's term, as the central character and a *mezzo-soprano* (like Maddalena in *Rigoletto*). In writing by women of this period, Neera's short story "Falena" (1893) also depicts the figure of the prostitute with great sympathy; the word "Falena" in Italian is a common noun used for various types of nocturnal butterflies.[39] Neera uses the butterfly as a metaphor to describe Falena's delicate body frame, her outward attractiveness, and her fleetingness and unattainability, for she, like Violetta, is also dying of consumption. However, feminist Sibilla Aleramo, writing in her autobiography *Una donna*, described the figure of the prostitute as "a monstrous being, against nature, created by a bestial masculine selfishness."[40] Though most women writers of this period were not emancipationists, and not all emancipationists were sympathetic to prostitution, cultural representations of the young, sympathetic, suffering female prostitute "with a heart of gold" had entered the collective imagination in Italy via France.

Education for Middle-Class Girls and Young Women

Before the Casati law, if women received an education at all they did so in a convent or in a private school, or, informally, from within the home.[41] The law, which applied to the whole peninsula after unification, marked the beginning of a slow campaign to grant women access to all levels of education. In practice, however, given that girls could only attend girls' schools, boys were more likely to receive an education than girls, since if new schools were built, they were provided for boys in preference to girls, and difficulties were encountered in enforcing the law in the south.[42]

During the nineteenth century, there was a heated debate surrounding the question of whether women should receive a secondary education. Prior to unification, women's education had traditionally been managed by the Catholic Church. Following the schism between Church and State, at the time of unification moderates and conservatives in the new Italy were fearful of educating the middle and lower-middle classes at secondary level and were hesitant to approve of the education of the upper classes. There was also the belief, or rather, excuse, among positivists such as Lombroso and Mantegazza, that women were pathologically too physically and mentally weak to receive an education, and that subjecting them to the strenuous task of learning would reduce them to a state of physical and mental decay.[43] Notwithstanding the divide between Church and State, politicians and clergymen in Catholic Italy were united in their opinion of women's "proper" role, that of "mother and husband's helpmate, with the attendant virtues of modesty, submission and sacrifice."[44] Typically, and according to the available evidence, it seems that middle-class girls who received state education finished their schooling between the ages of 12 and 16 years.[45] In terms of what girls were taught, we know from the 1850 *Programma delle materie di esame d'una maestra elementare* (Curriculum of Exam Subjects in Primary Schools) that teachers were required to know how to teach religious education, literature, language (domestic vocabulary), spelling, grammar, arithmetic, sewing, and knitting;[46] Serao's short story, "Scuola Normale Femminile" (Women's Teacher Training College, 1886), suggests that the national curriculum for girls then included arithmetic, Italian language, physics, biology, history, geography, geometry, religious education, art, pedagogy, French, calligraphy, and housework.[47]

Though Casati's law did not explicitly ban girls from entering middle and upper schools for boys, debates about whether girls and young women should receive an education and, if so, what the curriculum should include, financial considerations, and existing prejudices surrounding mixed schools, presented girls with a psychological barrier to entry.[48] This meant that the number of girls' secondary schools until the early 1900s was marginal: the first of these was founded in Milan in 1861, but others did not appear until much later. Coppino's revision of the Casati law in 1877 introduced fines for parents found guilty of preventing their children from going to school, although its exclusion clauses included families who lived at a distance greater than two kilometres from school, difficulties in travelling to and from school, and absolute poverty. In consequence, education for girls and boys between the ages of six and nine was free and compulsory. Official permission to enter the *ginnasi-licei* (secondary schools) and the *istituti tecnici* (technical schools) was finally granted to girls by the Ministry of Education in 1883. Not until 1889–90, however, do girls show up on the attendance figures (either there simply were no girls who attended schools, or they were not measured statistically). In that year, 44 girls against 8,282 boys are recorded as enrolled in the *licei*. In 1900, this number increased to 287, and in the *ginnasi*, 1,778 were enrolled against 148 in the *istituti tecnici*.[49]

In tertiary level education between 1877 and 1900, 257 women graduated, whereas seven years previously there had only been 38 women graduates.[50] (During the period 1881–90, 15,974 males were enrolled on university courses in Italy.) Following the 1875 royal decree which allowed young women entry to the universities, the first woman to graduate in the new Italy was a Jew of Russian origin named Ernestina Paper (1846–1926), who received a degree in Medicine from the University of Pisa in 1877 (though she was not permitted to practice her profession).[51] In spite of these moves, less than 4 per cent of university students were female before 1914 compared with some 15 per cent in England, and the professions women could pursue were limited. The debates on women's access to education – which took place in periodicals for women, such as *Il Giornale delle donne* and *Museo di famiglia* – lasted between 1860 and 1900. During this time, not one of the numerous bills and proposals for the modification of the secondary school system was brought to a successful conclusion. It was not without a struggle from campaigners for women's rights and liberal intellectuals of the day that the decade 1874–84 saw women finally gaining the legal right to all levels of formal education. Nevertheless, in 1901, in many areas of the south, four out of five women still did not receive an education,[52] and the census of that year revealed that women represented almost 62 per cent of the total of illiterates. Indeed, in 1904, nearly one-quarter of children still received no primary school education.[53]

Women's Employment

In spite of the significant lack of civil rights afforded to women, they made an extraordinary contribution to the national economy. In 1861, more women than men worked in industry,[54] but they were paid around a third of men's salaries. Italian workers in general were the worst paid in Europe and worked the longest hours; there was no legal limit to the working day and no legislation providing for breaks or weekly rest. In 1876 it was reported that the textile industries employed four times as many women as men, yet women were habitually sacked at their first pregnancy. If they were lucky enough to remain in employment, they had to return to work within a few days of giving birth, and many women died of tuberculosis as a result of the poor working conditions. A survey of industry conducted in 1880 by the politician Vittorio Ellena calculated that 80 per cent of industrial workers were female, and the 1881 census found that 5.7 million out of 11 million females aged ten or over were economically active.[55] The census of 1881 shows that the number of men employed in industry had become slightly greater than that of women (1,853,656 to 1,823,134), but these figures were inaccurate for they failed to account for women workers in the countryside who continued to be involved in industrial production on a discontinuous and seasonal basis and to work from home.[56]

In 1883, the first woman with a Law degree, Lidia Poët (1855–1949), was denied the right to practise at the Bar.[57] "Acceptable" professions available to women included bookkeeping, secretarial work, working for a small business which accepted female members of staff, philanthropic work, working as a telegraph operator, and most commonly, primary school teaching, while middle-class men typically trained to be physicians, lawyers, professors, and engineers. The enrolment figures recorded in the *scuole normali* (teacher training colleges) of 1881–82 show there were 7,482 young women compared to 1,383 young men, and the number of women teachers recorded in the 1901 census was 62,643.[58]

There were restrictions on professional middle-class women: they had to cease working if they married, as was the case also in Britain. The poet-improviser Giannina Milli (1825–88), who in the latter half of her career had become a teacher of history and geography, as well as the headteacher of a *scuola magistrale* (shorter duration teacher training schools established by local authorities) in Rome, renounced her post upon getting married.[59] While this all suggests that women's employment conditions were bleak (to say the least), gradual incremental steps were taken towards improving women's employment status. In 1886, thanks to the campaigns of emancipationists, and specifically, Anna Kuliscioff (1857–1925), a law was introduced prohibiting the employment of children younger than nine, and this was raised to 12 in 1902.

Conclusion

Middle-class women in united Italy were therefore strongly confined to the private sphere as mothers and wives; women were expected to "nurture" the nation's future citizens and to have a "civilising" influence on their children, an idea that was dominant in France following the revolution and which found expression in Mazzini's "patriot mother" prior to unification.[60] Pisanelli Civil Code of 1865 enshrined in law Italian women's subordination to men, positing femaleness and maleness as rigid binary opposites, and ensuring married women's obedience to their husbands at a time when marriage and motherhood were a young middle-class woman's ultimate goal. The arranged marriage (*matrimonio combinato*) was an integral part of Italian life for young women aged 15 and over until the first decade of the twentieth century: daughters left their father's homes to marry and to enter their husband's homes, taking with them their dowry, while sons took home a wife and her dowry. The Code introduced the *maritalis auctoritas* (the husband's authority, abolished in 1919) which meant that women were unable to carry out financial transactions without their husband's permission, except where there were extenuating circumstances (e.g., if they were high-earning female performers or writers). Women could be educated, but only enough to be able to teach their sons to read and write; it was believed that an education offering reasoned thought was of no use to women because, according to one critic in 1886, in women, "sentiment prevails," and giving women an education only increased young women's tendency for their imagination to wander.[61] The dominant attitude towards girls and education held much in common with views put forward by priests, politicians, intellectuals, and physicians on reading naturalist or *verista* novels (after *verismo*, the Italian literary movement pioneered by Giovanni Verga and Luigi Capuana which sought to depict the downtrodden in southern Italian culture as victims of their environment). It was felt that the prevalence of sentiment over reason in women – a perception reinforced by positivist scientists like Lombroso and Paolo Mantegazza

(1831–1910) – made them susceptible to agitation and nervousness with regard to the novel's associations with desire, eroticism, and sexuality, themes not unlike those with which women's theatre, opera, and film were concerned. Indeed, still in early post-unification Italy, although theatre- and opera-going were a rite of passage for adolescent girls and the primary means to introduce them on the marriage market, young women's attendance was perceived with ambivalence by traditionalists, who held that young women were impressionable and weak, so that exposure to theatre performances caused harm to their minds and bodies.

Until the 1880s, devotional literature such as prayer books and sacred stories were the only items that had large print runs.[62] Despite the ambivalence on the part of the dominant hegemony of priests, politicians, doctors, and intellectuals in Italy, by 1879 there were 180 professional, published women writers (in contrast to around 4,500 male writers),[63] and between 1871 and 1910, 1,894 new poems, novels, essays, conference proceedings, conduct books, translations, plays, and biographies were published by women (from 1881 to 1920, 949 new novels were published by Italian women).[64] It has been estimated that while in 1863 there were just 210 public libraries, by 1896 the figure had risen to 1,831.[65] Concomitantly, the period in question also saw the *topos* of the "woman who reads" impose itself in literature and iconography at the same time as women as social subjects (in education and the professions) were emerging "as the new and powerful constituency of readers who played a huge part in the success of the novel as a genre."[66]

Though Italian novels were mostly authored by men (the genre having been introduced into Italy almost a century after its French and British counterparts as late as 1827 via the first edition of Alessandro Manzoni's historical novel *I promessi sposi* (The Betrothed)), "from the end of the 1870s, and moreover in the '80s and '90s, the 'women's novel' ('il romanzo femminile') became a genre of popular consumption."[67] Written for women, about women and by women, novels that were first published in serialised form, as well as short stories, conduct books and etiquette books, began to emerge on the literary market for an engaged female readership. Though mainly publishing in the north, there were also successful professional women writers in the south, including Serao and Grazia Deledda (1871–1936), who won the Nobel Prize for literature in 1926.[68] Columns for women in weekly journals and journals for women also began to emerge, in which writers such as La Marchesa Colombi (pen name for Maria Antonietta Torriani, 1840–1920), Serao, and Neera discussed female actors, audience members, their fashions, and performances. Since schooling for girls finished between the ages of 12 and 16, many were self-taught, including these writers, who, as adolescents, read voraciously. Even though literacy rates were markedly higher in the north, in the south in 1871 literacy rates were between 25 and 35 per cent (as compared to more than 55 per cent in the north).[69] By 1901, official statistics reveal that female illiteracy had declined to 55 per cent. The increasing number of educated women (as both readers and writers), together with the increased affordability of the entertainment industry, meant that a mass female critical community with its own lexicon of cultural criticism by, and for women was beginning to establish itself. How this discerning and "affective alliance" expressed itself in life-writings – including in letters, diary entries, autobiographies, and biographies – is explored in depth in Chapter 3.

Notes

1 There are, of course, recent exceptions, including the televised series of Elena Ferrante's *My Brilliant Friend* tetralogy (2017) and Roberto Saviano's *Gomorrah* (2014).
2 See: www.operabase.com [accessed 24 February 2020]: Verdi's *La traviata* (771 performances) and *Rigoletto* (510); Puccini's *La Bohème* (577), *Madama Butterfly* (493), *Tosca* (473); Rossini's *Il barbiere di Siviglia* (497).
3 See: www.operabase.com [accessed 24 February 2020].
4 On the elitism of opera in contemporary Britain as a "cliché," see: www.theguardian.com/music/musicblog/2014/feb/11/elitist-opera-cliches-alexandra-wilson [accessed 27 July 2018].
5 It was not until the early 1980s that the majority of Italians claimed to be using standard Italian as their first or home language (in 1974 51.3% of Italians used "dialect" with their "familiari," whereas by 1982 this figure was down to 46.7%). See: Claudio Marazzini, *La lingua italiana: profilo storico* (Bologna: Il Mulino, 1998), pp. 403-4. I am grateful to John Charles Smith and Martin Maiden for drawing my attention to this data.
6 Antonio Gramsci, *Letteratura e vita nazionale* (Turin: Einaudi, 1950), pp. 69–70.
7 Antonio Gramsci, "People, Nation and Culture," in *Selections from Cultural Writings*, ed. by David Forgacs and Geoffrey Nowell-Smith (London: Lawrence & Wishart, 1985), p. 204.
8 Carlotta Sorba, *Teatri: L'Italia del melodramma nell'età del Risorgimento* (Bologna: Il Mulino, 2001), p. 28.
9 *Ibid.*, p. 26; p. 33.
10 William Ashbrook, "The Nineteenth Century: Italy," in *The Oxford History of Opera*, ed. by Roger Parker (Oxford: Oxford University Press, 1994), pp. 114–37 (p. 115).
11 Sorba, *Teatri*, p. 95.
12 Ann Hallamore Caesar, "Crossing the Public/Private Divide: The *Salotto* and the Theatre in Late-Nineteenth-Century Italy," in *Theatre, Opera, and Performance in Italy from the Fifteenth Century to the Present: Essays in Honour of Richard Andrews*, ed. by Brian Richardson, Simon Gilson and Catherine Keen (Leeds: Maney, 2004), pp. 216–29 (p. 20).
13 See Gibus del *Mattino*, *Saper vivere: norme di buona creanza* (Naples: Tocco, 1900), pp. 284–85. Italics my emphasis; and, Francesco Bontempi, *La donna e la legislazione italiana: raccolta delle disposizioni contenute nei codici relative alla donna* (Turin: Tipografia del giornale, 1871), p. 30. Men had to be 18 years old in order to marry.

14 Anna Vertua Gentile, "A teatro," in *Come devo comportarmi? Libro per tutti* (2nd edn.) (Milan: Ulrico Hoepli,1897), pp. 301–3 (pp. 301–2).
15 *Ibid.*, p. 301.
16 Gibus del *Mattino*, *Saper vivere*, p. 289. Italics my emphasis.
17 Sorba, *Teatri*, pp. 97–8. Beggars and *contadini*, typically, could not afford the cost of a theatre ticket. See: John Rosselli, *The Opera Industry in Italy from Cimarosa to Verdi: The Role of the Impresario* (Cambridge: Cambridge University Press, 1984), p. 45:

> "Contemporary statements that 'the people' or 'the lowest class' were to be found in the gallery suggest, more than anything else, the restrictive definition of 'the people' common in the early nineteenth century. Labourers, peasants, beggars were not 'the people.'"

18 Rosselli, *The Opera Industry*, p. 45 and ftn. 26; p. 188: "Admission to the La Scala gallery in carnival seasons from 1823 to 1831 varied from 0.65 francs to 0.87 francs: the daily wage of a builder's labourer in those years was 0.77 francs." See, also, p. 181: "[A]fter 1814 the Piedmontese (ultimately Italian) lira was officially at par with the franc, though in practice there were very minor fluctuations." Discounts applied to the Austrian military.
19 Rosselli, *The Opera Industry in Italy*, p. 178.
20 *Ibid.*
21 Sorba, *Teatri*, p. 87.
22 See http://archiviostorico.teatrolafenice.it/ricerca.php [accessed 20 July 2020]. From 1880 to 1915 at La Fenice in Venice, seasons included performances of Ponichelli's *La Gioconda* (1885); Verdi's *Aida* (1886, 1908); Serponti's *Leonora* (1886); Bizet's *Carmen* (1888, 1907, 1913); Mascagni's *Cavalleria rusticana* (1891); Lozzi's *Emma Liona* (1895); Ponichelli's *Marion Delorme* (1886); Catalani's *Edmea* (1887); Donizetti's *Lucia di Lammermoor* (1887); Leoncavallo's *La Bohème* (1897); Puccini's *La Bohème* (1899, 1910, 1911); Mascagni's *Iris* (1900); Verdi's *La traviata* (1901, 1905, 1908); Dupont's *La Cabrera* (1908); Puccini's *Tosca* (1905, 1906); Catalani's *La Wally* (1906); Mascagni's *Amica* (1907); Cilea's *Adriana Lecouvreur* (1907); Giordano's *Marcella* (1908); Mascagni's *Iris* (1909, 1910); Verdi's *Aida* (1909); Puccini's *Madama Butterfly* (1909); Ponchielli's *La Gioconda* (1911, 1915); Bellini's *Norma* (1912); Mascagni's *Isabeau* (1912); Merli's *Melisenda* (1912).
23 See www.theguardian.com/stage/2020/feb/18/live-shows-get-your-heart-racing-scientists-prove-it [accessed 19 February 2020].
24 It was not until 1969 that the Roman Catholic Church formally revised the canonical definition of Mary Magdalene, conceding that there was no evidence in the Bible that she had been a prostitute and Jesus Christ's lover. See: Mary Haskins, *Mary Magdalen: Myth and Metaphor* (London: Harper Collins, 1993), p. 25.
25 Lucy Bolton, "Beautiful Penitent Whore: The Desecrated Celebrity of Mary Magdalene," *Celebrity Studies* 11:1 (2020), 25–42 (26).
26 *Ibid.*, p. 26.
27 Peter Brooks, "Melodrama, Body, Revolution," in *Melodrama: Stage, Picture, Screen*, ed. by Jacky Bratton, Jim Cook and Christine Gledhill (London: British Film Institute, 1994), pp. 11–24 (p. 22).
28 Danielle Hipkins and Katharine Mitchell, "*Le traviate*: Suffering Heroines and the Italian State Between the 19th and 21st Centuries" in *Prostitution*

and Sex Work in Global Visual Media: New Takes on Fallen Women, ed. by Danielle Hipkins and Kate Taylor (London and Basingstoke: Palgrave Macmillan, 2017), pp. 195–297 (p. 196).

29 Discussing Verdi's *oeuvre*, Rutherford draws attention to Violetta's "paean to the pleasures of sexual liberty and independence" in Act I of *La traviata* that constituted "a provocation to the period's conservative ideas about women." See Susan Rutherford, *Verdi, Opera, Women* (Cambridge: Cambridge University Press, 2013), p. 111.

30 *Giacomo Puccini Epistolario*, ed. by Giacomo Adami (Milan: Mondadori, 1982), p. 165. The quote derives from a letter Puccini addressed to his librettists for *Turandot*, Simoni and Adami on 23 October 1919, whom he requested they produce something that would "make the world weep."

31 See Kirsten Pullen, *Actresses and Whores: On Stage and In Society* (Cambridge: CUP, 2005), p. 2:

> "At particular historical moments, the body of the actress (assumed to be an object onto which male desires were projected) and the body of the prostitute (assumed to be an object onto which male desires were enacted) slipped discursively into one: whore/actress."

32 See: Catherine Clément, *Opera, or, The Undoing of Women*, trans. by Betsy Wing with a foreword by Margaret Reynolds (London: Tauris, 1997).

33 The short story "La lupa" was originally published in the Neapolitan *Rivista nuova di scenza, lettere ed arti* on 15 February 1880 and added to the first edition of Verga's collection of short stories, *Vita dei campi*, in the same year. The play premièred in Turin at the Teatro Gerbino on 27 January 1896 and was staged by the *Compagnia* Andò-Leigheb with Virginia Reiter in the lead female role.

34 Rebecca Stott, *The Fabrication of the Late-Victorian Femme Fatale: The Kiss of Death* (Palgrave: Houndmills, Basingstoke, 1992), p. xi.

35 Silvia Valisa has highlighted the prominence of performance and musical culture over literature in Italy during this period by showing how Merimée's *novella* arrived in Italy after Bizet's opera (first performed in Naples in 1879), as late as 1883, when the publisher Sonzogno brought out a translation in the *Biblioteca universal*e. See: Silvia Valisa, "Casa editrice Sonzogno. Mediazione culturali, circuiti del sapere ed innovazione tecnologica nell'Italia unificata (1861–1900)," in *The Printed Media in Fin-de-siècle Italy: Publishers, Writers, and Readers*, ed. by Ann Hallamore Caesar and others (London: Legenda, 2011), pp. 90–106 (p. 102).

36 Rutherford, *Verdi, Opera, Women*, p. 118.

37 On the "cult of the Madonna," see: Marina Warner, *Alone of All Her Sex: The Myth and Cult of the Virgin Mary* (New York: Knopf, 1976). On the invention of the myth of Mary Magdalene's promiscuity, Warner argues that, "The Madgalene, like Eve, was brought into existence by the powerful undertow of misogyny in Christianity, which associates women with the dangers and degradations of the flesh," p. 225.

38 Mary Gibson, *Prostitution and the State in Italy, 1860–1915* (New Brunswick and London: Rutgers University Press, 1986), p. 147.

39 Neera is the pseudonym of Anna Radius Zuccari (1846–1918).

40 Sibilla Aleramo, *Una donna* (Milan: Feltrinelli, 2020), p. 116.

41 The law was first promulgated in the Sardinian states and in Lombardy before being gradually enforced in other regions. The following two sections draw on material already published in Katharine Mitchell, "'Sorelle in arte (e politica)': The 'Woman Question' and Female Solidarity at the *Fin de Siècle*," in *Women and Gender in Post-Unification Italy: Between Private and Public Spheres*, ed. by Katharine Mitchell and Helena Sanson (Oxford: Peter Lang, 2013), pp. 197–223 (pp. 202–5 and pp. 211–13).

42 See: Dina Bertoni Jovine, *Storia dell'educazione popolare in Italia* (Bari: Laterza, 1965), pp. 141–3.

43 Anna Vertua Gentile published an article in *Vita intima* on 24 June 1890 in which she cited the case of a woman who fell seriously ill after devoting herself to the kind of study "appropriate" only to men.

44 Percy Allum, "Catholicism," in *The Cambridge Companion to Modern Italian Culture*, ed. by Zygmunt G. Barański and Rebecca West (Cambridge: Cambridge University Press, 2004, 2nd edn.), pp. 97–112 (p. 103).

45 Carmela Covato, "Educate ad educare: ruolo materno ed itinerari formativi," in *L'educazione delle donne: scuole e modelli di vita femminile nell'Italia dell'Ottocento*, ed. by Simonetta Soldani (Milan: Franco Angeli, 1991, 2nd edn.), pp. 131–47 (p. 138).

46 Bertoni Jovine, *Storia dell'educazione*, p. 134.

47 Matilde Serao, "Scuola normale femminile," in *Il romanzo della fanciulla*, ed. by F. Bruni (Naples: Liguori, 1985), pp. 146–85 (p. 150).

48 Covato, "Educate ad educare," p. 138.

49 Dina Bertoni Jovine, "Funzione emancipatrice della scuola e contributo della donna all'attività educativa," in *L'emancipazione femminile in Italia: un secolo di discussioni 1861–1961*, ed. by Comitato di associazioni femminili per la parità di retribuzione (Florence: La Nuova Italia, 1963), pp. 223–75 (p. 239).

50 Soldani, "Premessa," in *L'educazione delle donne*, pp. vii–xxi (pp. xii–xiii). The *Sommario di statistiche storiche* (Summary of Historical Statistics) *1861–2011* records the number of male graduates from 1926 only.

51 For comparison, the first degrees awarded to women in England were in the summer of 1880 by London University. See: Jane Robinson, *Bluestockings: The Remarkable Story of the First Women to Fight for an Education* (London: Viking, 2009), xxii.

52 Soldani, "Premessa," p. viii.

53 Denis Mack Smith, *Italy: A Modern History* (Ann Arbor: University of Michigan Press, 1969), p. 55.

54 Simona Ortaggi Cammarosano draws attention to a book published in 1868 by Enrico Fano entitled *Della carità preventiva e dell'ordinamento delle società di mutuo soccorso in Italia* (On Preventive Charity and the Organisation of Mutual Aid Societies in Italy, Milan: G. Civelli), in which Fano had highlighted the importance of the role that working-class and peasant women played in the economic life of the nation. He stated that for every 100 male artisans there are 123 females. See: Simona Ortaggi Cammarosano, "Labouring Women in Northern and Central Italy in the Nineteenth Century," in *Society and Politics in the Age of the Risorgimento: Essays in Honour of Denis Mack Smith*, ed. by John A. Davis and Paul Ginsborg (Cambridge: Cambridge University Press, 1991), pp. 152–83 (p. 156).

55 Martin Clark, *Modern Italy 1871–1982* (London and New York: Longman, 1984), p. 22.
56 Ortaggi Cammarosano, "Labouring Women," pp. 176–7.
57 Lucienne Kroha, *The Woman Writer in Late-Nineteenth-Century Italy: Gender and the Formation of Literary Identity* (New York and Lampeter: Mellen, 1992), p. 8. The first practicing female lawyer was Lina Furlan (1903–2000), who began her career in 1930.
58 Soldani, "Premessa," *L'educazione delle donne*, p. xvi.
59 Gualberta Alaide Beccari, "Giannina Milli," *La donna*, 30 October 1876, p. 2583.
60 Michelle Perrot, "Women, Power and History," in *Writing Women's History*, ed. by Michelle Perrot, trans. Felicia Pheasant (Oxford: Blackwell, 1992), pp. 160–74 (p. 161).
61 Oreste Bruni, *Le nostre donne. Considerazioni d'un direttore di scuole femminili* (Florence: Barbera, 1886), p. 240.
62 Ann Hallamore Caesar, "Women Readers and the Novel in Nineteenth-Century Italy," *Italian Studies* 56:1 (2001), 80–97 (83).
63 Angelo De Gubernatis, *Dizionario biografico degli scrittori italiani* (Florence: Le Monnier, 1879), cited in Michela De Giorgio, *Le italiane dall'Unità ad oggi: modelli culturali e comportamenti sociali* (Rome: Laterza, 1992), p. 377.
64 Gilda Corabi, "Scrittrici dell'Ottocento," in *Atlante della letteratura italiana* III, ed. by Domenico Scarpa (Turin: Einaudi, 2012), pp. 162–76 (pp. 170–1).
65 Erminia Irace and Adolfo Scotto Di Luzio, "Le istuzioni culturali del regno d'Italia (1861–1945)," in *Atlante* III. pp. 438–47 (p. 438).
66 Olivia Santovetti, "The Cliché of the Romantic Female Reader and the Paradox of Novelistic Illusion: Federico De Roberto's *L'Illusione* (1891)," in *The Printed Media*, pp. 49–62 (p. 49).
67 Corabi, "Scrittrici dell'Ottocento," p. 174.
68 Corabi estimates that 60 per cent of editions were published by publishing houses based in Milan and Florence (p. 175).
69 Irace and Scotto Di Luzio, "Le istituzioni culturali," in *Atlante*, p. 445.

3 The Private Female Gaze

We saw in Chapter 2 how the "deep images" (*figure profonde*) of sacrificing, suffering heroines/Fallen Women from around the 1830s, coupled with the arrival of the novel in Italy – which liberal-minded intellectuals associated with women readers – were circulating among the growing bourgeoisie, contributing to social formation, a new-found identity, and Italy's "nation-making" process. In this chapter, through an examination of a selection of diaries, letters, bio- and autobiographies belonging to middle-class women who attended and watched performances on stage and then on the silver screen in Italy from the 1870s onwards, I discuss the significance of friendships and solidarity among celebrated women performers and writers. I argue that as portents of modernity and intermediaries for women spectators, fans, and readers, female performers' and women writers' relationships were based on admiration and solidarity; and that these extended from them, to spectators, and back to performers, thereby constructing a continuous positive feedback loop.

Mark Seymour has recently suggested that opera and novels very likely played a part in shaping middle-class women's concepts of emotion and its expression during a period in which epistolary culture was at its height.[1] Traditionally considered the "best expressive form of the feminine voice," as Gabriella Romani has argued, in the *Ottocento*, letter-writing as an "emblem of the private" was "one of the most basic forms of writing available to women."[2] Nevertheless, and as Michelle Perrot cautions, "Nothing is less spontaneous than a letter," which applies even more so where *Ottocento* women's epistolary writing is concerned due to heightened norms of propriety and expectations of women's behaviour compared with men's.[3]

The "I" of a letter is different from the "I" of a diary. Whilst letters require an addressee, the addressee of a diary is its author and, sometimes, the diary itself (e.g., "Dear Diary"). Indeed,

> [t]he genuineness of the diary, as a record of inner life, has often been pegged to the absence of an addressee. Diarists are supposed to write only for themselves; they have no one to impress, no one to perform for, and thus can be quite simply themselves.[4]

DOI: 10.4324/9780429293511-4

Expanding on the semantic distinctions between letter-writing and diary-writing, Horace Porter Abbott further hypothesises that "the term 'diary' evokes an intensity of privacy, cloistering, isolation, that the term 'letter' does not."[5] Yet his (fictional) letter writer and diarist is predominantly male (in his analysis of ten authors of "diary fiction," only one – Doris Lessing – is a woman); as such, he unwittingly or otherwise subscribes to a notion of a unified, coherent, universal, Western, middle-class subjectivity, one in which the female voice is virtually silenced. For, as Linda Anderson reminds us, autobiography has been "implicitly bound up with gender"[6] since the end of the eighteenth century, even if women only began writing the story of their lives at the end of the nineteenth century. By association, so, too, has diary writing. And with Freud's recognition of the unconscious at the end of the nineteenth century, coupled with post-structuralist theories of autobiography (including Paul De Man's 1979 seminal essay, which deconstructed the Romantic notion of selfhood as unique, unified, and transcendent, arguing that all writing is autobiographical inasmuch as all knowledge, including self-knowledge, depends on figurative language or tropes), emphasis "shifted from women's experience as a given, to the complex construction of gendered subjectivities, [and] the field of autobiography has become a central preoccupation and testing-ground for feminism."[7] Taking account of debates in poststructuralism surrounding the impossibility of accessing subjectivity in writing, a reappraisal of Barthes's "The Death of the Author" on the importance of the authorial voice is more urgent than ever if we are to recover and interpret, in our time, the forgotten voices of women spectators.[8] If women have more psychologically fragmented selves – if we are still socialised to become more relational beings – then the content of the form of our private writings, of our speaking "I" will differ from men's. If "[w]omen [in the nineteenth century] were supposed to write in a simple and natural style, and the letter form seemed the genre most conducive to the expression of such qualities," this also applies to diary writing and autobiography.[9] These forms share common traits, as writing the story of one's life is itself an act in that story, "and like every significant new act it alters in some degree the shape of [one's] life, it leaves [one] different."[10] We can suppose that, in fact, any writing in the first person (nowadays a text message or an online blog) is an action that exerts an influence on the writer. In the same way as writing one's life changes that life to some degree, so the productivity and creativity of fandom – of being a fan – "can be read as a type of appropriation that borrows and repurposes existing cultural materials *to produce something new*."[11]

Where letter and diary writing diverge in the absence or otherwise of an intended addressee, autobiography is a more deliberately self-exposing, slippery form of writing the subject. (S)he writes to be published and read in a more or less lengthy narrative for general public consumption: (s)he, thus, undergoes more or less consciously, a continual process of self-censorship and censorship of others in writing their lives, too, in the knowledge that the private will become (at the time of publication) public, and open to critical scrutiny. And yet, aside from the few autobiographical female voices that were intended for public consumption, letter and diary writing remained in the private sphere of the home, whose care, as statesman Cesare Balbo wrote in 1844, was "assigned by 'natural order' to women" in Italy.[12] Indeed, the private, domestic sphere was considered women's "proper" place, particularly following unification and the introduction of Pisanelli's Civil Code. Yet, women's engagement in letter-writing and the reading of novels and conduct manuals, as well as journals for women, enabled them to participate in social and cultural activities that allowed them to reach beyond the home's confines. In recording in their diaries and letters their emotional responses to watching performing artists, women spectators were not only "becom[ing] prima donnas on their own operatic stages" as Seymour contends; they were also constructing their subjectivities as embodied, relational and discerning spectators.[13]

What now follows is an analysis of a selection of life-writings of a nascent feminine spectatorship-in-the-making, one which flew in the face of the stereotypes articulated by foreign visitors in their writings at the beginning of the nineteenth century of women attending theatre and opera performances "to flirt with their lovers." These life-writings show how women stage and screen performers shaped their performances to suit women spectators, thereby revealing evidence of a positive feedback loop that was akin to, and arguably a prototype for, the Italian feminist collective Diotima's notion of *affidamento*. This positive feedback loop was quite unique, and a result of a possible greater intimacy permitted through life-writing. Important female friendships existed between celebrity women writers and performers, and these were known to the general public. They included friendships among peers, such as between Eleonora Duse and Matilde Serao; Duse and Grazia Deledda; and Duse and the writer Gemma Ferruggia (1867–1930), as well as intergenerational friendships such as between Duse and Sibilla Aleramo; Adelaide Ristori (1822–1906) and Duse during the early stages of her career; Francesca Bertini and Serao; Aleramo and Giacinta Pezzana; and Pezzana and Duse. I argue here that their sisterhood, their "*sorellanza*" – by which I mean a secularised female solidarity – for female early capitalist consumerism, functioned as a model for everyday middle-class women spectators, who may have adopted similar close bonds and friendship ties in their everyday lives.

Of Female Fans' and Actors' Gazes at Performing Women

A single-authored monograph can only begin to scratch at the surface of a "female gaze" from a selection of life-writings, including monologues in diary and/or autobiographical form, as well as passages in biographies and letters. Nevertheless, an insight into one woman spectator's thinking can be gleaned from a set of letters written in the late 1870s, published as a collection in 1987 after they won the 1986 Pieve prize.[14] Known simply as "Emilia" from Milan, she was a nineteenth-century version of what became known as a "fan." Writing to her Italian infantry officer lover, Federico, who was based in Sicily, after an evening's entertainment watching the *Compagnia* Pietroboni in Milan in 1878, she describes the performers as "distinguished and all very good." (The *Compagnie* operated under an actor-manager system until the 1930s in Italy, with each actor-manager performing in the lead role of her/his own company, investing in her/his own theatre, hiring and firing actors, choosing the repertory and overseeing the wardrobe, among other tasks. Notable female actor-managers include Ristori, Pezzana, and Duse.) With the exception of their first production, Emilia writes that she "very much enjoyed the others," including the previous evening's, which she describes as "very moving and sad at the beginning. It ends well, however, to everyone's great satisfaction; and especially to us Women."[15] In the previous year, she had written to her lover that she wanted to see the opera singer Adelina Patti perform in Verdi's *La forza del destino* (1862) at La Scala: "What excitement there will be at La Scala; everyone is expecting great things and the cost of tickets is exorbitant."[16] Like the fictional Emma from Flaubert's novel *Madame Bovary*, Emilia was a devourer of French fiction: she read Dumas *fils* and George Sand (1804–76), though somewhat disappointingly does not pass comment on them.[17] In *Star Gazing* (1994), Jackie Stacey draws a link between the spectacle of the cinema screen and the shop window display in a discussion on cultural ideals of feminine beauty and women spectators' desires to imagine themselves as their favourite stars, presenting the desire for fashion and beauty embodied in the star as legitimate forms of female spectatorship.[18] Shifting her attention from spectating to considering her appearance on her evenings out, writing in 1879 Emilia describes how she has been working on a design for a black velvet dress she will wear "once" to the Teatro Manzoni, and "once" to La Scala. It had "a long train decorated with white lace; beautiful. The effect is wonderful for the way in which it is made," and she expresses regret he won't see her in it.[19]

Writing on fandom and media fan culture, Mark Duffett suggests that an aspect of fan attachment is that it can restructure notions of what is public and what is private. The sense of connection that each fan feels for a famous actor, singer, writer, or musician can alter and restructure their spatial experience.[20] This "sense of connection" experienced in writing a letter by hand to an idol has paradoxically never been more distant yet (bizarrely) close in an era of reality TV and social media platforms such as Twitter and Instagram, which supply an endless chain of "connection" to celebrities while simultaneously dismantling it through "fake," or PR-managed and curated celebrities' accounts. At the risk of romanticising the past, as with the experience of watching make-believe on screen compared with in a live auditorium, online screen "connection" feels far less intense and intimate than a handwritten letter, and more transactional and impersonal.

Of the letters mined for the purpose of this book, female fans' intensity of affect from watching women performers is striking and palpable.[21] So, too, is the emergence of a transnational and global female fandom for women performers. Among the 35,000 letters addressed to Ristori, for example, in a letter by two sister-admirers from Rio de Janiero in Brazil following Ristori's performances there of Vittorio Alfieri's *Ottavia* (1783) in 1869 at the Teatro Lírico Fluminense, they write of her "great artistic genius" and invite her back to South America for further performances in the near future.[22] Writing from Stockholm in 1880, the Swedish miniaturist and photographer Elise Zénaide Arnberg (1828–91) expresses *her* admiration referring to Ristori as her "idol," before begging to see her "just once" in order that she can finish her portrait.[23] Fandom is refracted through an epistemophilic gaze at the famous French tragedienne, Sarah Bernhardt (1844–1923) in a letter from La Marchesa Colombi (pseudonym for Maria Antonietta Torriani, 1840–1920) to her childhood sweetheart, Giovanni Marano, sent in 1882. On seeing Bernhardt perform Fédora in Victorien Sardou's 1882 play of the same name in Paris, she writes, "You cannot imagine the fascinating beauty and artistic talent of [Sarah Bernhardt]. No sooner [had] Patti earned my wholehearted admiration than the former aroused yet more enthusiasm in me."[24] Two years prior, Bernhardt had been engaged for several performances at the Teatro Carignano in Turin, and Duse had moved there from Naples to perform in Cesare Rossi's *Compagnia*. As the journalist Olga Signorelli (1883–1973) informs us in her memoir, Duse watched all of Bernhardt's performances, "enraptured [...] by the great French actress."[25] Duse had reportedly said: "Here is a woman who uplifts our work, who makes the audience respect what is beautiful, and bow before her art."[26] Inspired by her, when Bernhardt left Turin, Duse suggested to her actor-manager Ernesto Rossi (1897–1967) that they overhaul their repertory to include works that Bernhardt had successfully managed, including Dumas *fils*'s *La Princesse de Bagdad* (1881) and his *La femme de Claude* (1873), in which Duse was "triumphantly successful."[27] Duse clearly saw in Bernhardt a symbolic maternal figure and role model, and the feeling was mutual. In 1897, invited by Bernhardt, who was then director of the Théâtre de la Renaissance in Paris from 1893 to 1899, Duse performed Dumas *fils*'s *La Dame aux Camélias*, "even though Bernhardt was the acknowledged exponent of the part."[28] According to Signorelli, "when it came to the fourth act, with Eleonora's unrivalled performance as the suffering Marguerite, the play ended in delirious applause, among which Sarah Bernhardt's '*Bravo, bravo*' could distinctly be heard from her box."[29] Adoration for Duse was by now global – she was known and celebrated by both women and men for her novel and touching performances: for example, the Portugese Duchess, Maria Palmela (1841–1909), who befriended

Duse, writes to tell her from Portugal in 1901 that meeting her has been "life-changing,"[30] while the Chilean-born ballet-impresario, Georges de Cuevas (1885–1961), recalls the first time he saw Duse performing in Nice in Dumas *fils*'s La *Dame aux Camélias*:

> The audience's enthusiasm grew act by act in a *crescendo* till the third ... And I, too, felt crushed under the weight of the same human misery and a hopeless bitterness in the face of the agony of a heart wounded to death.[31]

The English writer George Bernard Shaw (1856–1950), who saw Duse perform in London, apparently "drew a moving word-portrait of her and defined her face, without make-up on the stage as off it, as the touchstone of her humanity."[32]

Evidence of a similar adoration on the part of a younger, less experienced female actor towards a more mature, fully realised one (in this case, Ristori), can be found in a letter written by the Modenese actor, Virginia Reiter (1862–1937), addressed to Ristori with an unknown date (though possibly around 1904). The letter reads

> From the moment the idea of becoming an actress was born in me, I have always associated with it that name: Ristori!
>
> That name, that image, that glory, has never left me, fascinating me with a light, however far, that was just as attractive!
>
> Her homeland, her Art, her genius, journeyed from Paris, to London, to the Americas, to Australia, to the Indies ... this is what equals a woman to the greatest of men![33]

The year 1873 was the year in which Reiter performed her first school play and in which her love for the theatre began (and when Ristori would have been her idol).[34] Reiter went on to become one of the most significant Italian female actors of the late nineteenth and early twentieth century in Italy, becoming famous for her roles in Verga's *La lupa* (1896) and Sardou and Moreau's *Madame Sans-Gêne* (1893). Her letter, in which each sentence ends with an exclamation mark, illustrates her utter enthusiasm and certainty about her idol. Writing in 1907 in "*Memoirs and Artistic Studies of Adelaide Ristori,*" the author Luigi Donato Ventura reminds us of what Duse had said of Ristori: "Adelaide Ristori; perfection in art, perfection in life."[35] Indeed, at the beginning of Duse's career in 1881, writing from her dressing room in the Teatro Argentina in Rome where Duse was listening to Ristori's performance of Paolo Giacometti's *Figlia e madre, o le storie intime* (Daughter and Mother, or Intimate Stories, 1865), and bespeaking the maternal symbolic theorised by the Diotima group, Duse had written to tell Ristori of her devotion and affection for her.[36]

These expressions of adulation and affirmation in fan letters by middle- or upper-class women, who were known in the public sphere to varying degrees, all display an exhilaration and a worship of their idol in their writings, whether through an exclamation mark or in the use of repetitive, expletive, affective language. The same use of language can be ascertained in the epistolary friendship between celebrated women in the public eye as actors and writers, who were marked out as exceptional for crossing boundaries in the eyes of polite bourgeois society between spheres that were delineated by masculine, dominant, hegemonic values.

Friendship Ties and Female Gazes between Women Performers and Writers

During the 1990s, scholars of theatre and women's writing drew attention to the forgotten contributions of women writers and female actors, re-defining Habermas's notion of the public sphere in early post-unification Italy as gendered.[37] Recent years have seen the publication of collections of uncovered correspondence between celebrated women writers and actors (e.g., between Serao and Duse, and between Pezzana and Aleramo).[38] According to Antonia Arslan, exceptional middle-class women cultivated female friendships and intellectual ties through the construction of a female solidarity.[39] As trailblazers in their time, the friendships between middle-class (frequently) self-taught women, who stepped out of the domestic sphere and built successful national and, subsequently, in some cases, international reputations, provided role models for middle-class married (or unmarried) women to mirror similar close bonds as wives and mothers in their daily lives. In practice, though, it may have been the case that celebrity female bonds were viewed as exceptional and as unattainable as the celebrities themselves, for there was a level of difficulty in establishing friendships among ordinary women due to domestic isolation, a lack of time, and the unavailability of comfortable public meeting places for women.[40] Yet it could also be the case that among some literate women in their correspondence with their female friends, ordinary middle-class women found something of the closeness they imagined was characteristic of celebrity female bonds. In *Tu che mi guardi* (1997), Adriana Cavarero claims that in exchanging life stories through letters, female friends effectively give each other, and celebrate, the desired unity of a recognisable and narratable gendered identity otherwise unattainable.[41] Moreover, Lucia Re has recently argued that through friendships with younger women, Duse contributed to fostering a sense of legitimacy for women's thought.[42] It may also be helpful here to invoke Gabriella Paolucci's concept of *rispecchiamento* (mirroring) in her 1991 essay, "Amiche" ("Female Friends"),[43] which is a fragmentary process that promotes a greater understanding of the whole self: emphasis is placed on differences between women, for these reveal the untapped in the reflected subjects. It does not imply a static mirroring of one individual to another, but rather a gradual discovery of oneself through, and made possible by, the other.

The Pezzana–Aleramo pairing is yet another example of *affidamento* retrospectively applied, though their mutual admiration for one another's art should not be dismissed. In spite of their 30 years' difference in age, in a letter to Aleramo sent in 1906, Pezzana tells her: "you are the first, and only Italian woman writer who has made a significant impression on me."[44] In the same letter, referring to the publication of her friend's controversial autobiographical novel *Una donna* (A Woman), the actor describes how she is full of admiration for her friend's straightforwardness regarding the issue of dignity for women. Evidence of an apparent threat posed by female friendship to white, male, middle-class hegemony is indeed presented in the novel when Aleramo is hired as a sub-editor to work in Rome (although in real life it was Milan), for the woman's journal, *L'Italia femminile*: her husband lets her relocate to Rome/Milan on the condition that she agrees not to strike up a close friendship with anyone. Aleramo defies him and becomes friends with "la buona madre," whom we know to be the Russian-born *salonnière*, emancipationist, and philanthropist, Alessandrina Ravizza (1846–1915), who introduced Aleramo to Pezzana.[45]

If the Pezzana–Aleramo pairing is an example of Diotima's *affidamento*, Duse and Serao's friendship is more representative of Paolucci's *rispecchiamento*. The friends were contemporaries, yet there was an inequality insofar as Duse, while regarding Serao a "good" person, reportedly said of her on one occasion that she found her superficial; on the other hand, Serao idolised Duse.[46] They were wives and mothers, though they both separated from their husbands and Duse had many subsequent relationships with both women and men, while Serao began a relationship with another man, with whom she had a child. They met in Naples during the early stages of their respective careers in the late 1870s, when Serao reached out to Duse, who was giving her first performances at the Teatro dei Fiorentini and was receiving excellent reviews; Serao was working as a telegraph operator and establishing herself as a writer, publishing short pieces in journals including serialised fiction. Their friendship was to last for around 50 years until Duse's death in 1924.

The examples in the letters that follow testify to an affirmative relationship between women spectators as celebrated professional writers and female performers, whose sense of self was enriched by an epistemophilic "female gaze" *as spectators*. Both writers and performers were well known among the middle-classes, and their friendships played a significant role in elevating their individual professional profiles. They provided one another with mutual emotional support, while concomitantly demonstrating to ordinary women the intrinsic value of female friendship within a deeply patriarchal society. Among Serao's recently published letters to Duse between 1921 and 1923, one in particular is illustrative of an epistemophilic gaze and arrives in the form of a note of gratitude

Figure 3.1 Eleonora Duse (left) and Matilde Serao on holiday in St. Moritz, 1895.

written in December 1921. Thanking God that, before dying, she was able to see Duse perform one last time on stage, Serao rejoices: "My dearest, yesterday evening, returning home still in tears, I thanked God for allowing me to see you still acclaimed for your genius and your tender and deep soul!"[47] Serao had most likely seen Duse act in Ibsen's *The Lady from the Sea* (1889), which she had performed in Turin during the same year. Duse passed away in Pittsburgh on tour in 1924, and Serao died three years later.

Aleramo also (albeit briefly) corresponded with Duse. Writing from Paris in 1922 to Duse in response to a telegram that she had received from her, Aleramo describes "one of the strongest impressions she ever had at the theatre" upon watching her in a performance of Chekhov's *The Cherry Orchard* (1904).[48] (By this point, Aleramo had left her husband and had had a relationship with the writer and poet Lina Poletti (1885–1971), whom Duse was also involved with romantically shortly after Aleramo and Poletti separated in 1910.) Aleramo was in Paris awaiting rehearsals of her play *Endymion* (1923) and expressed frustration about women's "jealousy," having received a poor review of her books by Mussolini's lover, the journalist Margherita Sarfatti (1880–1961), in the newspaper *Popolo d'Italia*. Aleramo lamented: "Women, my great Eleonora, what melancholy and mean things, when they are not You and our unforgettable Ravizza, or some other rare soul! What a shame …"[49] Losing her own mother to a mental asylum in her formative years may have pushed Aleramo (un)consciously to seek friendships with elective symbolic mothers like Duse, Ravizza, and Pezzana, and to particularly value friendships and relationships with women (and, therefore, to feel let down when they turned against her). Aleramo and Pezzana attended the same performance of Ibsen's *A Doll's House* (1879) at the Teatro dei filodrammatici in Milan in 1891, in which Duse played the role of Nora to great acclaim.[50] Pezzana's opinion about a play she was performing at the Teatro Argentina in Rome – she was Clymenestra in Aeschylus's *Oresteia* (458 BC) – is revealed in a letter to Aleramo sent in June 1906. Pezzana does not like the play, even though it contains "new and daring material."[51] In another letter to Aleramo around the same time, Pezzana discusses the "impeccable" performances given by the actors in Edoardo Boutet's *Compagnia* while criticising her own:

> Garavaglia was wonderful. Pieri father and daughter were stupendous. [Evelina] Paoli was faithful to the playwright. And me? I was very afraid of messing up my lines and I hope to do better next time. Absolutely everyone was enthusiastic. Men and women in the boxes and everyone in the stalls were all on their feet at the end of each Act, and there were five or six encores at the finale.[52]

A revealing example of Pezzana's critical acumen emerges in a letter she writes to Aleramo the following month from Vicenza. Pezzana mentions she has been reading a draft of a play by the feminist Jewish writer Virginia Olper Monis (1856–1919), which she had written as an entry for a playwriting competition jointly sponsored by Duse and the newspaper *La Stampa* (the prize was the sponsored production of the winner's play with a performance by Duse and her *Compagnia* at the Teatro Carignano in Turin, and 10,000 lire). Titled *Il castigo* (*The Punishment*), Pezzana describes the final act of Olper Monis's play in which the female protagonist, in a morbid psychological state, feels a burning desire to reveal how she poisoned her husband. Illustrating a similar bias against women exhibited by Aleramo, Pezzana suspects Olper Monis may have "stolen" some of her ideas from several novels, but concludes that while the public may not like it, it is a "bold final act" that "reveals Monis's resourceful mind for scenic inventions."[53] She says that "only Duse can pull off that kind of exceptional difficulty," before stating that she would have liked to play the character herself, but she is "30 years too old."[54] Indeed, Pezzana and Duse were part of the same *Compagnia* formed by Giovanni Emanuel in Naples in 1878 when Pezzana regarded Duse as very much her "pupil."[55]

Another woman writer with whom Duse corresponded was Ada Negri (1870–1945) from Lombardy, whose admiration for Duse as a performer becomes apparent from their correspondence. Negri sent Duse a copy of her autobiographical novel *Stella mattutina* in 1921, in which she reflects on her identity as a woman and mother. Negri tells Duse that she is exemplary in these roles, before suggesting they meet.[56] Duse's subsequent visit gives Negri "a renewed energy to live and work," as she describes her as "the most sublime female figure" of their time. Negri looks forward to seeing Duse perform that evening in her "perfect figuration of Poetry" as Ellida Wangel in Ibsen's *The Lady from the Sea* at the Teatro Lirico in Milan.[57] Subsequent letters to Duse describe her as "the first Woman of Italy" and as her "sublime Sister" who no longer belongs to life but to "Divinity."[58] Like Pezzana, who responded positively to Aleramo's request to ask the director of Pezzana's *Compagnia*, Eduardo Boutet, if he had read Olper Monis's entry to the Duse-*Stampa* competition,[59] Duse obligingly helped her women writer friends by using her connections to assist them as far as she could. For example, she writes to her friend the aspiring writer and noblewoman Laura Gropallo in 1898, suggesting that she might accompany her to Naples in June where Gropallo's work "would be welcomed by Serao with such justice and sweetness,"[60] and writing from Bologna in 1916 to her friend the writer Gemma Ferruggia, who had asked Duse to support her journalist husband's application to work in public office, Duse confirms she has spoken with the *salonnière*, the Contessa Carmelita Zucchini Solimei (1854–1936), "who immediately wrote to the Mayor of Milan, Ettore Ponti, warmly recommending" Ferruggia's husband.[61] In Ferruggia's biography on Duse, Ferruggia recalls how rapidly the "generous woman" had responded to the literary critic Giovanni Pozza's request to read Ferruggia's monologue, after which

Duse had rushed to go and meet her to discuss it, along with the writer Eduardo Calandra (1852–1911). Ferruggia recounts Duse's surprise visit using the language of religion and divinity, describing Duse as an "apparition."[62] Further evidence of Duse's altruism towards her friends and aspiring female artists is illustrated by the library she founded for women actors in Rome in 1914 (the "Biblioteca delle attrici"), with the aim of providing them with a space in which to read, discuss, rehearse, network, and educate themselves (it closed shortly after, due to underuse, an earthquake in Avezzano, and the onset of World War I).[63] The opera singer Gemma Bellincioni (1864–1930) also harnessed her celebrity status to benefit younger, aspiring female artists: writing from Berlin to a friend, she suggests he might wish "to finance several promising female pupils at [her] singing school" there.[64] Such examples are demonstrative of Arslan's "female solidarity" and the positive feedback loop, or "affective alliance," that shaped the relationship between female performer and spectator, whether as writer or aspiring performer.

Evidence of a transnational, epistemophilic "female gaze" on the part of women writers towards Italian female performers, in this case, Ristori, suggests that women writers' eulogies and expressions of solidarity with female performers were not limited to the peninsula. Writing from Rome, the English novelist and periodical writer Frances Eleanor Trollope (1835–1913) corresponded with Ristori, having seen her perform the role of Elizabeth in Paolo Giacometti's *Elizabeth, Queen of England*, which was written expressly for "Madame Ristori and her dramatic company," and published in 1866. Trollope praises emphatically Ristori's "magnificent interpretation of Elizabeth!," which she declares a "triumph,"[65] before commenting on her "glorious [...] voice, the tone of which has always stayed in [her] memory" from when she saw Ristori perform for the first time in London years prior: "Your lines were brilliant; not a gesture, a glance, or a syllable was lost," she continues, before telling her that her "face speaks!"[66] Trollope ends her letter by saying she will send a review of Ristori's performance to London, where she hopes it will be published in the newspaper *The Standard* (yet it was not until Ristori's visit to London's Theatre Royal in Drury Lane in 1882 for a run of performances of Shakespere's *Macbeth*, that her anonymous review was, indeed, published).[67] These are just a few of the many examples that bear testimony to the power of creative female friendships through writing.

Women Writers and Performers as Fans: Autobiography, Memoir

Discussing generic differences between memoir and autobiography, Helen M. Buss argues that "traditional autobiography makes the individual life central, while memoir tends to focus on the times in which the life is lived and the significant others of the memoirist's world."[68] Memoir is a much older and more accessible genre, existing at least as early as the sixteenth century, while the term autobiography was not used until the late eighteenth and early nineteenth centuries.[69] Elaborating upon the differences, Buss argues that: "Memoir writers are more concerned with making their lives meaningful in terms of the lives of others and in terms of their communities rather than in terms of individual accomplishments."[70] Drawing on Marcus Billson, she adds, "autobiographers are more concerned with 'becoming in the world,' memoir writers with 'being in the world.'"[71] Autobiography and memoir are slippery, elusive concepts; if a writer is always implicated in a piece of writing, then any writing may be judged to be autobiographical depending on how one reads it. Given its emergence in revolutionary times, and as a vehicle of expression for more individualistic narratives of the self, autobiography for nineteenth-century (male) writers became a way of attaining both literary legitimacy and a sought-after subjectivity, underpinning the centrality of masculine Western and middle-class modes of subjectivity.

Yet the genre's universalist assumptions were beginning to be questioned and unsettled. This was in part thanks to the explosion of women writers on the literary market in Italy in the 1880s, coupled with the publication of Aleramo's groundbreaking and controversial autobiographical novel *Una donna* in 1906. In addition, the increasingly cosmopolitan cultural and social climate at the *fin de siècle* contributed in some measure towards a heightened sense of awareness among middle-class women of their societally imposed oppressions and prescriptions of conduct through greater exposure to reading and spectating. At a time of greater discussion and visibility in public discourse in the printed media on the role of women and suffrage, better access to education, as well as the emergence in early capitalism and modernism of metafictional and self-reflexive styles of writing, autobiography and memoir such as Neera's *Una giovinezza del secolo XIX* (A Childhood of the Nineteenth Century, 1919) and, much later, Francesca Bertini's *Il resto non conta* (The Rest Does Not Count, 1969), could offer examples to middle-class women readers of a means to "reclaim" the female subject through life-writing. Such constructions of self-articulation are testimony to the affective and discursive ways in which exceptional women – as (inter) national writers and performers – articulated individual experiences of spectatorships. The extent to which Aleramo was moved by Duse's performance of Nora in Ibsen's *A Doll's House* is mentioned three times in Aleramo's published life-writings. The first is in *Una donna*, where she recounts how Pezzana, from her theatre box, had watched Aleramo "weep as Nora left her husband and child," as Aleramo herself was to do a decade or so later.[72] Pezzana and Aleramo were united in their appreciation of Ibsen's ending, which was apparently distasteful to Italian audiences, who protested about it vehemently:

> One evening, after all this, I went to the theatre. As I came out, I met the old actress. I was crying. I had never cried at a play before or,

> indeed, in response to any other work of art. There on the stage I had seen a poor doll made of flesh and blood come to terms with her own inconsistences, decide that she must leave her husband and children, for whom she was only a toy, an ornament. [...] [B]ut the public, admiring as they were of most of the play, had booed the final scene.[73]

She recalls "her great artist friend [Pezzana] with her still-magical voice," saying "if only I were a quarter of a century younger, I would have made [the Italian public] confront it!", after which Aleramo wrote that she "became all the more convinced [...] that it was up to women to defend themselves."[74] Writing some decades later in her diary in 1940, Aleramo reflected on how, in leaving her marital home and her son,

> Ibsen, in reaching [her], had not promised [her] joy, simply peace of mind: in calling upon [her] to take responsibility for [her] actions by being true to [her]self, he had given [her] the chance to exist as a new person, a newborn adult, an island [...].[75]

Several years later, Aleramo recalls how her husband's jealousy, while she was employed to write for the women's periodical *L'Italia femminile*, had meant she had to resign her post, and how she filled her time by reading and going to the theatre.[76]

In Neera's memoir, she reminisces about the "brief but *brillantissima*" Politeama Ciniselli where the Teatro dal Verme in Milan now stands, recalling fondly the "boxes resembling baskets of flowers full of beautiful women spectators."[77] Neera's desiring gaze at women performers is then revealed: recalling at the time (around the late 1860s) that circus shows with horses were very popular, a horse given to the *Compagnia* Ciniselli by the King had been admired and examined close up by Ciniselli's daughter and daughter-in-law, "both of them beautiful; the daughter was a flawless English-looking Amazon, and his daughter-in-law was a head-turner as she sat on the cantering horse."[78] There was a rival *Compagnia* – the Guillaume, she continues, which had two stars: the dark-haired Muller, who rode without a saddle and reigns, and "Miss Ella, who many presumed was a man due to the strength of her/his hamstrings and her/his ability to jump through three hundred hoops without stopping."[79] The androgynous Miss Ella, we are told, would typically wear a white veil and had a sister who (s)he never left behind, and who stood in the centre of the circus with a whip directing the speed of the rider; something that – according to Neera – was a task reserved for men only. Neera concludes that the *Compagnia* Ciniselli was the more elegant, and "high society's preference for that over the *Compagnia* Guillaume was justified."[80] Neera's father was a well-known architect and had helped design the theatre; from time to time, Neera would be taken there to watch shows as a girl, which she found to be "exciting" because they were an "open window onto the world."[81] An example of Neera's desiring, eroticised "female gaze" directed at men is revealed while at a conference held in the theatre, which she had attended with her father, who pointed out the journalist Leone Fortis (1827–96) interviewing the playwright Paolo Ferrari (1822–89). She recalls she "had opened her eyes wide to gaze at those two writers. Not even the King had made [her] heart beat in such a way."[82] Neera's father had also helped to construct the Fossati theatre, "a little people's theatre," which was opened to a packed crowd by the *Compagnia* Moro-Lin with Victor Hugo's *Angelo, tiranno di Padova* (1835). She recalls the performer Celeste Paladini (1845–1927) performing there in the early years of her career in the part of the *ingénue*, and remembers seeing Tommaso Salvini (1829–1915) perform in *I masnadieri* – he had asked whether she was afraid of gun shots from where she was sitting in the box, to which she had replied "no, which was a big lie."[83]

In 1969, silent screen diva and director Francesca Bertini published her memoir, *Il resto non conta*, which, like Aleramo, she dedicated to her son. It contains numerous examples of female spectatorship of theatre, opera, and film from the early twentieth century and of Bertini having met and socialised with the likes of Puccini, Picasso, D'Annunzio, and Marconi. Recalling the first time she saw the Lumierè Brothers' films, she describes them as "delightful,"[84] and later goes on to state that by *circa* 1918, the cinema had "become a part of [her]."[85] Reminiscing about the beginning of her career in 1910 as a stage actor at the Teatro Nuovo in Naples, where she worked for several months, Bertini describes how the famous *Compagnia* there attracted the literary *élite*, the "great and the good," including the journalist Eduardo Scarfoglio (1860–1917), who married Matilde Serao, and poets and playwrights such as Ernesto Murolo (1876–1939) and Salvatore Di Giacomo (1860–1934): "Each evening," writes Bertini, "there were half a dozen truly famous names, including, on occasion, D'Annunzio," by whose "refined elegance" she, along with other stage female actors, was purportedly "fascinated."[86] Even more great, she claims, was Di Giacomo. She recalls his "theatrical genius" in writing *Assunta Spina* (1904), in which Bertini performed the role of the ironer in Act 2 (staged by the *Compagnia* Molinari at the Teatro Nuovo in Naples); Bertini would later go on to adapt and co-direct the film version in 1915, which had "hundreds of screenings and was a great triumph."[87] She pays homage to the Neapolitan female actor in the play's lead role, Adelina Magnetti (1880–63), who she regarded as "a very good actor, very human, wonderful,"[88] describing how before becoming a silent film diva she "was always at the theatre, even when [she] didn't need to be [to act]; it was a habit to go anyway," remembering how she would arrive early in order that she could "read novels by D'Annunzio" that her parents had prohibited her from reading.[89] She reminisces about seeing a performance of Henry Meilhac and Ludovic Halévy's *Frou-Frou* (1870) with her mother in Rome around 1910, and says of the lead actor playing Frou-Frou, Tina Di Lorenzo (1872–1930):

> she was very beautiful, passionate and feisty, in love and sacrificing. I did not miss a moment of her lines as I sat in my chair; I followed her with consternation and also with so much sympathy. She was brilliant and beautiful! The scenes vibrated inside me like a hurricane that demolishes a forest, so much so that after the final act, I was on my feet madly applauding the great Tina Di Lorenzo, *a highly intelligent and deeply elegant female actor who had moved and fascinated me*.[90]

In an extraordinary revelation that perhaps marked the beginnings in the film industry of the problematic power differentials at play in our #MeToo era, Bertini describes a scene in which she is "illicitly" reading Pierre Louÿs's novel *La Femme et le pantin* (The Woman and the Puppet, 1898) about a Spanish *femme fatale*, given to her by Matilde Serao's son, when she is interrupted by Di Giacomo, who tells her that her real name, Elena, "is suited to her beauty," and that her "dark eyes sometimes light up," after which he enquires whether Serao's son is in love with her.[91] Bertini apparently shrugged off the suggestion, at which Di Giacomo reportedly said he would also bring her a French novel. Bertini puts an end to any question in Di Giacomo's mind that she might be open to a relationship with him by stating that she "is not in love with anyone and has other things on her mind," that she is still a young woman, and she "will have time to fall in love later on."[92] It would seem that Bertini felt this was a defining moment in her career, because Di Giacomo invited her to appear as the female lead in Louis Gasnier's film version of Verdi's *Il trovatore* (Film d'Arte Italiana, 1910) released in Rome. On her first experience of acting for the silent screen, Bertini recalls her reaction to working for "the imaginary paradise [...] forbidden to so many young girls and perhaps the dream of so many others" and describes the women spectators as "very elegantly dressed in light clothes with their hair up and decorated with flowers and fruit according to the fashion then."[93] Bertini recalls them wanting to meet her after watching her on the silent screen, remembering the Duchess Ottavia Spinelli d'Aquara (1865–1936) as "very beautiful."[94] On her return to Naples, she reports having met Magnetti who asked her about acting for the silent screen. Bertini remembers having said that "being beautiful, having a perfect face that is photogenic and expressive, and a good figure, is all very important," but that "one cannot compare acting for the stage to acting in the cinema since they are two very different things."[95] On the same visit, Bertini reports being invited to sit in Di Giacomo's and Murolo's box to watch a performance (she does not name which). She writes, "[I]t was ideal for me to be, once and for all, a female spectator" and how "it was a *coming-of-age*" for her; she no longer felt she was a little timid, sad girl, but that she was "becoming someone."[96]

Bertini was also an avid opera-goer. Summoned to Rimini to take part in filming for Gerolamo Lo Savio's *King Lear* (1910), during her stay she was invited to scc a sold-out performance of *Madama Butterfly* (1904) by Puccini, which she describes as "perfect" and "fascinating."[97] She confesses to being a great fan of Puccini's operas during a passage in which she recalls "the magnificent evenings" she spent at the Teatro dell'Opera in Rome, "in which great female singers triumphed: from Rosina Storchio (1872–1945) to Gabriella Besanzoni (1888–1962)," who she recalls was "an amazing Santuzza [from Mascagni's *Cavalleria rusticana* (1890)], who delighted her spectators."[98] Remarking on the women who were in attendance at the Teatro dell'Opera, Bertini reinforces the stereotype of the woman spectator who went "to show off [her] luxurious clothes and jewellery" frowned upon by Vertua Gentile in her *Come devo comportarmi* (How I should Behave), while Bertini instead "went to gain relief from trying days at work" and "always left before the end of the performance."[99]

The large extent to which the worlds of theatre and cinema collided in this period is exemplified in a discussion that reportedly occurred with Duse on their merits and pitfalls. Recalling the première of Giuseppe de Liguoro's and Gustavo Serena's *Fedora* (1916) – the film she confesses to having enjoyed working on the most – at the Teatro delle Quattro Fontane with Duse in attendance,[100] Bertini reports that "the spectators were enthusiastic, and the audience applauded the love scene *wildly*. Spectators were entranced by the drama of the last act in which the dying Fedora asks Loris for an embrace," and that "Duse continued to applaud when the lights came on, and was emotionally moved."[101] Bertini claims Duse had said to the director Alfredo De Antoni: "Fedora's death moved me profoundly. Francesca Bertini interpreted it with so much grace. Please, do tell her how much I admire her, and that I would be delighted to meet her."[102] Feeling anxious about meeting the "great actor," Bertini went to see Duse in her hotel room, which she describes as "one of the most beautiful moments of [her] life."[103] They expressed their mutual appreciation and admiration, and Duse purportedly said she "watched [Bertini's] interpretation and did not miss a second of it, believing that what [she] saw was not cinema but theatre." A conversation on the merits or otherwise of performing for the stage and screen then apparently ensued, and Duse enquired as to why Bertini had not pursued a career as a theatre actor; she hesitated, however, stating (according to Bertini) that "Theatre has irreplaceable values and strengths that will never die, but it also has many difficulties. On reflection," she continued, "I think you are right. The silver screen is better: a new art that, I am sure, will make big in-roads. And you will be its greatest expression," to which Bertini responded that cinema is her passion, and she dedicates all of herself, her soul, to it.[104] Bertini tells Duse – for whom D'Annunzio wrote his play *Francesca da Rimini* (1901) – she would have liked to have seen Duse perform the title role, and Duse reportedly began reciting some lines from the play. Bertini then asked which of Duse's repertory she preferred performing and which character, to which Duse responded: "Nora in Ibsen's *A Doll's House*."[105]

Another symbolic maternal figure for Bertini was Duse's friend Serao, whom Bertini recalls noticing in a box at the Teatro Costanzi in Rome for the première of an unnamed Russian ballet. At this point in her career, Bertini was editing and co-directing the films in which she starred, including *Tosca* (directed by Bertini and Alfredo De Antoni, 1918) based on Sardou's play, the première for which Serao was in attendance. According to Bertini, Serao spoke enthusiastically about the film at the première,[106] and went on to publish a "magnificent" review in her newspaper column "Mosconi" in *Il Giorno*, the daily newspaper she founded in 1904 and directed until her death.[107] In it, she claimed she "had never seen such a well-dressed and beautiful Tosca," adding that she had "seen many, including Sarah Bernhardt's [version] in Paris."[108] Commenting on Serao, Bertini describes her "astute observations" and "innate taste for elegance."[109] Similar to the mutual appreciation she expressed towards Duse, Bertini describes Serao's "passionate and spontaneous affection" towards her, which was apparently mutual, and her own deference, unlimited admiration and devoted affection for the gifted writer, confessing that "her novels had peopled her Neapolitan years with dreams" before they even met.[110] For Bertini, Serao was an "exceptional woman, not only for her indisputable genius, but also because of her temperament and her brilliant conversation," adding of her cosmopolitanism, "Serao had met the most illustrious people on her many trips abroad, and so her conversations were rich in anecdotes."[111] Bertini regrets that she was never able to work with her on a film version of her play, *O Giovannino, o la morte* (Giovannino, or Death, 1888), adapted with Murolo for the stage in 1912. Serao had reportedly written to Giuseppe Barattolo, the director of Caesar Films, about how happy she would be to see the female protagonist, Chiarina, performed by Bertini, but they had apparently never reached an agreement.[112] On hearing of Serao's death in 1927, Bertini writes that her sense of loss was profound; she had lost an "illustrious and great friend," whom she had loved "as *if she were her daughter*."[113] Such insights into women writers' and actors' ties and affective bonds reveal momentary traces and examples of cross-disciplinary female spectatorships in which exceptional women were moved, inspired, emboldened, and uplifted by one another in their careers. Further examples of these traces can be found in biography.

Women Writers as Fans: Duse's Women Biographers

Biography shares similar characteristics with historiography insofar as, like history, and as Ruth Hoberman suggests, it is "non-fictional and narrative, with the passage of time playing an important part in its structure."[114] Hoberman argues that biography resembles fiction "in its effort to evoke its subject's inner life, as well as in its literary 'realism', that is, its use of anecdote and description to make its subject 'come

Figure 3.2 Matilde Serao and Francesca Bertini on the beach in Viareggio, July 1917.

alive,'"[115] while Margaretta Jolly suggests that "[b]iographies have been important as genealogical, religious, and didactic forms since the start of recorded literature."[116] The writer Gemma Ferruggia, who was an avid theatregoer, was ten years younger than Duse, and their friendship lasted 35 years.[117] In her biography *La nostra vera Duse* (Our Real Duse), published following the actor's death in 1924, Ferruggia describes herself surrounded in her office by letters from Duse, who she says was "sublime," "passionate," "divine in her Art," "a Tragic Muse," and "the greatest Italian artist of our times."[118] On Duse's altruism, which has already been mentioned, Ferruggia writes: "She always gave and gave generously, never making an example of herself: every time she gave, she suffered for not being able to do more either as a woman or as a soul."[119] Describing her as "passionate and impulsive, a simple woman who was damaged by writers," she cites Ravizza as having described Duse as "a ray of sunlight" and also mentions Serao, whom Ferruggia refers to as "Duse's insurmountable and unrivalled 'sister.'"[120] Ferruggia likens Duse to a "gay and malleable Goldonian figurine: tragically animated by terror and fervour,"[121] but states that she always viewed "Duse 'the woman' as incomparably superior to Duse 'the artist', however extraordinary her fascination and intelligence (*ingegno*)," adding that "the collective joy and immense success of Duse's performances towards the end of her career were nothing in comparison to the prolific sparks she emitted when she wanted to console an individual soul."[122]

In a statement that contradicts Bertini's claim that Duse's preferred role was Nora in *A Doll's House* (thus signalling the potential for the unreliability of life-writing), Ferruggia writes that the "Latinate" Duse only performed Ibsen's work because she was pressured to do so, and found it "repugnant," referring to the play as "that horrible Norweigian brick," in which she played the role of Nora "with blood in her nose" (*col sangue al naso*).[123] Further on, Ferruggia reveals Duse's dismissiveness of Annie Vivanti's first novel, *Marion, artista di caffè concerto* (*Marion, Caffè Concerto Artist,* 1891), purportedly having said, "With a mentor like Carducci, I think she could have done better" (Giosuè Carducci (1835–1907) and Vivanti (1866–1942) were in a relationship at the time).[124] Writing to Serao in 1885 from Rio de Janeiro, where she was performing Sardou's *Fernanda* (1870) at the Teatro Imperial D. Pedro II, Duse purportedly told her friend that she felt it was the first time she had performed well, "very well," which she admits to telling her "because [she] does not make fun of people who 'speak highly of their own souls and intellect,'" she is instead "a good person," and "above" such behaviour.[125] Duse's influence over playwrights is presented in a letter published in Ferruggia's memoir addressed to Gallieno Sinimberghi, who was at that time in the process of writing *Il matrimonio d'Irene* (1886). Duse cautions Sinimberghi twice in her letter "not to write with a particular female actor in mind," and to "rid himself of any preoccupation he may have with writing for a particular actor or actress," on the basis that "today we are here, and tomorrow we will be no more."[126]

Writing on Duse as a stage artist, Ferruggia evokes Duse's early performances, claiming "she breathed life into the most inconsistent characters," and "where there was nothing, she created life. Even when she uttered banal sentences, she gave her spectators quivers that they will never forget."[127] Referring to Duse's performances in the title role in Sardou's *Fédora* (1882), Ferruggia emotes:

> Ah! How she accentuated her lines "And now he [Loris] tells of his punishment" in *Fedora*! After the gambling scene in his *Odette*

> (1881), how she uttered the words "child snatcher" to her husband! And we all remember clearly that happy and truly Goldonian Mirandolina: *that* truly seventeenth-century Pamela.[128]

Commenting on Duse's costumes in Dumas *fils*'s *La Dame aux Camélias* (The Lady of the Camellias (1852)), Ferruggia calls on her readers to remember how Duse was a "woman of personal intuition and a rare find," asking of them

> who, among us, does not recall Cesarina's hairstyle in the first act of Dumas *fils*'s *Moglie di Claudio* (The Wife of Claudio, 1881)? It was tied up in a dark silk red scarf in a bizarre manner that made her face look Satanic. And her dress in the final act? Cesarina seemed enveloped in snakes.[129]

Writing on Duse's voice, Ferruggia uses a capital "V" to describe "her unforgettable Voice," which "was human like no other; not bronze, not silver nor golden, but superhuman, a companion of the soul in search of perfection."[130] Discussing the previous generation of *grandi attori* (Ristori, Salvini, Rossi) and their perception of Duse, Ferruggia complains angrily that they "never gave Duse her due," suggesting they "were too different generationally, conceptually, and in terms of their personalities," a point that will be explored in more detail in Chapter 4.

Olga Signorelli's biography of Duse draws attention to her close friendships with women of her own generation. Writing on Duse's friendship with Serao, Signorelli states that "Matilde Serao was beside [Duse], supporting her like a sister in the first pangs of love. She, more than anyone, realised the hidden fragility under Eleonora's tenacity and will."[131] In contrast to Ferruggia's biography, Signorelli includes many images of the stage diva throughout her life's work, as well as of significant figures with whom she had a relationship. The tone is less personalised and more detached, but the biography's chronological structure is clearer and more coherent; though Signorelli met Duse in 1915, they were not friends. Signorelli includes in her biography oral history testimony from unidentified spectators who appreciated Duse's performances: "Every evening she seized your heart and squeezed it like a handkerchief" is a quotation from one such admirer.[132] Like Ferruggia, Signorelli cites Duse on several occasions in order to provide insight into Duse's personality. One such occasion is when, in Turin in 1880, Duse watches every evening of Sarah Bernhardt's performances. Signorelli writes

> Cesare Rossi [the director of the *Compagnia* in which Duse performed] gave over the theatre for several evenings to Sarah Bernhardt's company. For Eleonora, this was a revelation. "Here is a woman who uplifts our work, who makes the audience respect what is beautiful,

> and bow before her art", she said after she had watched, enraptured, every performance.[133]

Continuing, Signorelli reveals the powerful effect Bernhardt had on Duse and her creative and ambitious style of acting:

> When Sarah Bernhardt had left Turin, Duse suggested to Cesare Rossi that the repertory should be overhauled. She had realised more than ever the banality of the plays which, through habit and laziness, were then being offered to the public. Her energetically expressed wishes prevailed, and she attempted plays which then seemed absurd: she played in Dumas *fils*'s *Princesse de Bagdad*, which no actress apart from Sarah Bernhardt had managed successfully; immediately after it *La Femme de Claude*, also by Dumas *fils*, which no other actress had dared tackle since Desclée. And in both parts, she was triumphantly successful.[134]

Duse clearly saw in Bernhardt – her contemporary – a role model. Further on in her biography, Signorelli states that "a few years later [in the mid- to late 1880s]," when Duse began touring the world with her performances, "foreign audiences that did not understand her language were to understand her genius. The modest Italian actress was acclaimed throughout the theatres of the world by non-Italian speakers."[135] We are given a fascinating insight into what the actor is alleged to have said about the "comforting" Fallen Women she played:

> Those poor women in my plays have entered so far into my heart and into my mind that while I am doing my best to make my listeners understand them ... it is they who have, little by little, ended up comforting me![136]

According to Signorelli, Marguérite Gautier from *La Dame aux camélias* (The Lady of the Camellias)

> was one of Eleonora's favourite parts. [...] She loved [it] so much that when in 1897, she went to Paris and played at the Théâtre Sarah Bernhardt, she dared to start with *La Dame aux camélias*, even though Bernhardt was the acknowledged exponent of the part. And, of course, she acted in Italian, but had unequalled success.[137]

Another anonymous spectator of this performance (or was it Signorelli herself?) is quoted as saying

> [a]s the play advances [...] she binds us to her more and more, so that by the end of the fourth act one has hardly the strength to follow her. The joy of artistic participation is turned into profound suffering at that repeated "Armando, Armando" that enters the heart like a

> sharp knife. You want to cry out with pain, with despair, at a compassion that has turned to suffering.[138]

Revealing the extent to which Duse was a universal actor able to move audiences across the globe despite linguistic barriers, Signorelli cites a letter from Chekhov addressed to his sister after he had been present at the first night of a run of Shakespeare's *Antony and Cleopatra* (1607) in St. Petersburg, in which Duse performed the role of Cleopatra:

> I have just seen the Italian actress Duse in Shakespeare's *Cleopatra*. I don't know any Italian, but she acted so well that I felt I understood every word. What a superb actress! I've never seen anything like her. I looked at her and felt sad to think we have to educate our temperaments and tastes with such wooden actresses as ..., and others like her, whom we think great because we have seen none better. While I was watching Duse, I realised why one is bored at the theatre in Russia.[139]

Like Ferruggia, Signorelli takes umbrage at Duse's female detractors. Pauline von Metternich (1836–1921) – the organiser of Vienna's international drama festival in 1898 – purportedly "considered [Duse] lacked the international renown the programme demanded in its performers."[140] When Duse was invited to perform in Vienna following a rave review in the Austrian press of her performances in Russia, she consequently declined the invitation and accepted only the following year.[141] Whether she and Ferruggia used "fiction in [their] effort to evoke [their] subject's inner life, as well as in [their] literary 'realism,' that is [their] use of anecdote and description to make [their] subject 'come alive,'" we cannot know.[142] What we can be sure of is that the enthusiasm and *jouissance* (whether homoerotic or otherwise) of diva-worshippers, fans, and spectators of Duse's performances are clear examples of their spectatorial pleasures and admiration.

Female Gazes in Private Diaries

Together with the autobiographical genre and the modern-day letter, diaries have been widespread since the eighteenth century. Writing on the generic features of the diary, Rachel Cottam suggests:

> [I]t is an "elastic" – and expanding – stow, which a diarist often carries, and into which (s)he casts life's materials and loose ends, ostensibly without arrangement. Often, the diary is written in a compulsive attempt to "hold" and store literally all of the diarist's experience. [...] It is characterised by its hybridity and diversity. [...] It may be an intimate confessional or a family album; a collection of historical events; or an introspective attempt to capture mood; detached

> short notes [...]; or a narrative account of a particular life episode [...]. It may or may not be dated.
>
> While the diary is itself difficult to confine, it also unsettles the boundaries upon which other genre distinctions are usually made. Indeed, it lies on the border between life and its representation, supplementing both. It may be classified as art, or as document. On the one hand, it is continuous with the lived life: it is source material, used to explain the diarist's other writing (including other life-writing). It is an art*less* presentation of the self, a text that can be looked through, to catch a glimpse of undistorted life. On the other hand, it is an unfinished art form that engenders (but is subordinated to) the polished "work of art".[143]

Not all women took pleasure in going to the theatre, as we glean from an excerpt of a diary written by Silvia Ferro (1888–1965). A teenager from Genoa writing in her journal at the end of 1904 and reflecting on her year, she reveals how she was decidedly unimpressed with her first outing to the opera to see a performance of Verdi's *Aida* (1871):

> It was the first time in my life, at age 16, that I had gone to the theatre, to the Genoese Politeama, to see Verdi's *Aida*. But this entertainment doesn't appeal to me; with the money I spent on a ticket I would much rather buy myself many books.[144]

Reflecting several months later, she writes about how she overheard her school friends daydreaming about dances, theatre outings, and parties, which annoyed her given she does not feel inclined to join in because she does not know what to say (she had never attended a dance or a party, and had only been to the theatre once, at which her "friends laughed"). She remembers that it was her late mother who wanted to go to the theatre:

> The effect those artists on stage had on me was really very strange. They seemed like machines, and I felt sorry for them insofar as I thought: they sing all those verses, they sacrifice themselves to entertain others – a public that applauds and whistles – with the same indifference according to the effect the production has had on the spectators. I like the music, yes, I like it very much, and for this reason only I'd go back to the theatre, but for the rest I wouldn't spend a *quattrino*. I can enjoy good music elsewhere. If some of my friends and theatre buffs could hear me now!! ... What a telling off I would get!![145]

Ferro is more impressed years later upon watching William Cody's *Buffalo Bill's Wild West* (1883):

> So many people! It was a great show. So many English, who received huge applause when they arrived with their flag. A great show with

> horses and men [illegible] visible on their faces; Chinese, Japanese, Mexicans. Games of stamina and strength, pantomime. The whole thing was good. Behind us there were some Spaniards. We waited to see the carriages leave. What magnificent, colossal horses![146]

She also writes highly of Carlo Bertolazzi's *Il diavolo e l'acqua santa* (The Devil and the Holy Water, 1905), which she delights in seeing at the Teatro Nazionale in Genoa with her father, even though it confirms to her that she would not like to be an actor herself:

> Giusti [a family friend] performed the role of the Priest very well; I very much enjoyed watching the play, but I also see now that my aspiration is not to work in the theatre; indeed, I would like to do something entirely different.[147]

Ferro frequently watched amateur theatre. Describing her friend Corinna's performance (of what, exactly, is not mentioned) at the Istituto Vittorino da Feltre in Genoa, she observes that she "acted very well," and "received a lot of applause that was truly merited."[148] That same month, she describes Giusti performing Schiller's poem, "The dance of the dead," translated by Maffei, which Ferro describes as "splendid" and "very beautiful," and several days later she watches him perform Goldoni's *L'impostore* (1748) at the Teatro Nazionale, where "there were a lot of women in attendance" and "the performance was very good."[149]

Another diarist – upper-middle-class Rosina D'Amico (1878–1930) from Rome – writing on the last night of the year in 1893, after having been the previous night to a performance which she describes as "in general, good," records her happiness at having gone to speak to one of the women actors in the performance – a Signorina Vagnizzi – after the show, who expresses her pleasure in seeing and speaking to Rosina.[150] Another life-writer, Marcella Torretta (1881–1958), writing in her memoir from Turin, recalls how in 1900 she went to the Palestra Ristori to see amateurs perform Sardou's *Fédora* but that she "had hardly understood the play as her friend, who had recently returned from Montecarlo, was talking to her about her exploits throughout the performance."[151] She recalls her delight at the theatre one evening when an actor, whose name she does not recall, reminded her of her deceased father: "Suddenly, I thought I could hear my father speaking and I was so happy that I did not want the performance to end."[152] We are given an insight into the "tender gazes" that typified an evening out by the military officer, Bruno Palamenghi, the nephew of statesman Francesco Crispi (1818–1901), while based in Catania in Sicily. He writes that he has started to woo an unnamed princess during their evenings spent at the Teatro Pacini and at the Nazionale, and laments the fact he has to content himself with their "tender gazes" for the time being, since his friends, who could introduce them, are away on their summer holidays.[153]

Conclusion

As a repository for the emotions, the diaries of the Genoese Silvia Ferro and Roman Rosina D'Amico contained their innermost thoughts and feelings about everyday events, as well as their impressions of performances they had attended on their evenings out. Their diaries describe the world through their own eyes, and as such remain important social documents for gender and women's studies for what they reveal about the past and, in particular, female spectatorship. Recreating their voices and using their words enables us to temporarily glimpse and inhabit "the intimate dimensions of their lives."[154] In reading ordinary young middle-class female adolescents' diaries from the turn of the twentieth century, and in thinking about ordinary women's and adolescents' spectatorial pleasures, we can follow Saidiya Hartman in

> [S]peculating about what might have been, imagining the things whispered in dark bedrooms, and amplifying moments of withholding, escape [in the broadest sense] and possibility, moments when the vision and dreams [of middle-class teenage girls] seemed possible [and] recognise […] the utopian longings and the promise of a future world that [possibly] resided in […] the refusal to be governed.[155]

Affect is essential to becoming a fan; in a fan's admiration for a given performer, (s)he draws from felt and embodied responses towards the performer with whom (s)he may identify in a given role, and who provides her/him momentarily with escapism, an allusive sense of ownership and identification, and a sense of connection and shared feeling (with the performer or with other fans present). A fan may also maintain a critical distance from the performer as she performs a given role. As Nicolle Lamerichs has argued, "affect helps construct the identity of the fan," and "fandom is a way of making sense of the world through felt and shared experiences."[156] The examples in this chapter of the female gazes in life-writings by both exceptional and ordinary women reveal spectators' admiration for, and excitement (or, indeed, reservation) about how watching a performance of a play, an opera or, indeed, a film, is charged with emotional and affective currency by the use of exclamation marks, ellipsis, and short (occasionally one-word) sentences pronouncing their view on a particular performance, event, or performer. A female affective, critical community – an "affective alliance," to draw again on Grossberg – by and for women, was in the process of taking shape for a growing middle class that was becoming more educated and literate as the century drew to a close, and a new one was beginning. We now turn to the evidence of this feedback loop between women writers, performers, and spectators in published writings – in columns in women's journals and publications aimed at a female readership – and theatre, opera, and film reviews written by women writers in newspapers.

Notes

1 See: Mark Seymour, *Emotional Arenas: Life, Love, and Death in 1870s Italy* (Oxford: Oxford University Press, 2020), pp. 78–112. Seymour uses records of a dramatic 1879 Roman murder trial to develop a new paradigm for emotions history – the "emotional area" of social spaces – as a way of visualising and thinking about emotional cultures over time (p. 7).
2 Gabriella Romani, "Women Writing Letters: Epistolary Practices in Nineteenth-Century Newspapers, Manuals and Fiction," in *Across Genres, Generations and Borders: Italian Women Writing Lives*, ed. by Susanna Scarparo and Rita Wilson (Newark: University of Delaware Press, 2004), pp. 24–37 (p. 24).
3 *A History of Private Life: From the Fires of Revolution to the Great War*, Vol. IV, ed. by Michelle Perrot (Cambridge, MA: Belknap Press of Harvard University Press, 1990), p. 4.
4 Horace Porter Abbott, *Diary Fiction: Writing as Action* (Ithaca and London: Cornell University Press, 1984), pp. 9–10.
5 *Ibid.*, p. 11.
6 Linda Anderson, *Autobiography*, 2nd edn. (London: Routledge, 2010), p. 3.
7 Tess Cosslett, Celia Lury, and Penny Summerfield, "Introduction," in *Feminism and Autobiography: Texts, Theories, Methods*, ed. by Tess Cosslett, Celia Lury, and Penny Summerfield (London: Routledge, 2000), p. 2. See, also: Paul De Man, "Autobiography as De-Facement," *Modern Languages Notes* 94 (1979), 919–30.
8 Roland Barthes, "The Death of the Author," in *Image, Music, Text* [1968] (New York: Hill and Wang, 1977), p. 142.
9 Romani, "Women Writing Letters," p. 28.
10 Roy Pascal, *Design and Truth in Autobiography* (Cambridge: Harvard University Press, 1960), p. 183.
11 Nicolle Lamerichs, *Productive Fandom: Intermediality and Affective Reception in Fan Cultures* (Amsterdam: Amsterdam University Press, 2018), p. 17. Italics my emphasis.
12 Cesare Balbo, *Delle speranze d'Italia* (Florence: Le Monnier, 1844), p. 181.
13 Seymour, *Emotional Arenas*, p. 80.
14 The Pieve prize is a life-writing prize awarded annually by the Archivio Diaristico di Pieve Santo Stefano in Tuscany.
15 Emilia, *Le parole nascoste* (Milan: Rossellina Archinto, 1987), p. 131. Her capitalisation.
16 Emilia, *Le parole nascoste*, p. 101.
17 *Ibid.*, pp. 102–3.
18 Jackie Stacey, *Star Gazing: Hollywood Cinema and Female Spectatorship* (London and New York: Routledge, 1994), p. 197.
19 *Ibid.*, pp. 154–5.
20 Mark Duffett, *Understanding Fandom: An Introduction to the Study of Media Fan Culture* (London: Bloomsbury, 2013), p. 139.

21 The letters and diaries referred to in this chapter derive from collections of theatre and diary archives located in the following institutions: Fondazione Archivio Diaristico Nazionale, Pieve Santo Stefano; Museo Teatrale alla Scala, Biblioteca Livia Simone, Milan; Archivio Eleonora Duse, Istituto per il Teatro e il Melodramma, Fondazione Giorgio Cini, Venice; Museo Biblioteca dell'Attore, Genoa; Biblioteca Museo Teatrale Siae (Società Italiana degli Autori ed Editori), Rome; Biblioteca Italiana delle Donne, Bologna.

22 Letter from A. de Almedia and Rachele de Almedia to Adelaide Ristori, dated 23 June 1870, Fondo Adelaide Ristori, Archive of the Museo Biblioteca dell'Attore, Genoa.

23 Letter from Elise Arnberg to Adelaide Ristori, dated 27 October 1880. Fondo Adelaide Ristori, Archive of the Museo Biblioteca dell'Attore, Genoa.

24 Maria Teresa Cometto, *La Marchesa Colombi: la prima giornalista della Corriere della sera* (Turin: B. L. U., 1996), p. 162. Letter from La Marchesa Colombi to Giovanni Marano dated 2 March 1882. Housed in the state archive of Novara (Collezione Finazzi).

25 Olga Signorelli, *Eleonora Duse*, trans. by Isabel Quigly (London: Thames and Hudson, 1959), p. 26.

26 *Ibid.*, p. 26.

27 *Ibid.*, p. 28.

28 *Ibid.*, p. 46; p. 85.

29 *Ibid.*, p. 92.

30 Letter dated 5 November 1901, cited in Dora Setti, *La Duse com'era* (Milan: Pan, 1978), p. 233.

31 *Ibid.*, p. 47.

32 *Ibid.*, p. 73.

33 Undated letter from Virginia Reiter to Adelaide Ristori, held at the Biblioteca Museo Teatrale SIAE, Rome.

34 *Archivio Multimediale Attori Italiani* (Florence: Florence University Press, 2012), http://amati.fupress.net/Main.uri [accessed 16 July 2019].

35 Luigi Donato Ventura, *Memoirs and Artistic Studies of Adelaide Ristori*, trans. by Giorgio Mantellini (London: Doubleday, Page & Co., 1907), p. 246.

36 Letter dated 26 May 1881, held at the Museo dell'Attore, Genoa.

37 See, for example: Laura Mariani, *Il tempo delle attrici: emancipazionismo e teatro in Italia fra Ottocento e Novecento* (Doria: Mongolfiera, 1991), and Giuliana Morandini, *La voce che è in lei* (Milan: Bompiani, 1997). For Habermas, the public sphere is a masculine domain – an intermediary space between the intimate sphere of the family and the official sphere of the state, a space free from prejudice and separate from the government in which authority is held up to public scrutiny and where the common good of the people is debated. See: Jürgen Habermas, *The Structural Transformation of the Public Sphere: An Enquiry into a Category of Bourgeois Society*, trans. Thomas Burger, with the assistance of Frederick Lawrence, 9th ed. (Cambridge: Polity, [1969] 2006).

38 See, for example: *Lettere: Matilde Serao a Eleonora Duse*, ed. by Matilde Tortora (Naples: Graus, 2004) and *L'attrice del cuore: storia di Giacinta Pezzana attraverso le lettere*, ed. by Laura Mariani (Florence: Le lettere, 2005).

39 Antonia Arslan, *Dame, droga e galline: romanzo popolare e romanzo di consumo tra '800 e '900* (Padova: Cleup, 1977), pp. 23–4.

40 Michaela De Giorgio, *Le italiane dall'Unità a oggi: modelli culturali e comportamenti sociali* (Rome: Laterza, 1992), p. 119.
41 See: Adriana Cavarero, *Tu che mi guardi, tu che mi racconti: filosofia della narrazione* (Milan: Feltrinelli, 1997).
42 Lucia Re, "Eleonora Duse and Women: Performing Desire, Power and Knowledge," in "The Diva in Modern Italian Culture," ed. by Katharine Mitchell and Clorinda Donato, *Italian Studies* 70:3 (2015), 347–63 (354).
43 See: Gabriella Paolucci, "Amiche: figure dell'amicizia femminile e femminismo," *Memoria* 32:2 (1991), 18–27.
44 Letter from Pezzana to Aleramo, dated 16 June 1906. Housed at the Museo Teatrale alla Scala, Biblioteca Livia Simone, Milan.
45 Sibilla Aleramo, *Una donna* (Milan: Feltrinelli, 2020), p. 115.
46 Helen Sheehy, *Eleonora Duse: A Biography* (New York: Alfred A. Knopf, 2003), p. 27.
47 Letter dated 8 December 1921 from Matilde Serao to Eleonora Duse, cited in Tortora, *Lettere*, p. 23.
48 Letter dated 31 December 1922 from Sibilla Aleramo to Eleonora Duse. Housed in the Archivio Eleonora Duse, Istituto per il Teatro e il Melodramma, Fondazione Giorgio Cini, Venice.
49 *Ibid.*
50 See: Enza De Francisci, *A 'New' Woman in Verga and Pirandello: From Page to Stage* (Oxford: Legenda, 2018), pp. 42–8.
51 Letter from Pezzana to Aleramo dated 19 June 1906. Housed at the Museo Teatrale alla Scala, Biblioteca Livia Simone, Milan.
52 Letter undated from Pezzana to Aleramo. Housed at the Museo Teatrale alla Scala, Biblioteca Livia Simone, Milan.
53 Letter from Pezzana to Aleramo dated 2 July 1906. Housed at the Museo Teatrale alla Scala, Biblioteca Livia Simone, Milan.
54 *Ibid.*
55 Laura Mariani, "Giacinta Plays Thérèse," trans. by John Dean and Bianca Mastrominico, in *The Open Page* 8 (2003), 84–91 (90).
56 Letter from Ada Negri to Eleonora Duse dated 11 June 1921. Housed in the Archivio Eleonora Duse, Istituto per il Teatro e il Melodramma, Fondazione Giorgio Cini, Venice.
57 Letter from Negri to Duse dated 9 June 1921. Housed in the Archivio Eleonora Duse, Istituto per il Teatro e il Melodramma, Fondazione Giorgio Cini, Venice.
58 Letter from Negri to Duse dated 21 January 1923. Housed in the Archivio Eleonora Duse, Istituto per il Teatro e il Melodramma, Fondazione Giorgio Cini, Venice.
59 Undated letter from Pezzana to Aleramo, circa December 1905. Housed at the Museo Teatrale alla Scala, Biblioteca Livia Simone, Milan.
60 Letter from Duse to Donna Laura Gropallo dated 13 May 1898. Housed at the Museo Teatrale alla Scala, Biblioteca Livia Simone, Milan.
61 Letter from Duse to Gemma Ferruggia dated 24 January 1916. Housed at the Museo Teatrale alla Scala, Biblioteca Livia Simone, Milan.
62 Gemma Ferruggia, *La nostra vera Duse* (Milan: Sonzogno, 1924), p. 23.
63 Many of the books from Duse's library are now housed at Murray Edwards College, Cambridge, following their bequest by Duse's grandchildren in

1962. See: Anna Sica and Alison Wilson, *The Murray Edwards College Duse Collection* (Milan: Mimesis, 2012).

64 Letter from Gemma Bellincioni to unknown, dated 9 July 1912. Housed at the Museo Teatrale alla Scala, Biblioteca Livia Simone, Milan.

65 Letter dated 29 April 1881, held at the Museo dell'Attore, Genoa.

66 *Ibid.*

67 Eleanor Trollope, "Madame Ristori at Drury Lane," *The Standard,* 17 July 1882, p. 2.

68 Helen M. Buss, "Memoirs," in *Encyclopaedia of Life Writing: Autobiographical and Biographical Forms*, Vol. 2, ed. by Margaretta Jolly (London and Chicago: Fitzroy Dearborn, 2001) pp. 595–6 (p. 595).

69 Buss, "Memoirs," p. 595. The *Oxford English Dictionary* defines the genre as: "[A]ny personal record of events, not purporting to be a complete history, but treating of such matters as come within the personal knowledge of the writer," p. 595.

70 *Ibid.*, p. 595.

71 *Ibid.*, p. 595. See also: Marcus Billson, "The Memoir: New Perspectives on a Forgotten Genre," *Genre* 10 (1977), 259–82.

72 Sibilla Aleramo, *Una donna* (Milan: Feltrinelli, 2020), p. 118.

73 Sibilla Aleramo, *A Woman*, trans. by Rosalind Delmar (Berkley and Los Angeles: University of California Press, 1980), p. 156.

74 *Ibid.*, p. 156.

75 Sibilla Aleramo, *Un amore insolito: diario, 1940–1944* (Milan: Feltrinelli, 1979), p. 15. Entry dated 24 November 1940.

76 Sibilla Aleramo, *Dal mio diario (1940–1944)* (Rome: Tumminelli, 1945), p. 237.

77 Neera, *Una giovinezza del secolo XIX: Memorie* [1919] (Milan: Feltrinelli, 1980), p. 92.

78 *Ibid.*, p. 92.

79 *Ibid.*

80 *Ibid.*, p. 93.

81 *Ibid.*

82 *Ibid.*

83 *Ibid.*, p. 91.

84 Francesca Bertini, *Il resto non conta* (Pisa: Giardini, 1969), p. 16.

85 *Ibid.*, p. 118.

86 *Ibid.*, p. 20.

87 *Ibid.*

88 *Ibid.*

89 *Ibid.*, pp. 20–3.

90 *Ibid.*, p. 97. My italics.

91 *Ibid.*, pp. 24–5.

92 *Ibid.*, p. 26.

93 *Ibid.*, pp. 34–9.

94 *Ibid.*, p. 43.

95 *Ibid.*, p. 46.

96 *Ibid.* My italics.

97 *Ibid.*, p. 54.

98 *Ibid.*, p. 116.

99 *Ibid.*

100 *Ibid.*, p. 101. The film was accompanied by music written by Umberto Giordano.
101 *Ibid.*, p. 102. My italics.
102 *Ibid.*
103 *Ibid.*, p. 107.
104 *Ibid.*, p. 105.
105 *Ibid.*, p. 106.
106 *Ibid.*, p. 128.
107 *Ibid.*, p. 128. See, also: Matilde Serao, "Il grande avvenimento d'arte: *Tosca* al 'Maximum,'" in *Il Giorno*, 14 April 1918, p. 1.
108 *Ibid.*, p. 130.
109 *Ibid.*
110 *Ibid.*
111 *Ibid.*, p. 131.
112 *Ibid.*
113 *Ibid.*, p. 131. My italics.
114 Ruth Hoberman, "Biography: General Survey," in *Encyclopaedia of Life Writing*, pp. 109–12 (p. 109).
115 *Ibid.*, p. 109.
116 Margaretta Jolly, "Editor's Note: Aims, Scope, and Selection of Entries," in *Encyclopaedia of Life Writing*, pp. ix–x (p. ix).
117 See: www.treccani.it/enciclopedia/gemma-ferruggia_(Dizionario-Biografico)/ [accessed 9 December 2020].
118 Ferruggia, *La Nostra Vera Duse*, p. 14.
119 *Ibid.*
120 *Ibid.*, p. 21.
121 *Ibid.*, p. 22.
122 *Ibid.*, p. 23.
123 *Ibid.*, p. 25.
124 *Ibid.*, p. 27.
125 *Ibid.*, p. 40.
126 *Ibid.*, p. 45.
127 *Ibid.*, p. 47.
128 *Ibid.* Her italics.
129 *Ibid.*, p. 55.
130 *Ibid.*
131 Signorelli, *Eleonora Duse*, p. 24.
132 *Ibid.*, p. 20.
133 *Ibid.*, p. 26.
134 Signorelli, *Eleonora Duse*, p. 28.
135 *Ibid.*, p. 30.
136 *Ibid.*, p. 42.
137 *Ibid.*, p. 46.
138 *Ibid.*, p. 47.
139 *Ibid.*, p. 61.
140 *Ibid.*, p. 63.
141 *Ibid.*, p. 63.
142 Hoberman, *Encyclopaedia of Life Writing*, p. 109.
143 Rachel Cottam, "Diaries and Journals: General Survey," in *Encyclopaedia of Life Writing*, pp. 267–8.

144 Extract from the diary of Silvia Ferro (1888–1965), "Un secolo sta per morire," held at the Fondazione Archivio Diaristico Nazionale, Pieve Santo Stefano. Entry dated 31 December 1904.
145 *Ibid.*, entry dated 5 March 1905.
146 *Ibid.*, 16 March 1906.
147 *Ibid.*, 10 May 1907.
148 *Ibid.*, 19 May 1907.
149 *Ibid.*, 26 May 1907.
150 Diary entry 31 December 1893 from the diary of Rosina D'Amico held at the Fondazione Archivio Diaristico Nazionale, Pieve Santo Stefano.
151 Marcella Torretta, "In ricchezza e in povertà. Autobiografia, 1886–1953," held at the Fondazione Archivio Diaristico Nazionale.
152 *Ibid.*
153 Bruno Palamenghi, entry dated 1 August 1886. Held at the Fondazione Archivio Diaristico Nazionale. See, also: *Patria mia. Scritture private nell'Italia unita*, ed. by Massimo Baioni (Bologna: Il Mulino, 2011), p. 129; p. 211; p. 267.
154 Saidiya Hartman, *Wayward Lives, Beautiful Experiments: Intimate Histories of Social Upheaval* (New York: W.W. Norton & Company, 2019), p. xiii.
155 *Ibid.*, pp. xiv–xv.
156 Lamerichs, *Productive Fandom*, p. 19.

4 The Public Female Gaze

This chapter examines the linguistic strategies adopted by women writers to draw their women readers into the theatrical, cinematic, and/or operatic event about which they were writing. I argue that a mass, female, critical community of spectators, with its own lexicon of cultural criticism by and for women, was being established thanks to women writers' interventions in journalism addressed to a female readership. Through their commentaries on theatre-going in columns in journals for women, and theatre reviews in periodicals addressed to a female readership, women writers were inviting women spectators to watch and listen with a combination of critical acumen, emotional engagement, and surrender to pleasure. As intermediaries and critics, women writers were consciously educating and initiating women spectators – who were also readers – in how to be critically engaged with the new national language on their evenings out (e.g., through their use of hyperbolic language and responses of affect, ellipsis and exclamation, as well as through commentary on fashion, beauty, people-spotting, and in discursive pieces). Plays and screenplays, whose themes included adultery, betrayal, and transgression of societal norms, and whose performers belonged to a growing circulation of cosmopolitan, internationally renowned female Italian stars from the 1880s and 1890s onwards, were inviting women readers and spectators to look increasingly inwards, thus becoming self-questioning, self-aware, and self-determined, with a more developed sense of self as spectators.

In spite of the stereotypes advanced by the likes of composer Franz Liszt – that female spectators went to the theatre and opera to flirt with their lovers as "lovers of love itself," and were not at all engaged with the action taking place on stage – which, at least in French culture, were still very much embedded discursively in the 1880s – there is evidence in Italian women's print culture to suggest that exceptional upper-class women from the early nineteenth century who received an education did engage.[1] Gioseffa Cornoldi Caminer's *La donna galante ed erudita* (The Gallant and Erudite Woman), which appeared in Venice in 1786, was the first journal in Italy to address a predominantly female readership and published features on theatre, while Giuseppina Mascari's recent study

DOI: 10.4324/9780429293511-5

of Carolina Lattanzi's Milanese women's journal *Corriere delle dame* (1804–18) reveals that some learned, upper-class and aristocratic women were critical consumers of the performances they attended.[2] However, only exceptional women – members of the aristocracy and the upper-middle classes – published critical theatre and opera reviews in columns on theatre-going in journals during the Risorgimento.

Unlike in neighbouring European countries such as France and Britain, where the woman writer of the modern novel emerged *en masse* in the eighteenth century, middle-class women writers of the modern Italian novel began to establish themselves from the mid- to late 1870s onwards. Concomitantly, they also began writing commentaries and columns on theatre and opera-going in women's periodicals and in newspapers. Though women readers would have undoubtedly read, and been influenced by generations of women writers whose works were translated into the vernacular (e.g., novels by Jane Austen, George Sand, and George Elliot), the absence of an identifiable genealogy of "Italian" women writers prior to the mid- to late1870s suggests that the roots of what Elaine Showalter calls a "female literary tradition" were only then being established thanks to the favourable literary and cultural climate.[3] Thus, because of the influx of women writers writing critically about theatre and opera performances from the 1870s onwards, and the emergence of a sizable female readership following the rise in female literacy, women spectators began to watch and listen to stage and screen performances in a more critical, discerning, and self-conscious way. For example, Gualberta Alaide Beccari's emancipationist periodical *La donna* (1868–91), which presented itself as an "educational periodical compiled by Italian women," published eulogies praising the work of renowned women performers frequently, as well as many critical reviews too numerous to mention here. Yet, at the risk of essentialism, as we shall see in this chapter, reviews written by men differed insofar as they drew on more scientific, detached language, while women writers' observations were more freely subjective and openly emphatic about affect.

Moreover, as if driven by a sense of duty to guide and instruct their female readers on how to be a modern spectator, women writers intervened subjectively in their commentaries and reviews, guiding their female readers to observe, participate, and feel moved, interacting with them as if they were present. In their 2004 book on women and journalism, Silvia Franchini and Simonetta Soldani note in relation to women journalists the creation at this historical juncture in Italy of "a new type of writing, one which draws considerably upon less formal editorial forms: a rapid, 'imperfect' writing [...] of linguistic forms that are more direct and closer to the spoken language."[4] Women writers consciously adopted a personalised, subjective voice that deliberately and directly engaged the reader in order to initiate her as an intermediary in new modes of spectating. We now look at a selection of examples in letters to the editor published in women's journals in which examples of affect and idolatry towards female performers are presented.

The Female Gaze in Published Fan Letters, Interviews, and Columns

So practised and comfortable were women with the letter-writing format that it is hardly surprising to find evidence of the public female gaze in either published letters to the editor from readers in journals for women, or in columns whose titles bore reference to a personalised form of address, such as La Marchesa Colombi's "Lettera aperta alle signore" (Open Letter to the Ladies) in the *Corriere della sera* in 1877–78, and Matilde Scrao's "Per le signore" (For Women) from the *Corriere di Roma* in 1885–86. Writing to her friend Beccari in 1868, Leonia Cinotti called upon *La donna*'s women readers to contribute articles on "literature, the arts, politics, history, *theatre*, criticism, jokes," arguing that:

> [E]verything is, after all, at our disposal. Everything that men feel, we can feel. If ancient civilisations erected temples to Beauty, today men can more reasonably erect statues of women, because women personify Beauty, Science and Virtue.[5]

Adopting a distant, impersonal voice to critique the finished product of a composition – in this case, an opera – in August 1872, the Torinese poet-improviser and intellectual Carlotta Ferrari da Lodi (1837–1907) published discursive pieces, including on Verdi's *Nabucco* (1842). Despite her distancing and objective stance, Ferrari da Lodi nevertheless uses the first-person pronoun, which has the effect of drawing the reader into her analysis and train of thought:

> It was in this opera that Verdi made a name for himself, opening up a new direction as a composer. I will begin by recalling the wonderful Introduction, which I will never be able to give all the praise it deserves [...] with its admirably incisive *Allegro*, whose rhythm and tempo imitate that of the clatter of horses with such truth and accuracy that one could not wish for better music. The content is magnificent; majestically delineated and executed with such effectiveness. That Introduction summarises the whole action of the drama; it foreshadows everything [...]. The part of Zaccaria is musically the most beautiful and characteristic of the drama [...].[6]

Ferrari da Lodi also draws on personal anecdote and uses the exclamation mark to express affect, most notably delight – a feature which appears to be absent from reviews by men. Recalling the first time she heard Zaccaria utter the phrase, "Del futuro nel buio discerno" (Of the Future in the Dark Discernment) as a young woman, she reminisces with feeling and enthusiasm about the affect it had on her while providing an insight into the harmonic passages at this moment in the opera:

> It produced in me such an artistic shudder that it nearly made my teeth chatter. Oh, what intense, indescribable pleasure in that shudder! While dark thoughts passed through my mind and stirred in my imagination! How the harshness of the eleventh chord – so favoured in religious music – expresses here the mystery of the dramatic situation, insisting on the third beat to then resolve on the fourth, on the dominant![7]

Writing to Beccari also in 1872, a woman by the name of "Anita" from Conegliano in the Veneto region gives her glowing opinion of Pezzana's performance with the *Compagnia* Zoli in Paolo Ferrari's *Amore senza stima* (1868):

> It is impossible to give you an idea of the impression this woman had on me; in the course of a few hours, I experienced so many different sensations that I felt worn out, as if I had made a huge effort [...]. I was moved, stunned; not even the clamorous applause from the spectators could bring me out of my blissful daze [...]. Pezzana performed her role with such truth and grace that she completely made you believe that Contessa Livia's virtues were her own.[8]

The extent to which Anita experiences the full range of emotions in watching Pezzana perform is self-evident, and her attempt at critiquing Pezzana's rendition of the role would surely have been appreciated by the editor and have been the reason she decided to publish the letter for her readers. Indeed, Beccari says as much in an issue in the following year. Reminding her readers that *La donna* had published a letter from a "dear young woman" who had seen the "*élite* and excellent" Pezzana in performance, Beccari writes how Anita had "spoken about the performance with such enthusiasm, or might one say delirium, and that some readers may have found it amusing," but that "one should certainly not speak with disapproval about it since she gave her true impressions that were certainly not marked by falsity or a Baroque style."[9] She then reproduces a dazzling review in the Spanish press of Pezzana's performance of Legouvé's *Medea* (1857) at the Teatro Principale in Barcelona, adding that "Pezzana knows how to fascinate with the power of her art and arouse in her spectators' hearts the highest of enthusiasm."[10] The review from the unnamed Spanish publication eulogises Pezzana and her "triumphant" performances of *Medea* to Catalan audiences, who, "from the first performance did not stop clapping"; indeed, so "enthusiastic and overwhelmed" were the spectators, that "[Pezzana] received 16 curtain calls, by the end of which the stage was literally covered in bunches of fragrant flowers."[11]

Beccari reported on Pezzana's *tournée* at home and abroad in letters of admiration from her readers throughout the 1870s and 1880s. Writing to Beccari following the star's performance in Jan Neruda's *Francesca di Rimini* (1860) at the Teatro Rossini in Venice in 1877, Adele Chiminello explains how she was so moved that she could not sleep:

> It is midnight, I have just returned from the Teatro Rossini, and I am finding it impossible to close my eyes before writing to tell you that I have just seen Pezzana perform in *Signora di Rimini.* I am overwhelmed, moved; I have suffered, I have admired, I have felt I do not know what in myself. The artist who reaches such heights, who succeeds in her art to hide it to such an extent that we believe it is reality, is a creator, a genius! [...] Signora Pezzana was applauded enthusiastically; she would have been applauded even more so if emotion had not choked the voices of many ... of the women at least, of that I am certain.[12]

The mention here that the women in the audience in particular were affected by Pezzana's performance to the extent that she took their breath away is intriguing, and the affect expressed by Anita is a feature to which Beccari sought to draw attention. Beccari would go on lauding and raising Pezzana's star persona in the publication well into the 1880s, reporting on her international successes and celebrating her as an embodiment of exceptional modern womanhood and an emblem of so-called *italianità*, who was also (and, most importantly during these years) a "good patriot." Introducing two reviews of Pezzana's performances from two Mexican newspapers during her second tour there, when she stayed for two years, and which praise Pezzana's performances very highly, Beccari hails Pezzana as a patriot, stating that the "great dramatic artist always thinks lovingly of her Italy, and yearns to return in the same way as a prisoner yearns for freedom."[13] Beccari's use of the possessive to refer to Italy here is in keeping with discourses on patriotism more broadly. She continues:

> And if it is true that her tour of the Americas has brought honour on Italy, two articles I have commissioned for translation from the Spanish and which I publish here for my readers prove it. [...] Giacinta Pezzana Gualtieri is one of our good *sisters*, and it is this woman who honours her sex, who, for her talent as an artist, for her mind nourished by hard and firm study, and for her virtues, is dear to all those who know her and esteem her.[14]

From the 1870s until the onset of fascism in 1922, both moderate and radical emancipationists (whether they were self-declared emancipationists or not) espoused *sorellanza* – a secularised solidarity among women in the public eye. Through their expressions of solidarity towards one another in newspapers and periodicals, contributors helped to strengthen the emancipationists' cause in effecting structural changes in legislation in favour of women's role in the new Italy. Indeed, women performers had perceptible influence in inspiring social change,[15] and women writers' interests in their works on non-biological bonds between women conceived of alternative constructions of motherhood for women readers.[16] Evidence of *sorellanza* and the celebration of female autonomy, self-determination, and talent among performing women by women writers can be found in La Marchesa Colombi's regular weekly column "Colore del tempo" (Sign of the Times) in Neera's Milanese cultural magazine for women *Vita intima*, which ran fortnightly from 1890 to 1891. Like her 1876 column on theatre "Cronaca" in the family journal *Museo di famiglia*, it included comment and analysis on current debates, cultural events, society life, and the latest fashions, and focused on depicting public spaces rather than on issues pertaining to the domestic sphere. La Marchesa Colombi addresses her readers respectfully in the third-person plural as "le mie lettrici" (my women readers), positing herself as an enthusiastic, candid, often tongue-in-cheek and sharp observer and spectator of the events she describes. Writing in 1890 on the "lovely" Virginia Marini's recent performance in Felice Cavallotti's play *Lea* (1889) at the Teatro Manzoni in Milan, La Marchesa Colombi praises Marini's ability in the role of Ida to assimilate the feelings and character traits of the roles she plays, which have "earned her applause and praise throughout her glorious career."[17] (For the Milanese theatre critic Giovanni Pozza (1852–1914) – who remarked that there were "very many women spectators present, also in the stalls"[18] – Marini's performance was "exaggerated, especially in the final act."[19]) Continuing to eulogise women performers, La Marchesa Colombi foresees shouts of admiration and resounding applause the following night when Eleonora Duse, whom she describes as a "very modern and intellectual artist," will be performing in Dumas *fils*'s *La Principessa Giorgio* (1874).[20] In an October issue, she writes candidly to complain that reruns of old repertoire are

> no longer attracting spectators. [...] The audience did not much like Carlo Chiappani's opera *Nerina* at the Accademia dei Filodrammatici Theatre [...] and at the Milanese Theatre, where [Giuseppina] Giovanelli's absence is still felt and who was its soul, they are always putting on the same plays that for the last ten years have been financing their repertoire,[21]

repeating her strident message the following month:

> Theatres are not offering anything new. Verdi's *Aida* and Ponichelli's *La Gioconda* are performing at the Teatro Dal Verme. They are two rather good operas, and their productions are well done, but

> they have been entertaining us for years, and our fire of enthusiasm for them has been extinguished; we are always moved by them, we always listen to them respectfully. But they already belong to our artistic heritage; we aspire insatiably to hear new works.[22]

Earlier on that month, she had admitted to being:

> a little pessimistic. But how can one wish for much from an accumulation of works of which the majority, as far as we know, do not distance themselves from old schools, from old conventions, in which old French plays are performed because the audience laughs without the least regard for the "real" or for the plausibility of the story or the characters, for example, Sardou's *Tosca*, which had a very bad reception despite Sarah Bernhardt's appearance.[23]

La Marchesa Colombi's outspoken critiques about the "same old repertoire" being staged by (male) directors, *impresarios*, and producers of plays and operas were bold and innovative for her time, and challenged her women readers to think and speak out similarly about Milanese theatre life. (They indeed bear a striking resemblance to criticisms on social media regarding present-day debates over remakes of Hollywood films and TV series from the 1980s and 1990s, such as *Home Alone* and *Friends*.[24])

The great French tragic actor Sarah Bernhardt is also the subject of an interview conducted by Matilde Serao in her daily *Il Giorno*. Her interview appeared on the front page on 21 December 1904, and Serao prefaces it with the following subheadings on Bernhardt, citing her friend, Duse: "Her love for Italy and the Italians – Always travelling and always working [...] – Her fraternal affection for Eleonora Duse."[25] Serao begins her interview by describing Bernhardt as a "universal" artist, who is "like one of those exceptional creatures who never ages, and whose magnificent vivacity consoles and animates the numbness of our daily lives."[26] Serao emphasises how Bernhardt is a "great friend of Italy," whom Serao profoundly respects and admires, adding that Bernhardt "did everything [she] could in Paris to ensure Eleonora Duse's success there was full of glory."[27] Bernhardt then goes on to urge Serao to write to Duse to invite her to perform in Paris: "I want her in my theatre as a *sister in art*! I love her so much you must tell her: I feel so much admiration for this woman so passionate in her art."[28] (Serao was to adopt Bernhardt's phrase "sister in art" 16 years later to refer to her writer friend Neera in the obituary she published in 1920.[29])

Sisterhood, or female solidarity, had indeed been invoked by Serao in her newspaper earlier on in 1904 in reference to her friend Duse. Having travelled to Genoa to be with Duse on her sickbed, Serao describes how Duse, whom she refers to twice in her article as her "sister," spontaneously began reciting the part of Mila di Codra (as she was to do for Francesca

Bertini nearly 20 years later, though this time from D'Annunzio's *La figlia di Iorio*, 1904):

> What an admirable performance! As if by magic, as soon as the first verses began echoing around the room, I saw [...] the fatal beauty of her face compose itself again [...]. We were alone: and there was no theatre: and there were no actors: and I knew nothing of Mila and her story of love and pain; and from the first moment we were nothing but two melancholy *soul sisters* [...]. What an admirable performance! [...] Mila di Codra, herself, alive, as the Poet wanted it and when the final cry was uttered by Eleonora Duse and by Mila di Codra: *the flame is beautiful, the flame is beautiful*, I broke into waves of tears that the emotion had caused in my heart and my eyes to cry![30]

In publishing the account of a very intimate moment between the two friends, Serao stands in for her women readers *as* spectators as if by proxy, giving them "permission" to feel the full range of emotions when watching the suffering Fallen Women on their evenings out, while concomitantly celebrating female solidarity and friendship. Yet further evidence of Serao's *sorellanza* can be gleaned in another article on Bernhardt in which Serao laments the fact that despite the "indefatigable artist" having just completed a tour of America "performing five or six plays per week" in front of four thousand spectators, having earned millions for her son, Maurizio Bernhardt, she has still "not been awarded the Legion of Honour medal!"[31]

Serao the Screenwriter

The year was 1906, and Italian cinema was about to make a name for itself with its epic ancient-world blockbusters such as *Gli ultimi giorni di Pompeii* (The Last Days of Pompeii, 1908), *L'inferno* (1911), and *Cabiria* (1914). Serao was *the* first intellectual to write about film in her article, "Cinematografeide!" (meaning "Cinematitus!"),[32] describing the new medium disparagingly in apocalyptic terms as a virus that is "infecting" Naples.[33] By 1909, the film company Film d'Arte Italiana had established itself in Rome, and Naples had become the major centre for specialist film journals such as *Il Café-Chantant* and *Lux*.[34] Like many writers and journalists of the time who were initially suspicious of the new cinematic medium, thanks to its expanding success among a growing number of spectators, as well as its remunerative potential as a new industry for entertainment, Serao was later to write enthusiastically about film; specifically, on the first public projection of *L'inferno* by the Milano Film company in Naples, first screened at the Teatro Mercadante and directed by Francesco Bertolini, Adolfo Padovan, and Giuseppe de Liguoro. She proclaims that: "*L'inferno* has rehabilitated the cinema for us. For anyone, this film will be a real thrill of curiosity and emotion."[35] On seeing another historical epic, Enrico Guazzoni's *Quo Vadis?* (1913) on its release, Serao writes excitedly:

> It's a spectacle never before seen; cinema has never created anything like this. Yes, it's a world that Cines films has reconstructed; a world of beauty that enchants and thrills, of which Licia is the great poetic sun. The dances, the fires, the banquets, the landscapes, the orgies, the horrors, the terrible scene of the fire in Rome, all of which have never before been portrayed in a similar way, arouse unspeakable impressions and emotions. [...]. We will soon see this new, original and surprisingly grandiose show at our Mercadante theatre. Naples is one of the first cities to screen *Quo Vadis?* And what will be the crowd at such an event? And what will be its earth-shattering affect, its delirium?[36]

Writing on Giovanni Pastrone's forthcoming screening of *Cabiria* (1914) produced by Itala Film, Serao ponders the reaction of the film's spectators:

> What will be the greatest emotion among the immense crowds that will fill every theatre where Gabriele D'Annunzio's *Cabiria* is being screened? And who will have the deepest and most profound emotion? Of all those women who God has blessed in their great mission as parents, and of all those mothers who have small and adult children; and even of all those women who have no such sweet mission, who, deprived of the title of "mother" love even more ardently all that is a child or a young adult. [...] Everyone will admire [the film], everyone, even those who do not know the story, for they will see it again in vibrant scenes of light, of flame; all those who are ignorant of cinema will admire it, understanding that this is a sublime attempt; and all those who know the secret of the cinema and see that all the secrets in *Cabiria* have been surpassed will admire it.[37]

Cinema halls in Naples were well attended and included the Sala Cattaneo, the Sala Roma, the Olympia, the Salon Parisien, Krumans, and the Moderno.[38] Serao also wrote a (lost) screenplay for Monopol Film – *La mia vita per la tua!* (1914), first shown in December at the Cinema Modernissimo in Rome and directed by Emilio Ghione (1879–1930), who starred as the male lead – describing it as an "attempt at a cinematographic novel."[39] According to the critics, it was unsuccessful, even though Maria Carni (1880–1957) playing the role of Elena di Soubise was purportedly "very taken by the film, which had not happened often" to her, and eulogised Serao's ability to write a film that was "truly cinematic."[40] Discussing with the interviewer of the journal *La vita cinematografica* the extent to which Carni is fully immersed in the role of Elena, she marvels at how Serao's character has been a portent enabling her to experience new emotions:

> In impersonating the passionate and bizarre heroine imagined by Serao, I have actually experienced some subtle new sensations and indescribable emotions, as if I were myself the protagonist of the narrative. [...] Evidently, the great Italian writer had felt in her own soul the tremors and throbs of the characters of her imagination; which is why the lyricism of the drama is so penetrating and why, by necessity, it must move us as actors who, for the most part, are only a means of realising the film.[41]

Carmi concludes her interview by stating that the film is a "great, truly human drama" in which "passions are laid bare and the most ineffable pain is expressed in swift, dense and decisive action."[42] Its première was purportedly an important social event for the elegant and cosmopolitan *élite*, including leading artists, writers, and critics. According to Ghione in his memoirs, Serao was delighted with the film when she first saw it, "expressing her joy with that Neapolitan familiarity by planting several noisy kisses on [his] cheeks."[43]

Serao wrote a very favourable review of the first silent diva film, *Ma l'amor mio non muore* (Everlasting Love), featuring Lyda Borelli and released in 1913. Writing in *La vita cinematografica* on 7 January 1914, Serao described Borelli as "radiant with beauty," and "an exceptional creature [...] so soft and dramatic, so sumptuous and elegant, never until now had [she] been so penetrated with truth in love and sorrow."[44]

In an interview published in *Lo schermo* a year before her death, Serao confesses to having stopped going to the cinema for years because she had "at least seven unpublished screenplays locked in [her] drawer [...] that no one ever asked her for,"[45] and yet, it would appear that the following Seraian novels and short stories are in fact the subject matter of films: *O Giovannino, o la morte*, 1915 (Gino Rossetti); *Addio, amore!*, 1916 (Alberto Carlo Lolli), *Castigo*, 1917 (Ubaldo Maria Del Colle); *Il doppio volto*, 1918 (Giulio Antamoro); *Dopo il perdono*, 1919 (Ugo De Simone); *La mano tagliata*, 1919 (Alberto Degli Abbati); *Temi il leone*, 1919 (Ubaldo Maria Del *Colle* from *Il delitto di via Chiatamone*); *Sterminator Vesevo*, 1921 (Giorgio Mannini); *Les Hommes sans peur*, 1941 (Yvan Noë from *La mia vita per la tua!*); *Via delle cinque lune* (Luigi Chiarini from "O Giovannino, o la morte!", 1942), and *Addio, amore!*, 1942 (Gianni Franciolini).[46] Moreover, Serao's short stories published in her collection *Dal vero* (1879) are "literally all" material for Roberto Roberti's *Napoli che canta* (1926).[47] As an intellectual, Serao thought deeply about the new medium, and in particular its spectators. In her article "Parla una spettatrice" (A Woman Spectator is Speaking), published in *L'arte muta* in 1916, she writes as a self-declared "spectatrix," reflecting in retrospect on "the reasons for [her] tears, [her] smiles, [her boredom]."

Figure 4.1 Still from *Ma l'amor mio non muore* (1914).

As a "creature of the crowd," she addresses poets, playwrights, and screenwriters and tells them "[i]t is *she* whom you should move, whom you should please."[48] Meditating on how new film productions can satisfy spectators, she counsels production teams to "include scenes with a lot of movement and scenes from everyday life."[49] Confessing how for months she has paid 8 or 12 *soldi* to discover which films would move and entice her, she states:

> I sat still in a corner in silence, like all the other spectators; and my anonymous and unknown being became just like that of other anonymous spectators [...]. And do you know what happened? I had exactly the same impressions of the film as my neighbour to my right who was perhaps a shop assistant; the same impressions as my neighbour to my left, who, I imagine, was a young woman from the countryside who had moved to the city.[50]

In this way – writes Serao – she has become "the perfect woman spectator," laughing and crying with the indiscriminate, homogenous mass in the darkened auditorium. Bespeaking the regressive state and "womb-like" sensations of watching cinema that were theorised by apparatus thinkers in the 1960s, she concludes that:

> [C]inema spectators are millions of simple souls who become so through one of the most bizarre miracles penetrating auditoria; indeed, the auditorium is a unique, simple soul.[51]

Thus, Serao became a self-declared and converted cinephile in the same way as her friend Duse, mocking the moralising the well-to-do (who targeted cinema producers, screenwriters, and divas) for arguing that the new modern invention is "immoral" and "trivial."[52] Earlier during the same year, as previously stated in Chapter 3, Serao had written positively about Francesca Bertini's and Alfredo De Antoni's *Tosca* (1918) produced by La Caesar Film at the Teatro Maximum in Rome (and based on Sardou's play), though not before mentioning Giuseppe Giacosa's and Luigi Illica's "wonderful" opera version (1900) that Puccini "skilfully, brilliantly, and sweetly" set to music, and from which it is also adapted.[53] Marvelling at the "scenic and artistic resources" that artists had access to thanks to the availability of camera technology, Serao observes how "scenes could be shot on location in monumental churches, the Palazzo Farnese and the Castel Sant'Angelo."[54] Describing the "fascinating" Bertini in the starring role, she mentions her "insuperable silent art" and her "splendid interpretation" of Floria Tosca alongside the "sublime" artists Gustavo Serena in the role of Cavaradossi, and Alfredo De Antoni as Scarpia. Predicting that the cinema auditorium will be packed full of Neapolitan spectators given the low cost of tickets and the speed with which they were selling, she describes the film as "the greatest work of cinematic art thus far."[55] Reporting that critics' reviews following its screening in Rome were enthusiastic, Serao announces that the projection will be accompanied by an orchestra and singers. Serao did not enjoy all film, however. We know from the work of Giuliana Bruno that Serao was not a fan of the *sceneggiata* realist films shot on location in Naples by the younger Neapolitan director Elvira Notari (1875–1946).[56] Though her company, Dora Films, repeatedly asked Serao for the rights to make films based on her short stories and novels, Serao refused, preferring instead to sell them to more lucrative and established film companies.

One final mention of Serao's involvement in the silent screen comes in the form of a very striking and modern acknowledgement of the importance of female desire on the death of the male star, Rudolfo Valentino (1895–1926), in 1926. Writing in *Il Giorno*, Serao considers his effect on women spectators; how, for millions of women, his "magnetic gaze" and image, what she terms his "fantasy," was *essential* for women spectators in order that they might manage the hardships of everyday life.[57] It indeed chimes with what Ien Ang has argued in relation to soap operas, that pleasure in fantasy is not necessarily derived purely from the contents (of a film, for example), but in the experience of fantasising, of playing with fictional worlds and imagined selves.[58] Further examples in women's periodicals earlier on at the turn of the twentieth century reveal how Serao was not exceptional in espousing a politics of pleasure, involving female desire for male performers. Writing in Beccari's *La donna* in 1881, an author with the pseudonym "Flora" describes the *grande attore* Salvini as "a handsome man,"[59] and the writer and journalist Ida Baccini (1850–1911) defines the composer Pietro Mascagni (1863–1945) in her women's magazine *Cordelia* as "much more than handsome," admiring his "very elegant physiognomy, like that of a runaway boy whose unwitting neglect of his brown hair and vivid flash of his thoughtful eyes mark him out."[60] Baccini makes no excuses for writing solely about Mascagni's appearance, declaring: "I am not going to give you a musical critique ... I ... will speak to you a little about Mascagni the *man*, Mascagni the *young* man who few observe, and whom very few study."[61] These are clear early examples of male *divi* becoming the subjects of erotic pleasure for women writers and commentators *as* spectators; and the very fact middle-class women were openly acknowledging their desire to their women readers gave these readers permission to do likewise.

Fashion, Beauty, People-Spotting

We saw in Chapter 3 how fashion talk is not necessarily disconnected from a valid experience of spectatorship; indeed, Stuart Ewen argues that women's relationship to consumer culture has been a central one since its emergence in the late nineteenth century when, through the advertising of cosmetics and beauty products, as well as the arrival of the first department stores, capitalism positioned women as key subjects in the commodity exchange.[62] Many of the women's journals circulating at the turn of the twentieth century in Italy, as elsewhere, included advertisements for cosmetics and beauty products with endorsements from well-known performing artists. For instance, *La donna: rivista quindicinale illustrata* from 1909 (not to be confused with Beccari's emancipationist journal of the same name which, by that time, was no longer published) advertised a product that prevented hair loss featuring the opera singer Celestina Boninsegna (1877–1947). A photograph of the diva is the centrepiece of the advert, which includes a handwritten statement of her endorsement of the product.

Later that month, singer Rosina Storchio (1876–1945) advertised the same product.[63] Hygienists, including positivist anthropologist Paolo Mantegazza (1831–1910), warned women against using make-up on the basis it was "poisonous"; in an entry on "Beauty" in the *Dictionary on Hygiene for Families* (1911) co-authored with Neera, he sympathises with "Poor dramatic artists, who are forced to use make-up which often contains lead, and who suffer a slow poisoning with headaches, rheumatic pains, paralysis and other illnesses."[64] Nonetheless, beauty, fashion, and desirous gazes were integral to the experience of spectating in the

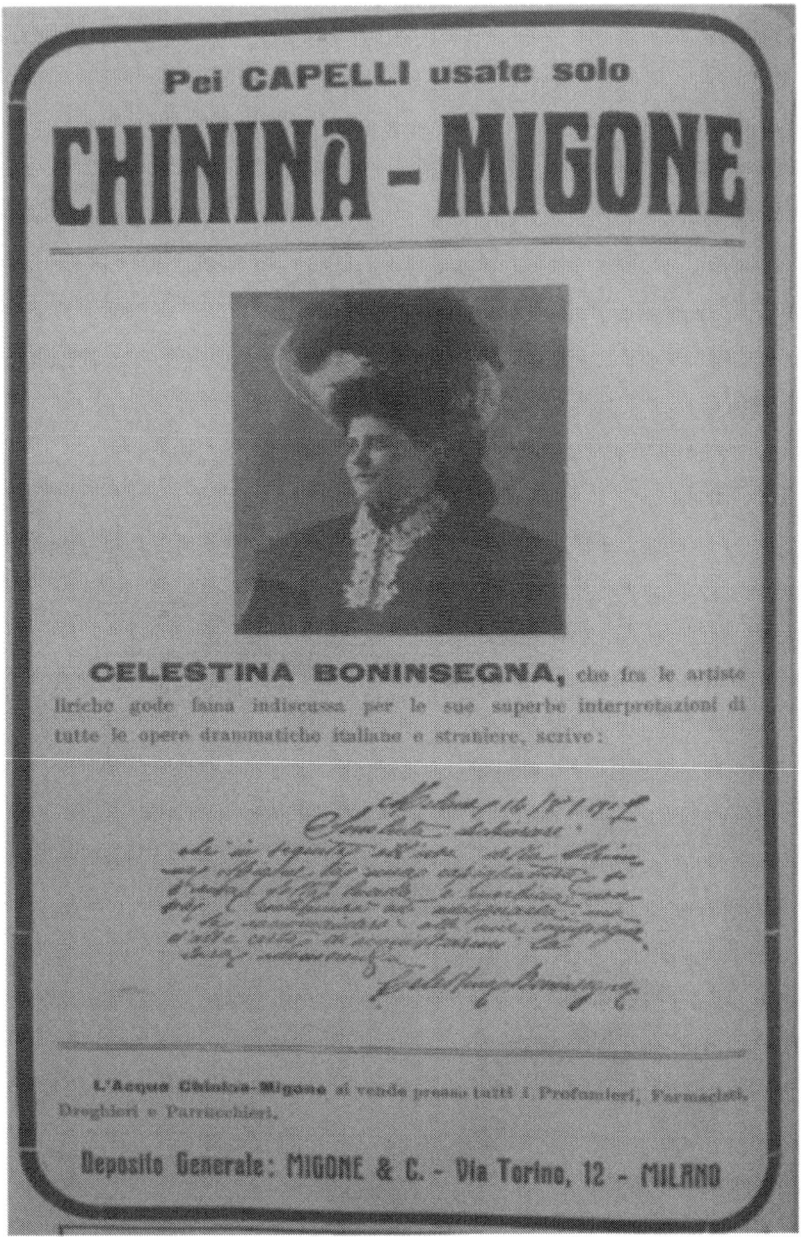

Figure 4.2 La donna: rivista quindicinale illustrata, 20 January 1909.

early previous century, when theatre-going was the sole preserve of the upper-middle classes. On his visit to Italy in 1817, Stendhal remarked upon female sexual assertion among audiences during his visits to theatre auditoriums in Rome:

> When a man finds favour in a woman's eyes, she will seldom seek to conceal her pleasure. *Dite a *** che mi piace* (*Tell him that I like him*) is a phrase which, in Rome, a woman may readily employ, with neither shame nor scruple.[65]

Remarking on a visit to the Teatro dei Fiorentini in Naples, Stendhal had also drawn attention to women spectators' sartorial sense of style: "[E]very box was [...] crowded with women radiant in their finery," and women had complained they are "too visible" and "find themselves perpetually 'on display.'"[66] Still in the late nineteenth century, divas and women spectators were all too aware of the need to be "beautiful," if not more so in the wake of early consumer capitalism. As Umberto Eco informs us, around this time a shift in perception occurred from thinking of the idea of beauty as tied to morality and virtue, to an emphasis on artifice;[67] and who better to promote this new conception of beauty and subject of female desire than the by now visually ubiquitous modern-day stage and screen diva, whose appearance was arguably implicit in her embodiment of the "divine?"[68]

Writing in *La Rassegna degli interessi femminili* (Review of Women's Interests) in 1887, the pseudonymous "Veritas" laments that "many of the divas from the *operettas* and *vaudevilles* owe their roles more to their beautiful eyes than to their singing abilities,"[69] and commenting in *Cronaca dei teatri* on the singer Linda Monti-Brunner (1862–1926), Emanuele Gaetani-Tamburini writes that she "has, all in all, everything that is necessary to obtain great success in whatever theatre: a beautiful, voice [...]; an attractive figure and expressive facial features."[70] Yet the standards women set for themselves were very high: an article published in Ida Baccini's magazine *Cordelia* in 1894 by a certain J. B. Laglaize, whose pseudonymic associations with "gazing" are not lost on readers, recalls the first performance of Donizetti's *Lucia di Lammermoor* (1835) at the Teatro San Carlo in Naples, when "women spectators *dressed up* to go to the theatre: a spirited person would say that they *stripped off*,"[71] before pronouncing that the combination of:

> colours, the iridescence of diamonds and rubies, and the brilliant white of arms and shoulders were – aesthetically speaking – far preferable to the ugly hairstyles of nowadays. While in those days garlands of fresh flowers were woven into locks of blonde, black and brown hair, today they are half hidden by obnoxious little hats. [...] Horrific![72]

Indeed, the desired beauty of the performer, and beauty in general, was celebrated religiously in print culture by both women and men, though the discursive construction of the Italian diva in this period was gendered: while beauty was an integral component of divahood for critics of *all* genders in the late nineteenth century, for male critics, how "beautiful" a performer looked mattered more to them than the extent of her artistic skills.[73] Nowhere is this crystallised more forcefully than in the autobiography written by the *grande attore* Tommaso Salvini in which he brutally pronounces Duse's celebrity as fleeting for her "monotonous" repertoire and that she will soon show signs of ageing:

> As soon as her first wrinkle appears on her forehead and her first hair turns silver, a great part of her prestige will disappear, and her star will no longer shine.[74]

Men writers' accounts of divas prioritise appearance over artistic talent. A critic who wrote with the pseudonym "Mazza," writing in the theatre journal *Comoedia* mentions that "Bianca Masnata, the beautiful, young and intelligent soprano, has triumphed in [Catalani's] *Wally* in Trieste."[75] The diva Bella Gorsky is reported in *Cronaca dei teatri* as having "on her very beautiful face a smile of sweet spring,"[76] while the Milanese journal *La frusta teatrale* reports on the singer known as "La Spezia" and her performance in Palermo, declaring she is "one of the most beautiful, dear and sweet *Traviate* of the era."[77]

Women writers' reviews and critiques bear witness first and foremost to divas' talents and artistry, while their aesthetic and physical attributes and clothes are typically mentioned secondarily. An anonymous (most likely woman) writer for the women's journal *Cornelia*, reviewing a performance of Ambroise Thomas's *Mignon* (1866) at the Pergola Theatre in Florence in 1876, states that:

> Mrs Maria Durand, an American, is the female protagonist. This woman is a singer gifted with unusual talent and resources. She is expressive, she has a dramatic, colourful method, a powerful voice, and she is attractive.[78]

Similarly, Serao, writing in her column in the Neapolitan daily newspaper *Il Mattino* on the musician Maria Felicità Tua, the Contessa Franchi-Verney della Valletta (alias Teresina Tua, 1866–1956), describes the "magic of her genius as a violinist, with her sparkling artist's smile, and her good, sweet and vivid gaze."[79] Writing on Duse's smile in the weekly Florentine literary journal *Il Marzocco* in 1901, Neera declares: "I wish to proclaim loud and clear the beauty of her smile"[80] having ascertained from a Neapolitan male colleague that Duse *is* "beautiful, in spite of the fact that her fragile and delicate beauty is not that of someone who might be brought to prominence on the stage" (read: she does not conform to contemporary notions of *la bella italiana*). By the same token, Serao comments on "the charming and fine singer Nera Marmora"; "the delightful, enchanting, special woman, Ettorina Mazzucchelli!"; "Maria Melato, who has depth and grace."[81] Though biased, women writers knew how to idolise and celebrate women performers' beauty. The reader of the emancipationist journal *La donna* mentioned in Chapter 3 – Adele Chiminello – upon watching Giacinta Pezzana perform Gualtieri's *La Signora di Rimini*, writes: "[Pezzana] was beautiful in her white wedding dress; but divinely beautiful in the final act in a black velvet dress with a white veil,"[82] and there is an announcement that her contemporary, Adelaide Ristori, "who as an actor never seems to age," will perform *Macbeth* and *Maria Stuarda* in London the following year.[83] Serao describes the actor and singer Lina Cavalieri (1874–1944) as an embodiment of beauty, referring to her "little face shaped like an apocryphal Madonna," which had a "pure shape and an adorable grace," while her chest "blossomed like a stalk," and her eyes "had a languor about them between sadness and *reverie*."[84]

From 1885 onwards, Serao would typically rave about the fashions and glamour of women spectators in auditoria in Rome and Naples in her column "Api, Mosconi e Vespe" (Bees, Flies, and Wasps) in her *Corriere di Roma*, *Corriere di Napoli*, *Il Mattino*, *La Settimana* (all co-founded with her husband Eduardo Scarfoglio), and *Il Giorno* under her pseudonym "Gibus," which was to endure for 41 years.[85] Presenting herself as a "fly on the wall" subjective observer of high society, and in many ways a mirror image for her women readers, her column covered observations on culture and current affairs and acted as a kind of gossip column for the well-to-do.[86] Writing on Gibus's aims, she is at pains to emphasise her column's mission to "always please" her women readers by giving them what they will like, mentioning the verb "to please" repeatedly, four times in succession in her entry of March 1892. This emphatic discourse of pleasure culminates in a final sentence in which she declares she will please her readers "even better and as much as possible" – her mission statement bears a striking resemblance to the ethics of pleasure previously discussed in her "Parla una spettatrice" (A Woman Spectator Is Speaking, 1916).[87] Serao uses a direct and honest language to report, comment on, and describe musical and theatrical performances taking place in Naples. Though she refers to a non-gender-specific audience in her descriptions, she explicitly draws attention to women spectators (*le spettatrici*). In March 1892, commenting on the tenor Francesco Marconi (1855–1916) and his performance in a salon, she writes:

> Marconi sang in front of an indulgent audience [...]. Among the celestial women spectators, the host wore a black dress, rich with wonderful lace ... Umberto Mazzone played the piano: a nocturne and a delicate *minuet* played with finesse and confidence. Checco Marconi had a more than joyous evening: his hearty and vibrant

> voice ravished the auditorium in Palloni's two improvised excerpts in the aria of Giulio Cottrau's *Griselda* – a great success, and there was also an *encore*.[88]

Serao would typically comment on the performances of singers and mention women's fashions (thus corroborating the stereotype circulating at the beginning of the century), never failing to list names of certain important society women. In her entry on 30–31 March 1892, she comments on the soprano Gemma Bellincioni (1864–1950) and her "amazing hairpiece," which she likens to a butterfly. Such apparel exhibited by admired women performers were coveted not only by spectators, but also Serao's women readers, whose desire to copy performers' fashions was also triggered, though not exclusively, by Serao's endorsements.

People-watching – the act of watching people in a crowd without their knowing it – is integral to the event of theatre-going, particularly where the auditorium is lit, as was the case in the majority of Italian auditoria until the late 1890s, when electricity had replaced gas lighting, and would have been a major component of spectating practices, including flirtation. Without fail, Serao would report on who she spotted or who was in attendance, before providing a by no means exhaustive list of the names of Neapolitan aristocracy, royalty, and famous people, including literary figures. In an entry in March 1892, Serao recalls seeing:

> Signora Errera, the Countess Anguissola, Signora Premoli to cite a few ... Delightful music [...]. Signora Cucini sang the *Medieval Serenade* passionately; I have never heard it sang better. Signorina Lombardi sang the *Chanson de Barberine*, which reawakens in the soul all the memories of lost love.[89]

In the following month at the Teatro San Carlo in Naples, Serao equates the intrigue of the spectacle on stage to that in the audience.[90] Similarly, describing an engaged and transfixed audience in a later entry, she comments on "the highly intellectual spectators" of the previous night at the Teatro dei Fiorentini, describing them as "so attentive, and so vibrant at every spiritual moment on stage. I noted: Signora Hermann Stevens – as elegant as always in a black dress; Signora Laura Schettino in a Russian velvet dress [...]."[91] Thus, the women spectators became the celebrities themselves, the subject of gossip and commentary as in modern-day women's magazines and tabloid newspapers. The mention in her column here of, for example, a "Russian velvet dress," or a "hairpiece shaped like a butterfly," connected Serao's readers to elegant high-society spectators and the performers they were watching, thereby giving them an illusion of being part of a female critical and affective community by, and for women. The fashion objects were commoditised for female desire, fascination, and consumption by Serao's women readers, who may or may not have been in attendance themselves.

In 1911, Serao was also the director of the Florentine weekly fashion journal *La moda del giorno* (Fashion Today), which she edited alongside the emancipationist Florentine writer Donna Paola (pseudonym for Paola Baronchelli Grosson, 1866–1954).[92] The journal published pieces on fashion, including new designs and photographs of clothes and accessories, alongside fiction (short stories and serialised novels) written by women. Assuming the role as an educator of "proper" behaviour in the manner of an author of conduct literature, in the first issue of the magazine Serao cautions her readers to "love fashion, providing it suits your beauty and charm; and reject it if it doesn't agree with you," counselling them to adopt a pragmatic attitude in matters of glamour and taste.[93] Indeed, Maria Teresa Mori highlights a contradiction at the heart of Serao's attitude towards fashion – on the one hand, she is seduced by it at the theatre; but on the other, she is also moralising and judgemental of excess and glamour.[94] This is apparent, for example, in her article from the issue on 28 May 1911 ("Dove arriveremo?" (Where will we get to?) p. 2) which is critical of women who indulge in luxury and shun a sense of moderation.[95]

Divas' Published Gazes

A feature of turn-of-the-twentieth century print culture in Italy was the occasional intervention in periodicals and newspapers by women performers. This was a time when actors – particularly in the Italian theatrical world – were often managers of their own *Compagnie*, and, in many cases, the authors, publicists, and PR representatives of their arts. Readers were fascinated by accounts of their esteemed performers' comments on, and impressions of their performances and everyday life, which contributed significantly to the sale of the various publications based on growing audience demand to read of, and understand, their heroines' inner lives. Performers occasionally very consciously intervened in periodicals and newspapers to take a moral stance on issues about which they felt very strongly; as managers of their own *Compagnie*, they influenced their reception, harnessing their agency, freedom, and scope to intervene as and when they saw fit. One such example of this is triggered by a journalist from the Venetian newspaper *Il Tempo*, who contacted Duse with a request for her biography, which Duse declined to provide. The newspaper consequently printed her response, which was re-printed by Beccari's emancipationist journal *La donna* under a pseudonym, thus bringing Duse's affirmative action and moral high ground to the attention of women readers who could celebrate the artist's self-preservation. Duse's letter read:

> If, before I became an *actor* no one was interested in me, why should I reveal the *woman artist* I am today? I do not feel obliged to, and nor will I ever do so ... and to put an end to it, I might add that of

> all the biographies written about me, none of them is accurate – they are all prying. And by way of putting an end to all of this, try judging the only part of me that belongs to you – that is, my art … the rest belongs to no one else, and here I am signing off.[96]

Another example of a stage diva taking an ideological stance and leveraging her position to influence her moral cause is illustrated by Beccari, who makes no secret of her close friendship with Giacinta Pezzana. Beccari publishes a letter in her journal from her friend on the occasion of the death of the socialist politician, Salvatore Morelli (1824–80), who, eight years prior to the publication of the philosopher John Stuart Mill's seminal essay on *The Subjection of Women* (1869), had published *Women and Science, or the Solution to the Human Problem* (1861). In this, he propounded the idea that in order to create a harmonious world, women should be equal to men in law.[97] Pezzana tells her friend,

> I think it is our duty as women to honour the memory of Salvatore Morelli. He supported women's rights and spoke out against the injustices of the Civil Code and against society in which women are victims. […] Perhaps we could raise money for a plaque with which we could remember *our friend*

before asking Beccari to appeal to "the hearts of Italian women" in her journal and ask them to contribute to a fund. (The plaque appears not to have been erected.)[98] Finally, an example of the "feedback loop" between women writers and performers, and their spectators and readers, can be gleaned from a letter written by the opera singer Adelina Patti and published initially in *Il Figaro*, in which she says how she has never forgotten the first time she performed Donizetti's *La sonnambula* (1831) at the Théâtre Italien in Paris because the "Parisian spectators welcomed [her] so warmly."[99] Upon reading the letter, a reader of the women's journal *Cordelia* identified only by the initials "G. G" sends it in, and it is printed by the journal's director, Ida Baccini (1850–1911).

Taking the public moral high ground – a position which in today's "call-out" culture on social media is now available to everyone with literacy and access to the Internet – was once the sole preserve of an elite few in the public eye. What happened, though, when two well-known women performers in the spotlight took the moral high ground against one other? Mirella Schino in her book *Il teatro di Eleonora Duse* (1992) draws attention to Italian actors' intergenerational conflict; in this case between Duse and Ristori, a rift that was mentioned by the biographer, Gemma Ferruggia, and referred to previously in Chapter 3.[100] In 1897, Ristori was interviewed by Leone Fortis for *L'Illustrazione Italiana* (the interview was re-printed in *Cordelia*). This interview is revealing for what it tells us about female solidarity – or lack thereof, on this occasion – among some women in the limelight at this time and for the interest (or *Schadenfreude*?) some journalists and the reading public took in what was essentially a "spat" between two powerful public female figures from different generations in defence of their art: Ristori wrote of her admiration for Duse's ability to "intrude on the spectator and command her/his attention by transporting her/him with her overexcited nervousness," before calling her the quintessential "'*Modern Woman*', with all her nervous illnesses and *anaemia*, and with all its consequences," and joining with Salvini in criticising her for not having attempted the heroic roles from Classical theatre (from which Ristori made a career), for her "repetitive repertoire," and for "never having truly created anything of significance in her repertoire."[101] In fact, it would appear from a reading of Olga Signorelli's biography of Duse that she herself was conscious of, and frustrated by her "more or less dreary repertoire," which Duse is said to have mentioned in a letter to her father on 6 October 1881.[102] However, Ristori made further public comments regarding Duse as a performer, which were to bring to an end the long correspondence and relationship she had with Ristori.[103] In 1902, on the occasion of Ristori's 80th birthday, Ristori was interviewed in St. Petersburgh by a correspondent from Rome working for the Russian newspaper *Novoye Vremya*. The *Corriere della sera* published the interview, and in this Ristori is reported to have expressed her disappointment at Duse for performing "D'Annunzio's monstrous plays."[104] Duse responded with a long letter in French addressed to the editor of the Parisian newspaper *Le Gaulois*, which had previously published a letter from Ristori to the nobleman, collector, and photographer Giuseppe Primoli (1851–1927) in May 1897, around the time Duse was making her Paris début and in which Ristori had also expressed her aforementioned views on Duse.[105] Duse is very respectful of Ristori in her letter, reiterating her view of the *grande attrice* as "Perfection in Art; Perfection in Life," though according to Schino, Duse's tone is detached and reserved, and no further correspondence took place between the two performers.[106] It was not until Ristori's death that "Duse *spettatrice*" came to the fore through her opinion on Ristori's acting, when theatre critic and historian Silvio d'Amico (1887–1955) published his interview with Duse in the early 1920s.[107] In the interview, Duse said the only role she had seen Ristori perform was Lady Macbeth, before revealing an intriguing insight into her opinion on Ristori's performance:

> I remember that she played the sleep-walking scene with a classic dignity mixed with a curious kind of realism: composure, clarity, with a crown on her head, her eyes fixed on the stage lights: and, between one phrase and another, I heard the light wheeze of someone sleeping: he was snoring! [...] It was a performance of regal composure. When I returned home, I *felt the need to tidy my bedroom.*[108]

Despite the swipe at Ristori, "Duse *spettatrice*" had in fact made an appearance in public prior to the early 1920s in the form of a curious article written by Serao and published in the American periodical *Current Opinion*, which had re-printed it from the *Boston Evening Transcript* in 1917. Excited at the news that the great tragic actor was reported to have made a film (*Cenere*, 1916), the article, entitled, "Can the Camera Immortalise the Melancholy Mask of Eleonora Duse?," features Duse's views on the new medium and on the silent Italian film divas. According to Serao, Duse:

> [A]dmires and loves those who, men and women, have already given their personality to the mute stage. Recalling them in conversation with [her], [Duse] spoke of certain interpretations of Francesca Bertini, of Leda Gys [pseudonym for Giselda Lombardi (1892–1957)], and her judgement was sincere, well pondered. Just. And always, with her beautiful, vague eyes, gazing off into the distance – who better than she has known how to dream of the infinite? – she exclaimed in a voice which came from a mysterious interior world: "Oh, so much can be done, ... so much can be done with the cinematograph."[109]

Current Opinion goes on to report what it claims to be Serao's words in which she reveals that Duse:

> has herself written sketches of dramas, of dramatic cinematographic episodes, she has put on paper her visions of art [...]. To see Eleonora Duse on the film of any writer must be a fascinating spectacle. But what would not be our emotion if Eleonora Duse should appear to us in a dream of her own making?[110]

Despite the lack of trace of the original article, the fact that this was published at all – and for a North American readership – testifies to an interest at the time in Duse *as a spectator*.

Conclusion

Thus far, we have seen how women spectators in Italy began to watch and listen to women's theatre, opera, and film in a more self-conscious and discerning way thanks to the influx of women writers across the peninsula writing critically about theatre and opera performances from the late 1870s onwards. As the women social media influencers of their day, writers and performers as spectators were configuring and signalling in multifaceted ways, for increasing numbers of women readers and spectators, the various forms of spectatorships available to them. Women writers and performers were "writing" the central roles of women's opera, theatre, and film in their realisations of the Fallen Women *trope*,

CAN THE CAMERA IMMORTALIZE THE MELANCHOLY MASK OF ELEONORA DUSE?

AMONG the younger generation of American theater lovers there are few who have ever had the opportunity to judge for themselves the enigmatic art of Eleonora Duse. Much has been written of this Italian woman who, according to the most discriminating critics of Europe, surpassed Bernhardt in subtlety, who inspired Gabriele d'Annunzio to his finest efforts, whose celebrated blush in her performance of Sudermann's "Heimat" inaugurated an endless controversy among the critics, and whose retirement at the very pinnacle of her success some years ago made of her a disputed semi-mythical figure. Now, through the medium of the celebrated Italian novelist, Matilde Serao, comes the news that Duse's art may after all be preserved for us and future generations.

In the "movies," of course! The actress whose epigram, "To save the theater, we must destroy the theater," has circled the globe, takes a deep interest in the newer form of expression. For more than a year, writes Matilde Serao, the great actress has been studying the art of the cinematograph. Signora Serao's interview is printed in the Boston *Transcript:*

"She believes firmly that from this mute stage, which has in its favor the rare and enviable element of the approbation of the most numerous and humble portion of the world's population, in the dark and crowded halls, new expressions of esthetic beauty and moral beauty may manifest themselves; she believes, nay, knows, that altho the fundamental laws which govern the representations on the white curtain must be respected, yet a singular dramatic greatness may be given to the cinematographic art, a horizon where all the valkyries of human passion can do battle, conquer, perish among the rolling clouds, seated on great white horses.

"Eleonora Duse, consenting yet once again with spontaneous abandonment to the fatigues of representative art, who retired still young from the stage, has not only faith in herself but in that cinematographic art which embraces the most complex as well as the most simple manifestations—this woman, who has been without vanity during the whole of her life, this woman whose only pride is in poetry and art, admires and loves those who, men and women, have already given their personality to the mute stage. Recalling them, in conversation with me, she spoke of certain interpretations of Francesca Bertini, of Leda Gys, and her judgment was sincere, well pondered, just. And always, with her beautiful, vague eyes, gazing afar off—who better than she has known how to dream of the infinite?—she exclaimed in a voice which came from a mysterious interior world: 'Oh, so much can be done, . . . so much can be done with the cinematograph.' "

We gather that Eleonora Duse had planned to appear on the screen in a scenario based upon one of the novels of Grazia Deledda. Matilde Serao writes:

"The austere and powerful talent of Grazia Deledda, those sculptured figures of women with primordial and profound feelings were, perhaps, not suitable for Eleonora Duse. The great actress listened to me and agreed. And then she revealed a secret to me which filled me with wonder and delight. Eleonora Duse is so penetrated with this cinematographic art that during her long days of workful silence she has herself written sketches of dramas, of dramatic cinematographic episodes, she has put on paper her visions of art. . . . Now, any one knowing Eleonora Duse in close intimacy knows that she possesses a magic pen and that her thoughts, in their written form, assume a strong and marked originality. . . . To see Eleonora Duse on the film of any writer must be a fascinating spectacle. But what would not be our emotion if Eleonora Duse should appear to us in a dream of her own making?"

"Her beautiful hair is all silvered and falls naturally in lines and waves, but it is shining silver and preserves on the forehead that slightly sinuous line, between the forehead and the temples, that makes so esthetic a frame. Her unforgettable eyes have ever that internal depth of poignant melancholy which she made as penetrating as a subtle sound."

RODIN'S SOUVENIR OF LA DUSE

The French sculptor named this arresting memory of the greatest of Italian actresses "Inquietude." Certain of her Italian critics fear that the enigmatic Eleonora has passed the age at which she might safely face the "movie" camera.

Figure 4.3 Current Opinion, 1 July 1917 – courtesy of HathiTrust.

positioning themselves as intermediaries and role models for their women spectators and readers.

The complex and self-affirming ways in which women writers and performers articulated and responded to narratives played out on stage and screen, which – more often than not – included themes of sexuality, sacrifice, betrayal, romantic love, loss, and (very often) death, guided their readers and spectators on how to respond to screenplays and performances cerebrally and with affect. The public declarations of friendships between women writers and performers (e.g., Gualberta Alaide Beccari's close friendship with Giacinta Pezzana; Matilde Serao's tie with Eleonora

Duse) – *exceptional* women in the spotlight as exemplars – were fundamental to ordinary women readers' and spectators' self-perceptions and friendships with their peers, which they may have attempted to imitate, to copy. Their enduring *sorellanza* – their close, long-lasting celebrity ties and mutual expressions of admiration and solidarity – was important symbolically for middle-class women's own personal friendships, insofar as it encouraged their nurture of otherwise more or less isolated mothers, wives, widows, and single, childfree women. We now turn to an examination of the "female gaze" in realist fiction, in which women spectators are also represented as looking increasing inwards, thus becoming self-questioning, self-aware, and self-determined, with a more developed sense of self as spectators.

Notes

1 A commentary written by an author using the pseudonym "Louis" in the French weekly publication *Le Méphisto: Journal artistique, littéraire, satirique*, argues that:

> Women love the theatre, because there they are loved. [...] As spectators, they become actors, and as lovers of love itself, they cannot be impartial in the love scenes that play out on the stage before them. Illusion dominates them. They are interested in the plot, and they often mix their real tears with pretend ones like those of the actors.

See: Louis, "La femme au theatre," in *Le Méphisto: Journal artistique, littéraire, satirique*, 25 January 1882, p. 2.

2 Giuseppina Mascari, "'Donne all'opera.' La voce del pubblico femminile Milanese attraverso le pagine del *Corriere delle dame* (1804–1818)," in *Il genere del pubblico: questioni per una storia della ricezione femminile nelle arti della scena*, ed. by Annamaria Cecconi in *Nuove frontiere per la storia di genere*, ed. by Laura Guidi, Maria Rosaria Pelizzari (Salerno: Università degli Studi di Salerno, 2013), pp. 199–206.

3 See: Elaine Showalter, *A Literature of Their Own: From Charlotte Brontë to Doris Lessing* (Princeton: Princeton University Press, 1977).

4 "Introduzione," in *Donne e giornalismo. Percorsi e presenze di storia di genere*, ed. by Silvia Franchini and Simonetta Soldani (Milan: Franco Angeli, 2004), pp. 24–5.

5 Leonia Cinotti, *La donna*, 31 May 1868, p. 30. Cinotti's italics.

6 Carlotta Ferrari Da Lodi, "Di alcuni luoghi insigni del Nabucco di Verdi" (On some distinguished parts in Verdi's *Nabucco*) in *La donna*, 10 August 1872, pp. 1117–9 (p. 1117).

7 *Ibid.*, 10 August 1872, p. 1117.

8 Anita, *La donna*, 10 May 1872, pp. 1030–1 (p. 1030).

9 Gualberta Alaide Beccari, "Giacinta Pezzana-Gualtieri," in *La donna*, 10 May 1873, pp. 1412–3 (p. 1412).

10 *Ibid.*, p. 1412.

11 Review from an unknown Spanish publication by an anonymous author published in Beccari, "Giacinta Pezzana-Gualtieri," *La donna*, 10 May 1873, p. 1413.

12 Adele Chiminello, letter dated 19 January 1877, cited in *La donna*, 30 January 1877, p. 2681.
13 Gualberta Alaide Beccari, "La donna e l'Arte," *La donna*, 30 November 1878, pp. 55–8 (p. 55). My italics.
14 *Ibid.*, p. 55. My italics.
15 Susan Rutherford has argued this in relation to celebrated women singers. See her *The Prima Donna and Opera, 1815–1930* (Cambridge: Cambridge University Press, 2006), p. 16.
16 Ursula Fanning has made the case for this in relation to Serao, Carolina Invernizio, and Neera. See her "Maternal Prescriptions and Descriptions in Post-Unification Italy," in *Women and Gender in Post-Unification Italy*, pp. 13–37.
17 La Marchesa Colombi, "Colore del tempo," in *Vita intima*, 30 December 1890, pp. 241–2 (p. 242).
18 Giovanni Pozza, *Cronache teatrali di Giovanni Pozza (1886–1913)* (Vicenza: Neri Pozza, 1971), pp. 69–72 (p. 69).
19 *Ibid.*, p. 72.
20 La Marchesa Colombi, "Colore del tempo," in *Vita intima*, 30 December 1890, p. 242.
21 *Ibid.*, 28 October 1890, p. 169.
22 *Ibid.*, 25 November 1890, p. 201.
23 La Marchesa Colombi, "Colore del tempo," 4 November 1890, p. 178.
24 See: www.telegraph.co.uk/news/2019/08/07/disney-remake-home-alone/ and www.telegraph.co.uk/tv/2020/02/22/cast-hit-sitcom-friends-reuniting-anniversary-special [accessed 9 March 2020].
25 Matilde Serao, "L'Artista Universale: Intervista di Matilde Serao con Sarah Bernhardt," in *Il Giorno*, 21 December 1904, p. 1.
26 *Ibid.*, p. 1.
27 *Ibid.*
28 *Ibid.*
29 Matilde Serao, *Ricordando Neera* (Milan: Fratelli Treves, 1920), p. 25.
30 Matilde Serao, "Figure di donne: Quella che tace," *Il Giorno*, 28 March 1904. My italics. It was not the first time Serao had journeyed to be with Duse on her sickbed: in January 1898, for the première of D'Annunzio's *La città morta* in Paris, Serao had travelled to Rome to "be with [her] great friend Eleonora Duse" as she awaited news of the outcome of the première. See Renée Lelièvre, *Le théâtre dramatique italien en France, 1855–1940* (Paris: A. Colin, 1959), p. 198, ftn. 98.
31 Matilde Serao, "Sarah Bernhardt," in *Il Giorno*, 25 July 1906.
32 Aldo Bernardini, *Cinema muto italiano*, vol. 2 (Rome and Bari: Laterza, 1980), pp. 20–1.
33 Matilde Serao, "Cinematografeide!," in *Il Giorno*, 30 March 1906.
34 Patricia Bianchi, "L'attrazione fatale dell'«arte muta», dal libro al teatro fino al cinema," in *Visibili, invisibili. Matilde Serao e le donne nell'Italia post-unitaria: materiali per una mostra*, ed. by Gabriella Liberati, Giuseppe Scalera, and Donatella Trotta (Rome: Centro Nazionale di Ricerca, 2016), pp. 149–64 (p. 160).
35 Matilde Serao, *Il Giorno*, 2 March 1911, p. 1.
36 *Ibid*, 4 March 1913, p. 2.

37 Matilde Serao, "Chi si commuoverà? Chi ammirerà?," in *Il Giorno,* 29–30 April 1914, p. 2.
38 Bianchi, "L'attrazione fatale," pp. 152–3.
39 Gina Annunziata, "Matilde Serao e il cinematografo," in *Non solo dive: pioniere del cinema italiano*, ed. by Monica Dall'Asta (Bologna: Cineteca di Bologna, 2008), pp. 249–54 (p. 250).
40 Author unknown, "Maria Carmi parla del 'soggetto' che Matilde Serao ha scritto ed ella ha interpretato per la MONOPOL FILM di Roma," in *La vita cinematografica*, 34–35, 15–22 September 1914, pp. 41–2.
41 *Ibid.*, pp. 41–2.
42 *Ibid.*
43 *Emilio Ghione, memorie e confessioni. Scritti sul cinematografo (15 anni di arte muta)*, ed. by Denis Lotti (Rome: Associazione Italiana per la Ricerche di Storia del Cinema, 2011), p. 60.
44 Cited in Bianchi, "L'attrazione fatale," p. 155. The article first appeared in Serao's newspaper *Il Giorno* on 6 November 1913, p. 2.
45 Author unknown, "Matilde Serao e il cinematografo," in *Lo schermo*, 17, 11 December 1926, p. 13.
46 Mario Sandri, "Gli uomini del giorno: Matilde Serao," *Modernissima* 37 (Milan: Casa Editrice Italiana, 1920), p. 28.
47 Annunziata, "Matilde Serao e il cinematografo," p. 252.
48 Matilde Serao, "Parla una spettatrice," in *L'Arte muta. Rassegna di vita cinematografica*, 15 June 1916, pp. 31–32, (p. 31). My italics.
49 Serao, "Parla una spettatrice," p. 31.
50 *Ibid.*
51 *Ibid.*
52 Matilde Serao, "Consiglio di Famiglia," in *Cin*, 12 May 1918, p. 2.
53 Serao, "Il grande avvenimento d'arte," p. 1.
54 *Ibid.*
55 *Ibid.*
56 Giuliana Bruno, *Streetwalking on a Ruined Map: Cultural Theory and the City Films of Elvira Notari* (Princeton: Princeton University Press, 1993), pp. 91–2.
57 Matilde Serao, "Fantasma," *Il Giorno*, 8 September 1926, p. 1.
58 Ien Ang, *Watching Dallas: Soap Opera and the Melodramatic Imagination* (London: Methuen, 1985), p. 134.
59 See: Flora, "Da Firenze. La lettura di Tommaso Salvini al Circolo Filologico," in *La donna*, 30 November 1881, pp. 40–2.
60 Ida Baccini, "Pietro Mascagni," *Cordelia*, 27 November 1892, p. 20.
61 *Ibid.*, p. 20. My italics.
62 See: Stuart Ewen, *Captains of Consciousness: Advertising and the Social Roots of Consumer Culture* (New York: McGraw-Hill Books, 1976).
63 *La donna: rivista quindicinale illustrate*, 5 March 1909, p. 2.
64 Paolo Mantegazza, *Dizionario d'igiene per le famiglie* (Sesto S. Giovanni: Casa Editrice Madella, 1911), p. 317.
65 Stendhal, *Rome, Naples and Florence*, trans. by Richard N. Coe (New York: John Calder, 1959), p. 468, entry dated 1 October 1817.
66 *Ibid.*, p. 351, entry dated 9 February 1817. My italics.
67 Umberto Eco, *Storia della bellezza* (Milan: Bompiani, 2007), p. 340.

68 See: Niccolò Tommasèo and Bernardo Bellini's *Dizionario della lingua italiana* (Turin: UTET, 1879), p. 916, whose entry on "Bellezza" includes the definition "Divina."
69 Veritas, *La rassegna degli interessi femminili*, 15 January 1887, p. 307.
70 Emanuele Gaetani-Tamburini, "Linda Monti-Brunner: la sua carriera, i suoi trionfi, le sue interpretazioni," *Cronaca dei Teatri*, 15 December 1905.
71 J. B. Laglaize, "Nel mondo della musica: la prima rappresentazione della *Lucia di Lammermoor* al Teatro San Carlo a Napoli," *Cordelia*, 4 March 1894, pp. 224–5 (p. 225). The author's italics.
72 *Ibid.*, p. 225.
73 Katharine Mitchell, "Beauty Italian Style: Gendered Imaginings of, and Reponses to, Stage Divas in Early Post-Unification Literary Culture," in "The Diva in Modern Italian Culture," Special Issue, ed. by Katharine Mitchell and Clorinda Donato, *Italian Studies* 70:3 (August 2015), 330–46.
74 Tommaso Salvini, *Ricordi, anedotti, impressioni* (Milan: Dumolard, 1895), p. 396.
75 Mazza, "Ombre e riflessi," *Comoedia*, January, February, March issue 1909, p. 2.
76 Author unknown, *Cronaca dei teatri*, 15 February 1905.
77 Author unknown, "Teatri italiani," *La frusta teatrale*, 30 December 1862.
78 Author unknown, *Cornelia*, 16 February 1876, p. 47.
79 Matilde Serao, "Api, Mosconi e Vespe," in *Il Mattino*, 23–24 March 1892, p. 1.
80 Neera, "Il sorriso della Duse," *Il Marzocco*, 24 March 1901, p. 1. See, also: Stephen Gundle, *Bellissima: Feminine Beauty and the Idea of Italy* (New Haven and London: Yale University Press, 2007), p. xvii: *La bella italiana* had "regular, though not necessarily classically perfect, features, long, simply-styled dark hair and expressive eyes."
81 Matilde Serao, "In un teatro, tutti i teatri," *Il Giorno*, 9 January 1916, p. 1.
82 Chiminello, *La donna*, p. 2681.
83 Author unknown, "Cronaca femminile," in *La donna*, 30 November 1881, p. 46.
84 Vittorio Paliotti, *Il Salone Margherita e la belle époque* (Rome: Benincasa, 1975), p. 193.
85 The *Corriere di Roma* went bankrupt in 1887 and Serao and Scarfoglio returned to Naples where they founded the *Corriere di Napoli* with funding from the banker Matteo Schilizzi. In 1892, they merged the *Corriere di Napoli* and the *Corriere del Mattino* and set up *Il Mattino*, and in 1902, they established *La Settimana*.
86 Angela Sarcina, *La signora del Mattino con antologia dei* 'Mosconi' *di Matilde Serao* (Naples: La Conchiglia, 1995), p. 108.
87 *Ibid.*, pp. 106–7.
88 Gibus, "Api, Mosconi, e Vespe," *Il Mattino*, 22–23 March 1892, p. 1. Serao's italics.
89 *Ibid.*, p. 1.
90 *Ibid.*, 10–11 April 1892, p. 1.
91 *Ibid.*, 24–25 April 1892, p. 1.
92 Maria Teresa Mori, "La moda del giorno," in *Giornali di donne in Toscana: Un catalogo, molte storie (1770–1945) II, 1900–1945*, eds. by Silvia Franchini, Monica Pacini, and Simonetta Soldani (Florence: Leo S. Olschki, 2007), pp. 384–9. The journal ran from January to November of 1911.

93 Matilde Serao, "Essi non debbono aver ragione," in *La moda del giorno* 1, 1 January 1911, p. 3.
94 Mori, "La moda del giorno," p. 386.
95 *Ibid.*
96 Letter by Eleonora Duse to *Il Tempo*, cited by La Spigolatrice, "Spigolando," in *La donna*, 20 August 1885, p. 345. Duse's italics.
97 See: Salvatore Morelli, *La donna e la scienza, o la soluzione dell'umano problema* (Naples: Stab. tip dell'Ancona, 1861).
98 Gualberta Alaide Beccari, "Una proposta," in *La donna*, 25 November 1880, p. 213. Beccari's italics.
99 G. G, "Teatri di artisti (Frammento di lettera)," in *Cordelia*, 26 February 1893, pp. 213–4.
100 See: Mirella Schino, *Il teatro di Eleonora Duse* (Bologna: Il Mulino, 1992).
101 Interview with Leone Fortis, *Cordelia*, 6 June 1897, cited in Schino, *Il teatro di Eleonora Duse*, pp. 233–5. Ristori's views were printed again in a special issue dedicated to Ristori in *Cronache drammatiche*, 1 January 1899.
102 Olga Signorelli, *La Duse* (Rome: A. Signorelli, 1938), p. 38.
103 Schino, *Il teatro di Eleonora Duse*, p. 237.
104 Author unknown, "Un'intervista ad Adelaide Ristori," *Corriere della sera*, 17–18 January 1902.
105 Letter from Eleonora Duse to the editor of *Le Gaulois*, 29 January 1902, cited in Schino, *Il teatro di Eleonora Duse*, p. 244.
106 Schino, *Il teatro di Eleonora Duse*, p. 245.
107 *Ibid.*, p. 247.
108 Silvio d'Amico, "Colloqui con la Duse," in *Lo spettatore italiano*, 1 May and 15 May 1924, cited in Schino, *Il teatro di Eleonora Duse*, p. 247. Duse's italics.
109 Matilde Serao for the *Boston Transcript*, cited in (author unknown), "Can the Camera Immortalise the Melancholy Mask of Eleonora Duse?," *Current Opinion*, 1 July 1917, p. 27. See: https://babel.hathitrust.org/cgi/pt?id=njp.32101077879797&view=1up&seq=47 [accessed 5 May 2018]. Leda Gys was the stage name of the Roman silent film diva Giselda Lombardi (1892–1957).
110 Serao, cited in *Current Opinion*, p. 27.

5 The Imaginary Female Gaze

When nineteenth-century Italian women writers began to emerge on to the literary scene during the 1870s, a focus on middle-class female *ennui* and women's frustration at their limitations in the domestic sphere was a recurring motif of their domestic fiction. Writing about middle-class women for a rapidly growing female readership, and as middle-class (more often than not, self-taught) women themselves, writers created fictionalised women performers and spectators as their protagonists – as both adolescents, and young married women who were more knowing and experienced in the manner of Emma Bovary. Susan Rutherford has shown in relation to fictional portrayals of women performers in British, French, and American fiction by women writers, that their fiction became a "form of evidence of a specifically female perception or reading of the prima donna [or woman performer] both as stage artist and as a woman."[1] As will become apparent in this chapter, and at the risk (once again) of essentialism, so, too, did Italian women writers offer evidence in their fiction of a specifically *female* perception or reading of the woman spectator, one that foregrounded desire and admiration for the woman performer. Further, whereas Rutherford argues that "[women writers] offer a limited and oblique solution to the theatre historian's perennial problem: that is, the difficulty of accurate assessment of the spectator's response to the theatrical image,"[2] when read alongside the numerous non-fictional accounts and examples in life-writings detailed in the previous chapters, and in conjunction with an assessment of the spectator's response to the cinematic image, a "multifaceted, nuanced portrayal of post-unification Italian women" emerges.[3]

In the same way that women writers in periodicals and columns were configuring and signalling for increasing numbers of women readers and/as spectators how they could take on the various forms of spectatorship available to them, so, too, were women writers adopting similar strategies in their fiction. As Wanda De Nunzio Schilardi observes in discussing the differences between Giovanni Verga's narration compared with Matilde Serao's,

DOI: 10.4324/9780429293511-6

> [Verga] does not need to intervene in his material on the hostile reality that he regards as immutable, [whereas] on the contrary Serao [...] intervenes frequently in the first person to help the reader to observe, participate, feel moved and disapprove.[4]

In treating fiction *on a par* with non-fiction by adopting a new historicist approach, and taking into account theories presented by feminist film and literary critics such as Mary Ann Doane and Elisabeth Bronfen on the feminine gaze, in what follows I explore representations of realist fictional women spectators and performers in a selection of excerpts to demonstrate that – unlike men writers – women writers in this historical period foregrounded women spectators' desire for, and pleasure in watching women performers, regardless of their class, age, or race.

My aim in this chapter is to demonstrate the (albeit rigid binary) *gendered* fictional configurations of spectators and performers at this specific moment in Italy's cultural history; while men writers' fictional representations of women spectators present the *cliché* of the woman spectator as preoccupied with fashion, gossip and flirtation, and as uninterested in the on-stage action (e.g., as *not* self-reflexive, self-questioning, and "wanting to know"),[5] women writers' fictionalised (and non-fictional) presentations typically depict a modern, self-conscious, early capitalist woman spectator who, on first attending an opera as a naïve adolescent (read: *not* like Bovary), identifies vicariously with the drawn-out emotional age-old dilemma of either following her heart or being guided by reason; or, as a married, more experienced spectator, reflects cerebrally and discerningly on the woman performer's performance *from a female perspective*. I suggest that, collectively, women writers' realist fictional presentations of theatre and opera scenes (I have been unable to find fictional evidence of women watching silent films) were portents heralding a nascent, self-affirming, and emboldened imaginary "female gaze" at the turn of the twentieth century in the manner articulated by Serao as a *spectatrix* of the silent screen in 1916, in which she called upon dramatists, cineasts, and writers to "please her."[6]

Similarly, while both women and men writers present women performers in their realist fiction, they do so differently: male authors tend to mythify and other the woman performer by aligning her closely to the figure of the *femme fatale*, portraying her as rejecting motherhood, and are more inclined to emphasise her "all-engulfing, [...] emasculating" beauty, as well as her apparent hostility and rivalry towards other women performers.[7] Although they share characteristics with male writers' constructions of "fatal" femininity, there are also marked differences in women writers' representations of women performers. Like the "New Woman" in the British and North American context, the Italian female-penned performer in realist fiction is a self-respecting, independent career woman, who, beyond the imaginary world of fiction, displays solidarity towards similar financially independent women in the public sphere, including women writers, having traits in common with actual, successful women performers beyond the realm of fiction, such as Eleonora Duse and others.[8]

To illustrate these marked differences, I first historicise the emergence of the realist novel in Italy in order to locate the very different ways in which – in the realist mode at least – women and men writers were representing everyday life as a gendered experience. Following this, I then explore the concomitant emergence on the tragic opera stage of the Fallen Woman trope and the curious absence of the *femme fatale* on Italy's stage and screen at the *fin de siècle*, before turning finally to an analysis of representations of women performers and spectators in realist fiction.

Gendering Realist Fiction

The publication of Gustave Flaubert's realist serialised novel *Madame Bovary* (1856) presented for the first time in literary fiction a "Fallen," middle-class female protagonist: the materialistic, adulterous, and yet pitied (at turns by her creator and readers) Emma Bovary.[9] An artistic movement that began in France in the 1830s in the visual arts in reaction against Romantic idealism, realism sought to depict "objectively" and with accuracy, in minute detail, the ordinariness of everyday life as it appeared to the eye and the ear; typically, artists would produce paintings of ordinary labourers or seamstresses working long hours and in poor conditions.[10] In literature, writers sought to represent subject matter "truthfully," without artificiality or reference to the supernatural. Emma in Flaubert's novel watches a performance of Donizetti's *Lucia di Lammermoor* at the Opéra-Comique theatre in Paris, and initially participates vicariously in the action on stage, appearing to identify with the suffering heroine (who has been forced into a marriage for a political allegiance). However, in what could be construed as a symbolic rejection of Romanticism, Emma ultimately sees the tragic love story (Lucia kills herself) in a detached way as "an embodied fantasy, an ornament for the eye"; Lucia's mad scene is "little to Emma's taste," and Lucia "seemed to be overacting":

> Emma found herself back in the books of her youth, in the land of Sir Walter Scott [...]. Remembering the novel, she could understand the *libretto* without difficulty, and as she followed the plot, sentence by sentence, elusive thoughts came back to her, to be dispersed immediately by the thunder of the music. [...] Gravely, Lucy entered upon her cavatina in G major. She plained of love, she longed for wings. So, too, Emma would have liked to escape from life and fly away in an embrace. [...] The heroine's voice seemed simply the echo of her own consciousness, and all this fascinating make-believe a part of her own life. [...] But, of course, such happiness must be a fiction, invented to be the despair of all desire. *She knew now the littleness*

> *of those passions that art exaggerates.* Accordingly, Emma strove to deflect her thoughts, to see no more in this reproduction of her sorrows than an embodied fantasy, an ornament for the eye.[11]

This degree of insight into a *bourgeois* female character's psyche had previously not been a feature of literary fiction; indeed, Flaubert – who was tried (and later acquitted) for writing an "obscene" novel – heralded a tendency to focus increasingly in literary fiction on middle-class characters' interior worlds, their psychological states. This gave vent for the first time in modernity, and since the French Revolution, to an exploration of ordinary middle-class female characters' imaginary worlds as a form of flight from the humdrum of a typically domestic, monotonous existence in the home (much in the same way as reading "dangerous" French novels was a form of escapism and saw the beginnings of a critique in literary form of (not only) women's social condition). Feminism, it can be argued, owes much to Flaubert.

The first edition of Alessandro Manzoni's historical novel *I promessi sposi* (The Betrothed, 1827) established the arrival of the modern novel in Italy, which came almost a century after its French and English counterparts. This was due in part to the absence of a sympathetic cultural climate and a nation state, as well as low literacy levels. By the end of the nineteenth century, the novel had a wide readership, yet it continued to be viewed with suspicion by members of the ruling class – priests, politicians, physicians, and intellectuals – who saw it, along with attendance at theatre or opera performances, as harmful to women's supposedly fragile minds, and as bringing about social risks for women by exposing them to themes of female desire, eroticism, and sexuality. Though women in the north of Italy in particular were reading French novels, including Flaubert's *Madame Bovary* and novels by Émile Zola, by the 1870s the publication of Luigi Capuana's *Giacinta* (1879) had marked the arrival of *naturalismo* in Italy. This can be defined as the representation of a believable everyday reality that grew out of the French realist novel and the naturalist school pioneered by Zola through his portrayal of the dark harshness of everyday life, as we see, for example, in his *L'Assommoir* (1877). Writing on the differences between *naturalismo* and *verismo*, Gino Tellini argues that while naturalism analyses in a seemingly detached way the political and social struggles of the subjects it describes, the narrator of *verismo*, rather than remaining outside the narration as a "detached" observer, is inside it as an embedded reporter, as a voice that belonged to the environment (s)he is describing.[12] Yet, the narrator, in her or his role as observer and/or as reporter, *always* writes subjectively, even while (s)he may aspire towards objectivity. *Verismo* as a literary school is commonly associated with Verga's short stories and novels, which represent social critiques of the oppression, poverty, and neglect of the south of Italy. Nevertheless, the modes and concerns of *verismo* allowed – and even required – women writers to present themselves as detached observers of the events about which they wrote, thereby positioning themselves as disengaged authors of the events they faithfully described.

Neera's narrative fiction complies with the principles of *verismo*, focusing on female experience.[13] This is also the case in the domestic fiction by Serao and La Marchesa Colombi, as well as in the realist fiction that documents female experience among the lower classes, such as La Marchesa Colombi's *In risaia* (In the rice fields, 1878). Serao explores the exploitation of female workers peripherally through her frequent portrayal of servants who nevertheless remain at the margins of their respective narratives, and so, too, does Neera through her portrayal of the prostitute, Falena (mentioned in Chapter 2), in her short story of the same name. In Italian domestic fiction, the embedded reporter/narrator from *verismo* is internal to the events taking place in the fiction. This is given credibility by virtue of the writers' sustained attention to the representation of the daily experience of middle-class women, which makes the fiction – partly influenced by the naturalists – unique. Women writers' use of language, notwithstanding its claims to objectivity and impersonality as realist, was, albeit in fictional form, the personal voice of certain women in spite of centuries of male-dominated literary discourse. The woman narrator tells the story of "real" women from *her* point of view. As if to recover hundreds of years of a majority of silent female voices, an all-female world is depicted in the texts.

In Neera's *œuvre*, the reader gains insight into the eponymous protagonist's state of mind in her *Teresa* through an account of Teresa's *feelings* upon having danced the previous night for the first time with a young man: "On awakening her first thought was of him; but instead of being a gay and happy thought, it came almost like a pain, like a sharp thorn in her skin."[14] Women and men authors of realist fiction differed in their depictions of female characters: women writers emphasised the life cycles of female characters, which provided the plot and were crucial to the ways in which the stories were told. The language of writings by women from this period is often simple and direct; it is not the language of Verga's *contadini*, nor is it the language of D'Annunzio's aristocrats. Instead, women writers of realist fiction inject feeling into their writing, expressing *sympathy* for their protagonists' thoughts and emotions pertaining to their circumstances (much in the same way as Verdi and Puccini express sympathy in their music for their suffering heroines). Women writers describe characters from different social groups through the personal voice of the woman narrator who empathises with the characters' situations. As Ann Hallamore Caesar explains:

> Where *veristi* writers look to create the appearance of truth, *vraisemblance*, by giving readers the illusion that they are looking directly on the world without having recourse to an authorial lens, … women writers … develop an aura of truth by making very visible their own hand in the development of the narrative […].[15]

Italian women writers of the late nineteenth and early twentieth century follow the example of their British and French foremothers and counterparts, such as Jane Austen, George Eliot, and Charlotte Brontë, who, in the words of Sandra Gilbert and Susan Gubar, were "[p]arodic, duplicitous, … all this female writing is both revisionary and revolutionary, even when it is produced by writers we usually think of as models of angelic resignation."[16] They were aware of this subversiveness in their style of writing, which was partially a consequence of the fact that many were, of necessity, self-taught. In La Marchesa Colombi's novel *Un matrimonio in provincia* (A Small-Town Marriage, 1885), the narrator gently mocks the protagonist's father's enthusiasm for the classics in Latin, Greek, and Florentine, pitting his knowledge and ability to recite these works to his daughters against their ignorance on their daily walks:

> He was the one who, from time to time, taught us to read, write and do arithmetic. And during our walks he gave us our literary education. At least this is what he believed, because he told us the stories of the *Iliad*, the *Aeneid*, and *Jerusalem Delivered* … Our poor father came over all anxious and in a sweat, as if he had performed those exploits himself.[17]

Similarly, Neera writes in her *Una giovinezza del secolo XIX* (An Adolescence of the Nineteenth Century, 1919) that, "among the classics I found in my father's library, I read not even one; I judged them boring and cold."[18]

Through a series of readings of nineteenth-century realist novels, Catherine Belsey has demonstrated that these texts perform the ideological function of bringing their readers into being as subjects. In *Critical Practice* (1980), Belsey puts forward the view that realist novels offer themselves for interpretation on the principle that it is above all character that governs social action.[19] In drawing upon Louis Althusser's view of ideology, Belsey shows how the reader of realist fiction is asked to read from the subject position of the omniscient narrator. She demonstrates how the reader is required to make sense of the text as if from within the subjective experience of one of the characters and is directly asked to take up the position of a subject. The ideological function of realist fiction contributes to the reader's belief that (s)he is the centre of her or his own thoughts and actions, and able to make sense of, and determine, her or his own life.

In realist fiction by women writers from late nineteenth-century Italy, whose narratives repeatedly feature female characters as passively accepting their prescribed roles as wives and mothers or as single women, this presents an interesting paradox: the female protagonists are entirely conventional and recognisable to their women readers. While the protagonists may entertain thoughts of transgressing their desired role as "good" wives and mothers, and in some cases carry out these transgressions, the narratives conclude with their protagonists passively accepting their fates, thereby seemingly upholding the *status quo*. This is the case in La Marchesa Colombi's *Prima morire* (Before dying, 1887) – a reworking of Flaubert's *Madame Bovary* from a female perspective – in which the protagonist, Eva, a devourer of novels, leaves her husband and daughter for a musician whom she soon abandons to return to her husband and child upon learning of her daughter's illness, turning the (masculine) "*cliché* of the woman reader" as romantic and "Bovarystic" on its head.[20] The same is true of Serao's short story "La virtù di Checchina" (Checchina's Virtue, 1883), in which the protagonist accepts an assignation with the Marquis only to reject it for fear of bringing shame upon her and her physician husband's reputation.[21] Thus, on the one hand, late nineteenth-century Italian women readers (who were most likely also spectators) are afforded pleasurable identification with the narratives' protagonists. Readers were interpellated into the narratives *as subjects* able to make sense of, and able to determine, their own lives; and yet, on the other hand, the narratives' prevailing ideology is seemingly one that repeatedly upholds and perpetuates their conservative social roles in the new Italy as middle-class wives and mothers. Yet, however conventional the subject matter of individual narratives may seem, by reading them it becomes apparent that the same contemporary social issues with which its female readership was intimately connected are addressed repeatedly, revealing *sympathy*, esteem, and respect on behalf of women writers, not only for ordinary middle-class women readers, but also for their protagonists as performers and spectators, as we shall see. And while one must be cautious about making claims that there existed an Italian women's writing in the late nineteenth century, it is important to acknowledge the distinctions between women and men writers insofar as how they were received at this juncture in history, as well as their use of subject matter, the differences in their tone and use of language, and their very different experiences of everyday life.

Gendered Representations of Imaginary Women Performers

Formulating a notion of men writers' constructions of women performers in realist fiction enables us to understand some of the ways in which male authors' perceptions and attitudes were reverberating and circulating beyond the printed page, in the everyday. An apparent fear of femininity on the part of (some) men casts the *femme fatale* as other – as different from what is familiar and accepted; male artists' and writers' perceptions of women as other have forced them to understand and control the category "woman" since Classical Antiquity as either "good" women – as passive, self-sacrificing, and submissive, as Coventry Patmore's "Angel of the House," in contrast to the so-called "Whore" – the seductive *femme* who takes control of her destiny, as in the figure of Medea in Greek mythology.[22] "Fatal" femininity can be understood in terms of

Bram Dijikstra's landmark 1986 interdisciplinary study mentioned in the Introduction, in which he shows that women were seen as static and un-individuated, as sexual and valued above all for their reproductive function, whereas men were considered to be intellectual and rational, undergoing an evolutionary process towards a disembodied spiritual essence. This was, after all, a paradoxical period, one in which male intellectuals, politicians, clerics, and middle-class parents all agreed that the confinement of women to the domestic sphere as wives and mothers was a *sine qua non* for the creation of a better and new society; at the same time, there emerged the "New Woman" in Britain and North America, and the same period saw the emergence of modern feminism, and imperialist, white, male, supremacy was beginning to establish itself throughout America and Europe; indeed, what Dijikstra's study fails to account for, and what books by Tracy Davis on the British context, Kirsten Pullen on American culture, and John Stokes, Michael R. Booth and Susan Bassnett on the European context bring to light, are the many (actual) professional, talented female performers who provided their own powerful artistic interpretations of the Fallen Women they performed, and who were the objects of desire of a multitude of (also) female desiring gazes.[23] The ambiguity of the period, then, arguably created a sense of acute anxiety and (unconscious?) fear among the majority of (middle-class) men and the many reactionary women concerning the gradual shifting of traditional gender roles.

Following the publication and circulation of Darwin's ground-breaking ideas of superiority and inferiority among the species, sexes, and races in his landmark study *On the Origin of Species* (1859), positivist scientists and thinkers in Italy, such as Cesare Lombroso and Paolo Mantegazza, aimed to prove that female moral and intellectual functions were tied to "natural" factors, particularly the reproductive function, constituting women's subordination in society as a law of nature. Positivist scientists' studies asserted both the natural inferiority and sexual passivity of women, thereby affirming their role within the family as wives and mothers, and the home as the place for female sexuality, destined solely for the purpose of reproduction. France had seen the establishment of the first professorship of psychiatry, and Charcot began to deliver his first Tuesday lectures on female "hysteria" at La Salpetrière Hospital in 1870 in Paris. Unable to locate organic lesions in his patients that might help him explain the malfunctions they exhibited, he attributed psychic trauma as a significant agent in the production of hysteria and used hypnosis to get his patients to reproduce their physical symptoms in order that physicians might study these.

In Italian realist fiction, "fatal femininity" is presented by *both* female and male writers, as is illustrated in the eponymous "hysterical" protagonist of Iginio Tarchetti's *Fosca* (1869) mentioned in Chapter 2, in Antonio Fogazzaro's Marina in his *Malombra* (1881), in Serao's Lalla in her *Cuore infermo* (Frozen Heart, 1881) and her Lucia in *Fantasia*

(1883), as well as in Gabriele D'Annunzio's Ippolita from his *Il trionfo della morte* (The Triumph of Death, 1894). In D'Annunzio's *Il fuoco* (The Flame, 1898) and Verga's realist stories *Eva* (1873) and "La serata della diva" (An Evening with a Diva, 1894), as well as in Luigi Pirandello's "Lumie di Sicilia" (Sicilian Limes, 1910), women performers are portrayed as cousins of the *femme fatale* insofar as it is their "fatal" effect upon male characters, told from the male narrator's point of view that characterises them as "threatening" according to *fin de siècle* norms of bourgeois morality and social propriety. Typically, they share facial features: dark, intense eyes, a dark complexion, and a made-up face with bright red lipstick. Similar to Zola's Nana, a singer from his eponymous novel (1880), Verga's ballerina, Eva, in his long story of the same name (1873), is described by the male protagonist, Enrico, as an "Amazon," a "Siren," and a "Goddess," "a splendidly nude and beautiful woman" with "daring eyes."[24] Enrico, Eva's "victim," tells his readers of his feelings of abuse and hatred towards Eva brought on by her lack of interest in him: "I hate her! I despise her! I want to bite her, slap her! ... I'd like to stamp on her,"[25] and in D'Annunzio's *Il fuoco* (1898) set in the early 1880s in Venice, the male protagonist, Stelio, describes his lover, Perdita, a female actor (the character is based on Duse with whom D'Annunzio was in a relationship for ten years from 1894), and the singer, Donna Arvale, as "temptresses."[26]

Describing French and Anglo-American women writers' fiction from the nineteenth century, specifically that of George Sand (1804–76) and George Eliot (1819–80), Susan J. Leonardi and Rebecca A. Pope draw attention to how:

> [d]ivas in women's texts [...] tend to redress *prima donna* stereotypes and revise the representations of female singers we find in many texts by men. [...] The Diva in this tradition is neither *femme fatale* nor happy handmaiden to what is finally a male muse. She is, rather, a *hardworking* woman more interested in music than marriage, in empowering women than seducing men.[27]

Indeed, yet again, the tradition begins in France with the renowned and exceptional French woman of letters, Madame De Staël (1766–1817), who, as we saw in Chapter 1, was an avid theatre-goer. Her most famous novel, *Corinne, ou l'Italie* (1807), which was based partly on her own life and partly on that of the Piedmontese poet, playwright, and author, Diodata Saluzzo Roero (1774–1840), conforms to the way in which actual and fictional women performers are constructed in literary culture by Italian women writers at the end of the nineteenth century: that is, typically, as talented, exceptional, and celebrated professional performers, whose appearance, as nevertheless *bella*, is depicted as coming second to her skills as a performing artist. In the novel, upon enquiring what important occasion the city of Rome is preparing for, the male protagonist,

Oswald, is told that "the most famous woman in Italy, Corinne, the poet, the writer, the improvisor, and one of the most beautiful people in Rome, was being crowned that morning."[28]

The same is true for Italian women writers of the late nineteenth century: in Neera's *Fotografie matrimoniali* (Marriage Photographs), first published in serialised form in the Milanese literary journal *Il pungolo della domenica* (1898), when the newly wed Sofia asks her husband whether he is going to see "La Zaeo" perform at the Teatro dal Verme in Milan that evening, she replies: "They say she is really very good," before adding, "She is beautiful."[29] Nevertheless, occasionally, women performers are also similarly "othered" by women writers who adopt a masculine perspective. La Marchesa Colombi's character Vittoria, an actor in the short story "Teste Alate" (Winged Heads, 1879), is reportedly described by Gustavo on whom she has a "fatal" effect, as an "Amazon," with "very black hair, sparkling black eyes, a Greek profile [...] with a dark brown attractive complexion."[30] Carolina Invernizio's popular horror story *Il bacio di una morta* (The Kiss of a Dead Woman, 1886) pits the wronged wife Clara, a name which symbolises light, against the evil temptress, Nara, which echoes *nera*, meaning black. Similarly, in Annie Vivanti's *Marion, artista di caffè-concerto* (Marion: Caffè Concerto Artist, 1891) set in the world of theatre, one of the performers, a singer, named Giulia, is described as having "eyes that are outlined in black [...] indicating the irreparable loss of her virtue," and Marion wears make-up, has black hair and a dark complexion, while the blonde-haired and blue-eyed character Anna is pitted against her as an innocent victim.[31] Marion is also presented sympathetically to some degree, as akin to the archetypal Fallen Women from women's opera, theatre, and silent film: like Verdi's Violetta in *La traviata*, Marion is consumptive, and, like Puccini's Tosca in his eponymous opera, she is a murderer. Marion is also presented as financially and emotionally independent, and agentic. Indeed, reference to women financing their lovers in Vivanti recalls Violetta's predicament in Act II of Verdi's *La traviata*: having fallen in love with the bourgeois Alfredo, she finances their living arrangements in the country with her earnings as a high-class courtesan.[32] (Beyond the imaginary world, it is well known that Duse financed many productions and performances of D'Annunzio's plays on the international stage at the turn of the twentieth century.)

In La Marchesa Colombi's "Teste Alate," Vittoria is presented as an independent artist, monitoring her critical acclaim in the press and expressing enthusiasm and admiration for authors and female actors. Gustavo, who is in love with her, describes to his friend Vittoria's artistic predisposition with respect and esteem:

> She was excited about acting. She showed enthusiasm for authors, female and male actors; she wanted to get to know them, and she had the language and behaviour to express her admiration, revealing passion in her artistic soul.[33]

In Vivanti's *Marion*, upon seeing that her colleague, Gina, is unhappy in her role as a *caffè-concerto* singer, the eponymous protagonist allows herself to be kissed on the lips by her boss in exchange for Gina's release from her contract.

Solidarity between women performers in fiction by male writers, on the contrary, is non-existent; in fact, unsurprisingly, rivalry is positively encouraged: in Verga's "La serata della diva" (An Evening with a Diva), the omniscient narrator informs his readers that "the star female singer [...] exchanged a hostile look with the star female dancer," and in D'Annunzio's *Il fuoco* the actor, Foscarina (whom Stelio calls Perdita), feels rivalry towards the younger, more beautiful women performers whom Stelio admires.[34] Writers of fiction in *fin de siècle* Italy diverged in their presentations of the woman performer according to their gender: men writers presented her as an "other," and women writers as a "revelation of potential freedom from patriarchal and essentialist thought," to use a definition coined by Lucia Re and ascribed to Duse.[35] Female-authored women performers in realist fiction share features in common with this description of Duse, who, as Re argues,

> for many women especially (but not only in Italy) and Europe, [...] was a living symbol of the "new woman," and of a woman's potential to free herself, to take centre stage, to be independent and professionally successful, and to challenge patriarchal norms.[36]

Male-authored, and some female-authored representations of Italian "fatal" femininity, embodied in the *femme fatale* figure from Tarchetti onwards, posited her as a "sick" figure; "a symptom of the neurosis afflicting modern woman."[37] While women writers such as La Marchesa Colombi and Vivanti resisted identification as "new" women themselves, their fiction presented a positive image of womanhood, one that borrowed intertextually from the male-constructed Fallen Woman *trope* in women's opera, and recast it to construct fictional women performers who were emotionally strong, sexually desiring and assertive, self-respecting, and who knew their own worth. Moreover, women writers did not "punish" their female performer characters for rejecting motherhood as male writers often did by killing off *femmes fatales*; rather, women writers saw the profession of the female performer as incompatible with motherhood (although Duse, Pezzana, and Bertini all had children, and many other successful women performers were also mothers).

Gendered Representations of Imaginary Women Spectators

To recap, the sympathy and empathy felt by spectators, including male opera composers and film directors, who were watching and listening to the suffering heroine/Fallen Woman on stage and screen from the 1850s onwards, prompted an unprecedented engagement – particularly on behalf of women spectators. Their epistemophilic gazes, including erotic curiosity, identification, and desire, brought about their engagement as critical consumers of the performances they attended. As we have already seen, the male-authored view of women's responses to such hyperbolic outpourings of grief on behalf of suffering heroines, was that women spectators were preoccupied by fashion and by observing other spectators, rather than by the action taking place on stage. Verga, in his *novella*, *Eva* (1873), has his first-person narrator describe the spectators' appearance and behaviour prior to curtain-up at the Pergola Theatre in Florence during a performance by the eponymous ballerina:

> The boxes began filling up with beautiful women – at least, they were adorned with many flowers, jewels, ribbons, white and red, and in the half-light they all seemed beautiful. Among the men, there were those who were very well shaven and with such well combed, shiny and curly hair, that those beautiful women were sure to be looking at them with their eyes wide open, just as I looked at them, and instinctively hid my bare hands under my hat.[38]

The emphasis here is on beauty, glamour, and desiring gazes at the "beautiful women" in particular. In D'Annunzio's re-telling of his love affair with Duse in his *Il fuoco*, the poet-protagonist and D'Annunzio's *alter ego*, Stelio Effrena, anticipates the effect his performance will have specifically on the women spectators: "For my female spectators, the art with which my tie is knotted will be far more appreciated than the art with which I coordinate my sentences."[39] While D'Annunzio may well have had a different view of how women spectators responded to female performers, the implication here that women spectators were far more interested in fashion is consistent with Risorgimento stereotypes of women spectators' behaviour in the descriptions by Liszt, and also by Stendhal mentioned in Chapter 4.

In narrative fiction by women writers in late nineteenth-century Italy, women spectators are engaged in, and enthusiastic about, watching and listening to theatre and opera performances, in contrast to D'Annunzio's and Verga's male characters' views of women spectators. This new, middle-class, female-penned *spettatrice impegnata* (engaged woman spectator) in fiction offers mixed responses to watching performing women: some responses are critical, others are emotional; yet others are a combination of both. Denza, the lower-middle-class protagonist in La Marchesa Colombi's Piedmontese-based *Un matrimonio in provincia* (A Small-Town Marriage, 1885), is transfixed by the singer who performs the role of Marguerite from Gounod's *Faust* (1859) in Novara in Piedmont when Denza's more worldly female cousin takes her to the opera for the first time. Denza's response to Faust's declaration of love for Marguerite is to feel consumed by tenderness, as if he had addressed his song of love directly to her:

> Then the performance *really* began to interest me. How did he fall in love? Oh, how eagerly I waited for that moment! When Faust bent amorously towards Marguerite, murmuring sweet nothings to her in the softest of voices, I felt as though I were consumed with love, just as though he had murmured these things to me.[40]

The passage chimes with Teresa's response from Neera's eponymous novel (1886), who is, like Denza, a lower-middle-class adolescent growing up in the provinces, though in Lombardy. On her first outing to the opera, she experiences a similar epistemophilic and close emotional involvement: naïve, yet instructive (in matters of sex and love) with the unfolding of the narrative in Verdi's *Rigoletto* (1851):

> Teresa was enraptured. The beauty of art revealed itself to her heart already open to love. She anxiously followed the development of the dramatic action. The kidnapping of Gilda frightened her, she cried with Rigoletto, she had disrespect and scorn for the courtesans, and waited excitedly for Gilda's return to the stage.[41]

Such portrayals of adolescent girls watching the highs and lows of tragic realist opera – particularly in Denza's case – describe how the naïve literary protagonists respond vicariously to the tragic heroine's emotional suffering and feelings of romantic love, awakening in them their own newly discovered (hetero?)sexuality and educating them on how to relate to potential suitors.

A specifically gendered response to performances and screenings is a feature of many accounts published by women in late nineteenth-century Italy, one that for women is characterised by a visceral feeling of enthusiasm, wonderment, and delight; for more experienced middle-class women, their affect took on a more "knowing" and mature response. Feeling disappointed and underwhelmed at the everyday reality of being a wife in late nineteenth-century Italy, having had a *de rigueur* arranged marriage, in a letter to her female close friend in which she expresses disillusionment, Sofia, the protagonist from Neera's novel *Fotografie matrimoniali* (Wedding Photographs, 1883), is (perhaps somewhat masochistically) nostalgic for a time when, at the Teatro Dal Verme in Milan, she:

> melted with Rosina (from Rossini's *Il barbiere di Seviglia* (The Barber of Seville, 1816) at the sight of the handsome and poetic Almaviva, and would have given she knows not what to be kidnapped by him

after recalling the "delightful" opera singer Elena Varesi (1844–1920) performing the role of Rosina and her signature tune, "Una voce poco fa …"[42] (Rosina is being courted by Count Almaviva, who eventually succeeds in marrying her.)

In Serao's *Addio, amore!* (Farewell, My Love!, 1890) the women spectators are described by the third-person narrator seconds before the opening scene of Meyerbeer's *Gli Ugonotti* (1836) at the Teatro San Carlo in Naples as "Immobile, dumbfounded in their attention; the women in their boxes did not bat an eyelid, immediately won over in their sensibility by the wave of music."[43] Similarly, the third-person omniscient narrator in Vivanti's *Marion* mentions the women spectators' stunned response to watching the poet improviser, Mario, perform in Genoa:

> In the drawing room of the detached house in San Pier d'Arena, all the lights were on, and the women drank their tea, all still shuddering and moved by the verses that Mario had recited. "Sublime!", sighed Signora Astori. "What perfume! Such delicacy!", exclaimed the perfumed and delicate Marchesa Elisi, and with a childish onrush of enthusiasm she grabbed the hands of the poet and held them tight in hers.[44]

Conclusion

Male-authored "othering" depictions in fiction of performing women were a backlash against the emergence of increasing numbers of "knowing" and engaged female consumers as readers and spectators of popular culture: of novels, women's magazines, theatre performances, and screenings. Like the suffering tragic Italian opera heroines they were watching and listening to, and the fictional stage performers they read of, women spectators participated vicariously in the "transgressive" characteristics of *donne nuove*, of the transatlantic and British "New Women" playing out on stage and screen through the figure of the woman performer. While representing a threat to traditional masculine forms of power, privilege, and status, women producers and consumers of culture in Italy at the *fin de siècle* were not only taking ownership of their roles as producers of their art, but they were also articulating an early consumer capitalism – one which embraced choice and female embodiment, as well as the beginnings of gender equality.

We now turn to look beyond Italy to examine spectating and performing practices with regard to female-authored texts and screenplays that were exported to France, the United States, and Australia. As will be shown, the Magdalene archetype from Italian tragic opera was recycled in spoken theatre, and subsequently onto the silver screen from Naples, to Paris, to Boston and back.

Notes

1 Susan Rutherford, "The Voice of Freedom: Images of the Prima Donna," in *The New Woman and Her Sisters: Feminism and Theatre, 1850–1914*, ed. by Vivien Gardner and Susan Rutherford (Ann Arbor: University of Michigan Press, 1992), pp. 95–113 (p. 98).

2 *Ibid.*, p. 99.
3 Laura Salsini, "Private Lives, Public Letters: The Making of an Epistolary Heroine," *Italica* 88:4 (2011), 602–20 (616).
4 Wanda De Nunzio Schilardi, *L'Invenzione del reale: studi su Matilde Serao* (Bari: Palamor, 2004), p. 14.
5 Anna Vertua Gentile, writing in her conduct manual *Come devo comportarmi? Libro per tutti*, 2nd edn. (Milan: Hoepli, 1897), purposefully rejects this masculine stereotype, arguing that women who go to the theatre to receive visitors in their box and converse are "vain" and "disrespectful of the performing arts," p. 301.
6 Serao, "Parla una spettatrice," in *L'Arte muta. Rassegna di vita cinematografica*, 15 June 1916, p. 32.
7 Virginia M. Allen, *The Femme Fatale: Erotic Icon* (Troy, New York: Whitston Publishing Company, 1983), p. 193.
8 See: Sally Ledger, *The New Woman: Fiction and Feminism at the* fin-de-siècle (Manchester: Manchester University Press, 1997): "[The New Woman] had a multiple identity. She was, variously, a feminist activist [...] a popular novelist, a suffragette playwright, a woman poet," p. 1.
9 See: Gustave Flaubert, *Madame Bovary*, trans. by Geoffrey Wall (London: Penguin, 1995). The novel was published in serialised format in the *Revue de Paris* in 1856 and as a novel in 1857 by Michel Lévy Frères.
10 See, for example, paintings by Gustave Courbet (1819–77) and Jean François Millet (1814–75). Critics generally agreed that the first realist novel was Honoré de Balzac's *La Peau de chagrin*, published in 1831.
11 Flaubert, *Madame Bovary*, pp. 234–9. My italics.
12 Gino Tellini, *Il romanzo italiano dell'Ottocento e Novecento* (Milan: Bruno Mondadori, 1998), p. 184.
13 For recent work on Neera as a "literary mother," see: Catherine Ramsey-Portolano, *Nineteenth-Century Women Writers and the Woman Question: The Case of Neera* (New York: Routledge, 2021).
14 Neera, *Teresa*, trans. Martha King (Evanston: Northwestern University Press, 1998), p. 50.
15 Ann Hallamore Caesar, "Writing by Women in Post-Unification Literary Culture: The Case for De-segregation," in *Women and Gender in Post-Unification Italy: Between Public and Private Spheres*, ed. by Katharine Mitchell and Helena Sanson (Oxford: Peter Lang, 2013), pp. 225–44 (pp. 231–2).
16 Sandra M. Gilbert and Susan Gubar, *The Madwoman in the Attic: The Woman Writer and the Nineteenth-Century Literary Imagination* (New Haven: Yale University Press, 2000), p. 80.
17 La Marchesa Colombi, *Un matrimonio in provincia* [1885] (Novara: Interlinea, 1999), pp. 18–9.
18 Neera, *Una giovinezza del secolo XIX* [1919] (Milan: Feltrinelli, 1975), p. 119.
19 Catherine Belsey, *Critical Practice* (London: Routledge, 1980), p. 73.
20 See: La Marchesa Colombi, *Prima Morire* [1881] (Rome: Lucarini, 1988). Olivia Santovetti defines the *cliché* of the romantic woman reader as "bovarystic" for her emergence in Flaubert's protagonist Emma Bovary as "the Romantic dreamer [...] *par excellence*." See: Olivia Santovetti, "The Cliché of the Romantic Female Reader and the Paradox of Novelistic Illusion:

Federico De Roberto's *L'Illusione* (1891)," in *Printed Media in fin-de-siècle Italy: Publishers, Writers, Readers*, ed. by Ann Hallamore Caesar, Gabriella Romani and Jennifer Burns (Oxford and Bern: Legenda, 2011), pp. 49–63 (p. 49).

21 See: Matilde Serao, "La virtù di Checchina," in *La virtù delle donne* [1884] (Rome: Avagliano, 1999).

22 For an analysis of this dichotomy in French nineteenth-century literature, see: Lisa Downing, *Desiring the Dead: Necrophilia and Nineteenth-Century French Literature* (Oxford: Legenda, 2003).

23 See: Tracy C. Davis, *Actresses as Working Women: Their Social Identity in Victorian Culture* (London: Routledge, 1991); Kirsten Pullen, *Actresses and Whores: On Stage and in Society* (Cambridge: Cambridge University Press, 2005); and John Stokes, Michael R. Booth and Susan Bassnett, *Bernhardt, Terry, Duse: The Actress and Her Time* (Cambridge: Cambridge University Press, 1988).

24 Giovanni Verga, *Una peccatrice: Storia di una capinera; Eva; Tigre reale* (Milan: Mondadori, 1975), pp. 227–314 (pp. 240–98).

25 *Ibid.*, p. 233.

26 Gabriele D'Annunzio, *Il fuoco* [1898] (Milan: Mondadori, 1967), p. 73.

27 Susan J. Leonardi, and Rebecca A. Pope, *The Diva's Mouth: Body, Voice, Prima Donna Politics* (New Brunswick, New Jersey: Rutgers University Press, 1996), p. 74. My italics.

28 Germaine De Staël-Holstein, *Corinne, ou l'Italie* (Paris: Garnier Frères, 1869), p. 21.

29 Neera, *Fotografie matrimoniali* (Catania: Giannotta, 1900), p. 56. The novel was first published in nine instalments in 1883 between 18 March and 22 July in the Milanese Sunday literary periodical, *Il pungolo della domenica.*

30 La Marchesa Colombi, "Teste Alate," in *Serate d'inverno* [1879] (Ferrara: Luciana Tufani Editrice, 1997), pp. 64–5.

31 Annie Vivanti, *Marion, artista di caffè-concerto* [1891] (Palermo: Sellerio, 2006), p. 37.

32 *Ibid.*, p. 87.

33 La Marchesa Colombi, "Teste Alate," p. 77.

34 Giovanni Verga, "La serata della diva," in *Tutte le novelle* [1894] (Milan: Mondadori, 1979), pp. 753–65 (p. 764); D'Annunzio, *Il fuoco*, p. 197.

35 Lucia Re, "Eleonora Duse and Women: Performing Desire, Power, and Knowledge," in *The Diva in Modern Italian Culture*, ed. by Katharine Mitchell and Clorinda Donato, *Italian Studies* 70:3 (2015), 347–63 (p. 349).

36 *Ibid.*, p. 350.

37 *Ibid.*, p. 349. On the subject of female illness, see: Catherine Ramsey-Portolano, *Performing Bodies: Female Illness in Italian Literature and Cinema* (1860–1920) (Vancouver and Madison, NJ: Fairleigh Dickinson University Press, 2018).

38 Verga, *Una peccatrice, Storia di una capinera, Eva*, and *Tigre Reale*, pp. 239–40.

39 Gabriele D'Annunzio, *Il fuoco* (Milan: Mondadori, 1967), p. 32.

40 La Marchesa Colombi, *A Small-Town Marriage*, trans. by Paula Spurlin Paige (Evanston IL: Northwestern University Press, 2001), p. 23. My italics.

41 Neera, *Teresa*, p. 60.

42 Neera, *Fotografie matrimoniali*, p. 89.

43 Matilde Serao, *Addio, amore!* [1890] (Naples: Tommaso Villani, 1919), p. 60.

44 Vivanti, *Marion*, p. 126.

6 The Female Gaze Beyond Italy

This final chapter looks beyond Italy to explore women spectators' responses to Italian female-penned and performed works on stage and screen circulating in France, North America, Britain, and Australia at the turn of the twentieth century. In 1905, Matilde Serao adapted her sentimental novel *Dopo il perdono* (After the Pardon) for the Parisian stage with Pierre Decourcelle (1856–1926); it had a run of performances in 1907. In addition, Eleonora Duse (with Febo Mari (1881–1939) in *Cenere* 1916) and Francesca Bertini (with Gustavo Serena (1881–1970) in *Assunta Spina*, 1915) were both directors and divas of silent films that were shown internationally (Bertini had her own film company, Bertini Films).[1] These were the mainstay of Italy's silent film exports between 1910 and 1917, when the Italian film industry went bankrupt, irremediably damaged by a dramatic increase in Hollywood film exports. The earliest and most prolific Italian female filmmaker was arguably the Neapolitan Elvira Notari (1875–1946), who ran her own film company, Dora Films, and many of the films she produced were enjoyed by the Italian immigrant community in New York (it is estimated that around 4 million southern Italians emigrated, principally to the United States, between 1900 and 1910).[2] In what follows, I draw on theatre reviews by French women writers in the periodical press such as *Le Figaro*, *Les Annals politiques et littéraries*, *Le Temps*, *Le Journal amusant*, and reviews in American, British, and Australian periodicals of performing women whose star *personae* were also marketed and circulating in the Anglophone world through advertisements, *cartes de visites*, and postcards. I examine reflections among middle-class women spectators from Naples, to Paris, to New York, London, and Sydney, and demonstrate that these pointed towards an "exportable" Mediterranean, southern European, critical, and affective female spectatorship-in-the making, whose origins were nevertheless rooted in the specificity of the relationship between Italy's female performers, directors, and writers as critics and embodiments of modernity. Finally, I argue that women writers and performers personified a cosmopolitan and desirable southern European "exoticism" for their global readers and spectators as consumers.

DOI: 10.4324/9780429293511-7

Stage and Silent Screen Divas Abroad

As "agents and metaphors of changing gender relations," as "social texts" and media constructs, performers' public personae, popularity, and influence at the turn of the twentieth century shared common characteristics, roles, and (trans)national receptions.[3] In defining "national character" and "national identity," Silvana Patriarca acknowledges that "both notions are rather slippery and lend themselves to multiple definitions and uses," describing the former as "a set of distinctive moral and mental traits," and the latter as indicative of "a more subjective dimension of perception and self-images which may include a sense of mission and self-projection in the world."[4] Drawing on Patriarca's definition of national identity, I ask here to what extent Italian women writers and performers catalysed social and political change through the circulation and consumption of their "star text" at home and abroad? As mobile embodiments of Italian cosmopolitanism, to what extent were Italian divas received positively by women critics in the countries in which they gave performances, and what were the influences of their international tours and legacies? To what extent did Italian women performers and writers embody aspects of national identity when they travelled abroad for work? On their international tours, how far were they portrayed in newspapers and periodicals as models of celebrated femininity in ways that anticipated the star discourses that would later surround Hollywood film stars?[5]

In her discussion on the representation of European female stars in Australian periodicals, Julie Allen claims they "were far more likely to be mentioned by name and lavished with extravagant praise than their male contemporaries."[6] This was also the case for Italian stage and screen divas. What follows is a consideration of the international reputations from a female perspective of the most highly acclaimed Italian opera singer (Adelina Patti), theatre actor (Eleonora Duse), and silent diva (Francesca Bertini); they were each also managers and directors of their performances. As a celebrated writer, and by way of introduction to her play *Aprés le pardon* (After the Pardon), I also discuss Serao's international profile.

Adelina Patti (1843–1919), Opera Singer and Manager

Patti was a highly acclaimed *coloratura* soprano. According to John Rosselli, she was "[probably] the highest paid opera singer in history" in real terms.[7] Known to her fans as "the nightingale" for her pure voice, she was hailed by American and German critics as possessing "genius" for her performances as Lucia in Donizetti's *Lucia di Lammermoor* (1835).[8] Born in Madrid to opera singers, Patti spent much of her childhood in New York, touring Europe and the Americas during her working life before retiring in the early 1900s in Wales. She married three times. By the end of her career, she had mastered leading roles in 40 operas and had a wide variety of concert repertory, having performed in London's Covent Garden, Madrid's Teatro Real, Paris's Théâtre-Italien, St. Petersburg's Imperial Theatre in Moscow, and in Milan's La Scala, among others, managing all of her contracts and fees.

A search of her name in the American Periodicals digitised database in the available newspapers and magazines published between 1880 and 1916 yields 491 magazine articles, scholarly articles, and trade journals. (The tenor Enrico Caruso (1873–1921) features in only 105 over a similar length of time.) If we look to Australia during the same decades, the Trove Digitised Newspapers database captures Patti's name in 1,548 articles, and in Britain's Nineteenth Century Collections Online, a search yields 984 articles. While these "mentions" or articles are clearly proportionate to the number of digitised sources existing within each database, the figures nevertheless provide some evidence of the stage diva's stellar reputation and influence beyond Italy. The English novelist Ouida (pseudonym for Maria Luisa Ramé, 1839–1908), writing on "The New Woman" in the *North American Review* in 1894, mentions Patti in her discussion of "women of great genius or of great beauty."[9] Similarly, an anonymous woman writing of her memories of being in Vienna in the American periodical *The Cornhill Magazine* (reprinted in *The Living Age* in 1920) remembers Patti as "a bright musical star who shone upon us," who "thrilled [...] with her wonderful voice."[10] Writing in *Life* magazine in 1910 on Patti's retirement, an unnamed contributor states that Patti's rendition of Thomas Moore's "The Last Rose of Summer" would "make armies pause and break up the most solemn assembly of the world's greatest," and that "[w]e take off our hats to [her] – the greatest of them all."[11] During her last tour of the United States between 1903–04, she commissioned the American songwriter Charles K. Harris (1867–1930) to write a song entitled "The Last Farewell" for her American tour, and Americans claimed Patti as their own. The lyrics at the end of the first stanza include the phrase "Home, sweet home," and the first stanza of the second verse draws an intimate connection between Patti and the United States, where she spent her childhood: "It seems so sweet once more to meet/To know and feel your love is real/And here tonight, with faces bright/Your hearts have shown, I'm welcome home."[12]

Eleonora Duse (1858–1924), Actor, Manager, Film Director

A contemporary of Patti, Duse was one of the greatest actors of all time. Born in Vigevano in Lombardy to actor parents, as a *figlia d'arte* she gave her first performance at the age of four in the role of Cosetta in an adaptation of Victor Hugo's *I miserabili* (1862), and in 1873 she played the role of Juliet in William Shakespeare's *Romeo and Juliet* (1597) to great acclaim in Verona's famous arena. She married and had a daughter, but the marriage did not last long. She formed her own *Compagnia* in 1884 and went on to achieve international acclaim in France, Russia, South America, the United States, Britain, Spain, Austria, Germany, among others, retiring from the stage unexpectedly in 1909. Her interest in the new medium of cinema, which she regarded as a "different language" to theatre,[13] led her to finance the film *Cenere*, produced by Ambrosio films, in which she starred and directed.[14] Duse returned to the stage in 1921, first in Turin, then in London, Vienna, and the United States, where she died. She, too, had a reputation as a "genius" among her international critics and, in tune with discourses surrounding nation-making at the time, proudly embraced her national identity. Writing in the French daily newspaper *Le Gaulois* to the director in 1902 in response to the criticism directed at her by Adelaide Ristori mentioned in Chapter 4, Duse said:

> As a female artist and an Italian woman, I have the great honour of being able to give my name and my good will and effort to renew [Italian theatre]. As a female artist and an Italian woman, in my country I do my duty.[15]

Gemma Ferruggia, writing in her biography of Duse, recalls journalist and *impresario* Eduardo Boutet questioning whether, if she "truly lacked *italianità*, how is it she keeps returning to Italy every year she is away?"[16] Italians saw in Duse an ambassador of so-called *italianità*: wishing her well on her international tour of 1899, an anonymous writer signing with the initial "A" in the *Corriere dei teatri* from 10 June celebrates Duse on the front page, commenting:

> After her tour in Italy, the great actress will leave us for an extended tour beyond the borders of our nation. May our good wishes – which are the good wishes of the whole of Italy – accompany her; we are so proud to have in her such a strong and exquisite actress.[17]

The emphasis on "Italy's" good wishes is suggestive of a unified culture and people, yet, in reality, the majority of people, particularly in the south, felt neglected by the Liberal government, as Serao's direct address to the then Prime Minister Agostino Depretis (1813–87) testifies: her *Il ventre di Napoli* (The Belly of Naples, 1884) is an angry indictment of governmental neglect and a demand for intervention and subsidies following the Cholera epidemic of 1884.

Duse was lauded for her particular style of acting, which was regarded by many as effortlessly poetic, and for totally assuming the role of the female lead character compared with the apparently prosaic style of the majority of British and U.S. actors. A search of online digitised periodicals in Nineteenth Century Collections online, the British Library Newspapers archive, Nineteenth Century UK Periodicals and *The Times* Digital Archive yields a total of 710 "mentions," while a search in the Hathi Trust Digital Library produces 102 "mentions" in newspaper articles from North and South America. The Trove collection of the National Library of Australia, on the other hand, shows 481 results in a search of her name in newspaper articles. Duse was eulogised in particular by the likes of George Bernard Shaw, James Joyce, Anton Chekhov, and Charlie Chaplin. Her repertoire was predominantly drawn from the Italian nineteenth-century melodramatic genre; she would perform plays by D'Annunzio and Verga, though she was also known for her roles in the plays of Ibsen and Sardou. *The Woman's Home Journal* in Boston reports on how "the great Italian tragedienne, whose success has been remarkable" will appear at the Globe Theatre following "scores of letters from Boston's best people, begging the Rosenfeld Brothers to book 'La Duse' in Boston."[18] Indeed, she performed the role of Santuzza in Verga's *Cavalleria rusticana* (Rustic Chivalry, 1884) there several days later on 14 April.[19]

The British-born American stage actor Eva Le Gallienne (1899–1991), who wrote a biography of Duse, purportedly said of her:

> [Duse] is the greatest artist I've ever seen in the theatre. The Method people talk about how one should be real and true and simple – and they aren't, but Duse was. She would sit on the stage and would seem to be doing nothing. Yet you knew everything she was thinking, everything she was feeling. There was something that seemed like a ray that came from her and captured the house.[20]

Le Gallienne's description of the spectator being completely aware of "everything [Duse] was thinking" and feeling, as if the audience were not there before her, is evocative of a similar statement made of the opera singer Erminia Frezzolini (1818–84) and published in her obituary.

> [She] could never appear on stage without feeling an extreme painful and at the same time sweet emotion; but [...] this feeling disappeared immediately as [she] identified with her role, and until the end of the first act the spectators no longer existed.[21]

However, not all of Duse's critics were positive: the English novelist Maurice Baring, writing in *Vanity Fair* in 1923, said somewhat belittlingly that Duse's performance of Cleopatra in Shakespeare's *Anthony and Cleopatra* was unconvincing, and that she had looked like "a charming little Italian lady dressed as a queen," even though she was medium-sized.[22] Duse is said to have inspired the American poet Amy Lowell (1874–1925), as well as many contemporary younger women actors.[23] In July 1923, she became the first woman (and Italian) to be featured on the cover of *Time* magazine.

Prior to this, the *New York Times* reported on Duse's performance in Alexandre Dumas *fils*'s *La Dame aux Camélias* at the Daly's Theatre in London in 1894 as having been "received enthusiastically," and how "she was called repeatedly before the curtain,"[24] while in what could be regarded as a strikingly relevant modern-day "call out" at her male critics, the American silent film star Theda Bara (1885–1955), writing with considerable anger in the journal *Forum* in 1919, laments the fact of having been accused in her career of being a "vampire" compared with women stage actors who have not:

> To men who sigh to music and the long-limbed women who people these ghostlands of cerebral culture, [Duse] is another cursed product of the commercialism they despise [...] [A]lthough artists like Duse, Bernhardt, and other equally famous *tragediennes*, have given us characterisations in the theatre of complex women, *they* have not been accused of being vampires.[25]

In Britain, the author George Frederic William Lees, writing for *The Lady's Realm* in 1897 on "The Art of Eleonora Duse," recalls the moment as a young girl when Duse was inspired by watching Sarah Bernhardt perform in Turin (mentioned in Chapter 4), before describing her "genius" as an actor and

> the impression she creates upon her audience [that she] is not acting but [that] what is happening on the stage belongs to real life. Her mobile, expressive face has something about it which fascinates one, and her power of transformation is truly marvellous.[26]

Writing under the pseudonym "Sub Rosa" in *The Gentlewoman and Modern Life* and reviewing a book titled *Eleonora Duse* by Mme Jeanne Bordeaux and published by Hutchinson, the reviewer refers to "the inevitable struggle of [Duse's] passionate personality with the conventions of an art in which she was a genius."[27] In 1913, in an effort to foster inter-cultural exchanges and connectedness, the possibility of universal communication, and to promote the learning of foreign languages among its readers, *The Gentlewoman* published an article written in Italian summarising Duse's career thus far and pondering on whether or not she will return to the stage.[28]

There were, however, voices of mixed praise and dissent, too. The author Helen Zimmern (1846–1934), writing in June 1900 in London's *Fortnightly Review* on Duse, critiques her rendition of Marguerite Gautier in Dumas *fils*'s *La Dame aux Camélias*: "Splendid as is Duse's

Figure 6.1 *Time*, 30 July 1923.

rendering, beautiful in all its varying moods, it is, nevertheless, hardly the Marguerite Gautier as Alexander (*sic.*) Dumas painted her in the book and play," though she praises Duse's roles in "more genuinely Italian plays."[29] She continues:

> The popularity of the evenings in which [Duse] appears in Verga's *Cavalleria rusticana* [...] shows that, in England at least, her

> interpretation of her native dramatic literature is appreciated. The change from the unrestrained passion of Santuzza, where the actress has to start, as it were, on the highest note of tragedy, with no preliminary working up to the point, to the gay coquetry of Mirandolina [in Goldoni's *La Locandiera*], is evidence of the versatility of which she is capable, a versatility limited in so far as the character, whether of comedy or tragedy, appeals to and can be identified with her own nature and temperature. The representation of rustic life, or of the lower or middle classes, is that which suits her best; she has the passion and the power, but she has not the style, nor the presence necessary for the *grande dame*.

And further on, she gives even higher praise, commending her individualism:

> Whatever Duse is or is not, she is individual – artificiality has no part or lot in her. Her diction, her mimicry, are put to the service of an absolute veracity. And this veracity is always the truth as seen through the subjectivity of the actress [...] She is not one about whom it is easy to write, whose past may be picked to pieces for the gratification of the curious, the details of whose everyday life may be dragged into the commonplace belittling light of publicity. Eleonora Duse is one of those rare beings sent into the world for our teaching and our delight, to show us depths of poetry and passion.[30]

Following Duse's death, Alice Rohe (1876–1957), writing for the American periodical *The Independent*, reported on going to see Duse at the silent screen at Fourteenth Street Theatre in New York. She describes the screening as "a marvelous opportunity" and Duse as "the greatest actress of modern times."[31] In *Cenere* (re-released as *Madre* in America following her death[32]), which Duse directed for Turin's Ambrosio films, she plays a conflation of the roles of a *mater dolorosa*/Fallen Woman who abandons her son due to financial hardship (though in Grazia Deledda's novel on which the film is based, Rosalia abandons her son to be with her lover):

> First, there came an announcement telling of Duse's reluctance to make this film, her fear of age, her refusal to use make-up, her concealing her face behind a kerchief in the first half of the story when she portrayed a young woman.[33]

Duse deliberately avoids the overemphatic style articulated by the new silent divas of the next generation (e.g., Lina Cavallieri; Francesca Bertini; Pina Menichelli) in her film; rather, and as Maria Pia Pagani has argued, her naturalistic screen acting style embodies a kind of "anti-diva."[34] Rohe celebrates Duse as the director of her film:

> There are touches of inspiration in the direction – the shadow of the mother's raised arms, the eloquent hands, stretched toward the lonely little child calling "Mama." [...] The exquisite beauty of the pose alone stands out like a masterpiece [...] And always there are the hands – the most eloquently beautiful hands the stage has ever known

before referring to "The Duse craze," which she describes as "superlatively characteristic of America," since only "a handful of reverent Italians" were in the theatre auditorium.[35]

Francesca Bertini (1892–1985), Actor, Silent Diva, Director

Another female actor, one who would have no doubt been inspired by Duse and seen in her a role model, but who belonged to a new generation, was making her mark as a silent diva and director of her own film company, Bertini films.[36] Elena Seracini Vitiello, who is known better by her stage and screen name Francesca Bertini, began her film career working as a theatre actor in Naples at the Teatro Nuovo, as one of a number of Neapolitan-language actors under the director of Gennaro Pantalena (1848–1915). In 1909 she acted in Salvatore Di Giacomo's *Assunta Spina* at the Teatro Nuovo with Adelina Magnetti (1882–1963) in the lead role (which Bertini would herself go on to perform and co-direct with Gustavo Serena for the silent screen).[37] Her cinema début occurred in 1907 at the age of 15 in *La dea del mare* (The Sea Goddess). She was among three of the most famous Italian silent divas during the period around World War I, the other two being Lyda Borelli and Pina Menichelli. By 1915, Bertini had already directed over 50 silent films, as well as playing the lead character.

As Monica Dall'Asta has shown, Bertini's voice and acting style did not suit the advent of sound film, and during the 1920s the frequency of her appearances on screen began to decline.[38] In her women spectators, Bertini aroused curiosity, identification, admiration, and desire for her beauty and Grecian, statuesque poses, embodied in sophisticated, glamourous modernity, and cosmopolitanism. Julie K. Allen has shown how

> [t]he circulation of European silent films in Australia connected Australian audiences and society to the European continent in psychologically different ways. Unlike sound films, which segregated film markets by language, the lack of linguistic barriers rendered the circulation of French, German, Italian, Swedish, and Danish films in Australia in the early 1910s relatively uncomplicated,[39]

while Australian audiences comprised minority groups including immigrants from the South of Italy. Seeing close-up shots of silent divas like Bertini re-connected them, particularly women, to memories of their country of origin and a Catholic cultural heritage from a female perspective. Bertini's acting style was naturalistic – "intuitive, realistic, and measured."[40]

From a search in the National Library of Australia digitised newspaper database Trove between 1880 and 1916, Bertini is the subject of 16 advertisements and is featured in 15 articles, while the same search in the British Newspaper Archive during 1910–1919 yields 86 article mentions and features in England, 10 in Scotland, 3 in Ireland and 1 in Wales. The newspaper the *Mudgee Guardian and North-Western Representative* in New South Wales, Australia, includes an advertisement in 1915 with the heading "Francesca Bertini," who is billed as "Italy's leading and most highly paid actress," and reports on her starring role in "an enthralling drama entitled *Woman*" (not the original title – titles of Italian, French, and German silent films in English varied from place to place, and frequently changed for foreign distribution, which can make the films difficult to track – and not to be confused with Maurice Tourneur's film of 1918 with the same name).[41] In *The Times of India* from 1919, publicity for Bertini's principal role in De Liguoro and De Antoni's *Fedora* after Sardou's play is included. Bertini is described as a "*prima donna*," whose "powerful acting as Princess Fedora Romanoff, will come as a revelation to many,"[42] while Scotland's *The Scotsman* publicises Francesca Bertini's appearance in *A Modern Marriage* (not the original title and not to be confused with Victor Heerman and Laurence Windom's film of 1923) screening at the Princes' Cinema in Edinburgh in 1919.[43] In addition, *The Shanghai Times* looks forward to seeing "the clever Italian actress" in a screening of *The Masked Amazon* (*L'Amazzone mascherata*, 1914) in the role of Franca.[44] As Giorgio Bertellini reminds us:

> Italian-produced films found a vast audience in New York City theatres, encompassing motives of emotional longing and diasporic nationalism among immigrant spectators well into the 1920s.[45]

The Washington Post incorrectly refers to Bertini as "French" in its report on a screening of *The Woman Who Dared* (1914) in 1915 "featuring the famous beauty of France, Francesca Bertini."[46] As we saw in Chapter 4, one of the most intriguing examples of female spectatorship can be found in Serao's writings; in particular, her revelation of Duse as a spectator admiring the films that Bertini made.

Matilde Serao (1856–1927), Writer, Journalist, Theatrephile, Cineaste

The name Matilde Serao is known to most in Italy, who recognise her as the first woman in the new Italy to found her own daily newspaper, *Il Giorno*. Today, one can visit the tiny square from where she ran her newspapers: Piazzetta Matilde Serao, which is located in the centre of

Naples. Born in Patras, Greece, to a Greek mother of aristocratic origin, who was a teacher, and a Neapolitan father who was a freelance journalist, the family moved back to Naples in the 1860s, where Serao trained as a teacher, though her first job was as a telegraph operator. Introduced to the world of journalism by her father, she secured a post in Rome as editor of *Capitan Fracassa* in the early 1880s and began publishing serialised novels, short stories, and reporting on lifestyle for a growing female readership. By the 1890s, she had established an international following and reputation, having been translated into many European languages.[47] She is the author of around 40 works of fiction ranging from sentimental realist novels to melodramatic and gothic narratives. Highly regarded by Henry James and Edith Wharton, she dedicated her anti-romantic novel, *Dopo il perdono* (first published in 1905 in *Nuova Antologia*) to Duse, referring to her in it as a "Glorious Soul." Her passion for theatre-going is well documented in her "Mosconi" column as well as her interest in adapting *Dopo il perdono* and *O Giovannino, o la morte* for the stage in the early twentieth century (not to mention her eight screenplays discussed in Chapter 4). To give an idea of the breadth of Serao's reach, a search of her name in the Bibilotéque Nationale de France's online resource "Gallica" yields 335 newspaper and journal articles. Turning to Australia's Trove digitised collection, 111 "mentions" appear in an online search, while the British Library Newspaper Archive produces 223 articles on Serao from the 1860s through to the 1920s. A search of "Matilde Serao" in literary and women's journals and newspapers in the American Periodicals Online database between 1880 and 1927 yields 127 articles in which she features.

Matilde Serao's *Dopo il perdono/Après le pardon*

Dopo il perdono is set in contemporary times in Rome. An aristocratic woman in her thirties, Elena Bosco, having left her husband three years before to live with Marco Fiore, reluctantly admits that their once passionate love affair has reached its end. They separate in order that Marco can marry his cousin, Vittoria Colonna. Meanwhile, Elena returns to her doting husband who forgives her betrayal, humiliation, and abandonment. However, both Elena and Marco suffer the constraints of their respective marriages, and once again leave their spouses, meeting by chance in Switzerland, where Elena has been living for some months. The story ends with them deciding to live side by side in the knowledge that they will never again find the spark that once ignited their passion. With this novel, Serao had wanted to "narrate all love's brief and violent intoxications, its long, incurable sadness, just as it is, with the humility of a chronicler."[48] Speaking at a conference in Naples in 1895 on literature's obsession with love and women – how the modern world only deems women worthy of study in terms of their sexuality and in their relation to love; whether they love, or not; whether they *can* love, or do not want to love; whether they do not know *how* to love; whether they die loving; whether they die because of love – Serao had wanted to portray romantic love's shelf life.[49]

Her novel was translated into French by Georges Hérelle (1848–1935) for the *Revue de Paris*, where it appeared in instalments from February to April 1906 and was published as a novel by Calmann-Lévy in 1907. Having read the first three instalments in the *Revue de Paris*, the playwright Pierre Decourcelle proposed a collaboration with Serao on an adaptation for the French stage, though she already intended to write up her novel as a play; in an interview in 1904 with Antonio Catapano for *Il Secolo XX*, Serao is cited as having said she would soon be writing a play titled *Dopo il perdono* in four acts for four characters drawn from a novel she would write for *Nuova Antologia* and the *Revue de Paris*.[50] If Mario Sandri's account of her adaptation of her short story *O Giovannino, o la morte* (Giovannino, or Death, 1888) with playwright Ernesto Murolo (1876–1936) for the Italian stage in 1912 is anything to go by, that

> Serao thought up the action and structured it into various acts, dramatising it in a number of scenes, concluding it with an epilogue, and listening to the *denouément* scene by scene, modifying, and tidying up the intensity of the whole event; and Murolo, having completed a part of his work, read the manuscript aloud almost completely in dialect, and Serao would listen, adding certain sentences, completing a scene by making the effect of a dialogue more robust with reticence and suspense,[51]

then it is quite possible that she and Decourcelle collaborated similarly. *Après le pardon* had its first-night performance at the Théâtre Réjane in Paris on 20 November 1907, with Madame Réjane (1856–1920) – to whom Serao dedicated the French version of her novel – in the lead role. In the same month, the play was published in the *Illustration théatrale*. Following its Paris premiere, and in spite of negative press reviews by male critics,[52] Serao transposed the play to Italy, changed the name of the protagonist from "Elena" to the more pious "Maria," and moved the original Act II from Venice to Rome. The play had its Italian premiere at the Teatro dei Fiorentini in Naples on 5 February 1908 under the direction of the *Compagnia* Ruggieri, with Emma Gramatica and Ruggiero Ruggeri in the lead roles. Curiously, Silvio d'Amico's *Enciclopedia dello spettacolo* (Encyclopaedia of Theatre, 1957) includes no mention in either biography of them having taken part in the play. Playwright Eduardo De Filippo (1900–84), however, in an interview for *La Repubblica* in 1977, recalls the success of the play *O Giovannino, o la morte*, which was a hit "also thanks to Mariella Gioia's performance – she was the star of Neapolitan theatre," adding he "can still remember Ruggero Ruggeri and Emma Gramatica who acted in *Dopo il perdono*."[53] The play was published by Perrella in 1908, and in April 1919, the Roman film company La Gladiator Film released a cinematic version of *Dopo il perdono* in Milan directed by Ugo De Simone.[54]

Serao the "Spectatrix"

Serao was an avid theatre-goer and lover of the performing arts, and according to the journalist Ugo Ojetti (1871–1946), she never missed an opening night of a performance in Naples.[55] Indeed, De Filippo describes Naples as the capital of Italian theatre during the late nineteenth century, and Serao frequently mixed with travelling celebrity actors there, including Ermete Novelli (1851–1919), Ermete Zacconi (1857–1948), and Tina Di Lorenzo (1872–1930). According to Alfredina D'Ascenzo, "In Serao's writings there is not one work that does not refer to the theatrical world, and in some cases it becomes the genuine protagonist."[56] Serao's published musings on theatre-going begin with a rather wry, realist fictional account of Parisian nightlife in her first sentimental realist novel, *Cuore infermo* (Frozen Heart, 1881). The protagonists – a newly married aristocratic couple from Naples – are on honeymoon in Paris. Serao's omniscient narrator describes a typical evening's entertainment, revealing the author's wealth of knowledge on theatres, sociability, French playwrights, and actors:

> There are theatres [in Paris], above all, the *Opéra*, where you absolutely have to make yourself seen on certain days by hiring a box, being highly visible – the woman perfectly lit, her husband discreetly covered up in the shadows – to hear rather dated music sung by out-of-breath singers while you look through your binoculars at the Duchess's profile from her forehead to her hands. If you do not wish to reveal your lack of taste for high art, there is the evening you can spend at the Comédie-Française applauding plays by Got and Coquelin, as well as Molière, or where you can see Miss Croisette dying in Feuillet's *The Sphinx* and hear how Sarah Bernhardt says to Mounet-Sully in *Hernani*: "You are my handsome and generous lion!" Then, you can see Sardou's new play at the Gymnase, or Offenbach's new operetta at the Renaissance.[57]

Further on in the novel, the distanced narrator targets the *femme fatale* character, La Contessa Lalla D'Aragona, as adopting "sentences from French novels; from those really very hideous ones written by Montépin and Ponson du Terrail."[58] A specifically gendered response to live performances, one that for women sees them reacting enthusiastically, and is shot through with affect, is a staple of Seraian fiction, in which women characters are gripped by the action on stage, with which they identify, and/or the music of an opera. In her novel *Fantasia* (1883), at a musical performance at the Teatro Sannazzaro in Naples:

> The ladies became enthusiastic; they seized their opera-glasses and leant over the parapet of their boxes, while a thrill of delight moved the whole assembly [...] The ladies' gloves were torn to shreds in the storm of applause.[59]

In the same year as *Fantasia*'s publication, Serao met the nobleman Count Giuseppe Primoli, described by Alexandre Dumas *fils* as the "ambassador for French literature in Italy and for Italian literature in France."[60] Impressed with her writing, Primoli introduced Serao into literary circles in Paris. In a letter addressed to Primoli the following year, Serao revealed that she would like to adapt *Fantasia* into "a great pitiful and neurotic play."[61] Instead, having moved in 1882 to Rome, she began writing about theatre and opera-going in her column "Api, Mosconi e Vespe" (Bees, Flies, and Wasps) mentioned in Chapter 4. It was this column featuring in the *Corriere di Napoli* that, on a visit to Naples in 1891, so impressed the translator Georges Hérelle, that he took out a subscription.[62] He subsequently wrote to Serao in 1895 following the publication in her newspaper of D'Annunzio's *L'Innocente*, introducing

Figure 6.2 Federico Zandomeneghi, *At the theatre*, c.1895.

himself as D'Annunzio's translator and offering to translate some of her short stories into French.[63] However, French readers would have to wait until 1906 for Hérelle's first translation of *Dopo il perdono*; yet, prior to that date, Hérelle translated short stories, including *O Giovannino, o la morte*.[64] Serao expressed how she felt honoured and was "moved to tears" in reading his translation of *Dopo il perdono*, thanking him for their collaboration and friendship, which was to endure until 1914 when Serao's *Il Giorno* purportedly expressed Germanophile views and Hérelle severed ties with her (though, as a "pacifist," she vehemently declared those were not her own views and that she was at the mercy of shareholders' conservatism).[65]

Serao's French Women Translators

The extent to which French women readers were delighted and pleased by Serao's writings is borne out by the translations by middle-class French women translators – for, Hérelle was not Serao's sole translator. Among them was the wife of the French author Paul Bourget (1852–1935): Minnie. Primoli had introduced Serao to Bourget and Minnie in 1891, and Minnie became the first French translator of Serao's *Il paese di Cuccagna* (1901). Her translation appeared in serialised format in the *Revue hebdomadaire* with the title *Au pays de cocagne: mœurs napolitaines* in 1897, with a preface by Bourget in which he described Serao as "D'Annunzio's true rival," thus guaranteeing its quality and success.[66] The novel was published by Plon the following year. Despite Serao's confession to Hérelle in 1895 to having little faith in Minnie's translation,[67] writing in *L'Instantané* – the supplement to the *Revue hebdomadaire* in 1907, the critic Henry Bourdeaux praised Serao's "excellent" translator of *Il paese di Cuccagna*.[68] Moreover, in spite of Serao's initial reservations, in a letter to Primoli she wrote fondly of her first impression of Minnie on meeting her: "I can tell you that I loved her from the first day I met her, and that now I feel more bound than ever to this such sweet creature."[69]

Another female translator, and one whose name (and pseudonyms) would go on to be more linked to Serao's works than Minnie's, is Nelly Carrère – a "dear friend" of Francesca Bertini – who translated under the pseudonyms "Madame Charles Laurent," "Mme Jean Darcy," and "Mme Jean Carrère."[70] Carrère was the first translator of a Seraian novel, *Addio, amore!* (Farewell, Love!, 1890), which Serao had suggested in a letter to Primoli in 1894 so that it could be printed in the *Revue de Paris*.[71] Five years later in 1899, Ollendorf published Carrère's translation of *Cuore infermo* (Frozen Heart, 1881), which was re-issued in 1927 together with another of Carrère's translations of *Addio, amore!* (reissued in 1900 and 1907). Subsequent translations of Serao's novels and short stories by Carrère included: *La conquista di Roma* (The Conquest of Rome, 1900); *La virtù di Checchina* ("Checchina's Virtue,"

1900); *Fantasia* (1901); *Castigo* (Punishment, 1902; 1927); *Nel paese di gesù* (In the Land of Jesus, 1903); and *Il pellegrino appassionato* (The Passionate Pilgrim, 1909).

Serao on Italian Theatre

Serao was first introduced to the French reading public through an article by Jules Claretie, published in the newspaper *Le Temps* in 1884 – the year she wrote to Primoli expressing her wish to be made known to readers in France.[72] 10 years later, she would make her first of 11 trips to Paris.[73] The supplement "Feuilleton du temps" from *Le Temps* of 29 August and 5 September 1904, entitled *L'Année théâtrale Italienne* (The Theatrical Year in Italy), contains a fascinating essay by Serao, introduced by an unknown writer who signs with the pseudonym "X," and is translated into French from the original manuscript by an unknown translator bearing the initials "L.G.". Calling attention to Serao's "eminent" role in Italian literature, it refers to her as a "Latin genius" and part of a "remarkable group of brilliant writers, including D'Annunzio, Fogazzaro, and Deledda." "X" describes her as a "passionate journalist" with "an unbelievable number of articles" to her name, before introducing her *c.*2000-word instructive piece on contemporary Italian theatre and the closing season in two instalments.[74] Serao compares the typical Parisian playwright who "knows precisely who he is writing for," to one in Italy who must "seduce 16 different kinds of audiences in the 16 principal theatres (Milan, Turin, Venice, Rome, Naples, Genoa, Florence, Bologna, Palermo and Trieste)" and the "less prestigious" theatres (which she names as: Siena, Brescia, Parma, Ferrara, Livorno, Catania), appealing for readers' sympathy for the "poor Italian playwright. Imagine this unfortunate, lonely dramatist […] if he allows his imaginative gaze to wander across to the overcrowded boxes decorated with women spectators!"[75] Further on in the article, and with hindsight, we discover the probable reason why (as if to litmus test her skills as a playwright) only *after* her Paris début did Serao bring the adaptation of her novel *Dopo il perdono* to the Italian stage:

> In the great Parisian capital, an opening night is always decisive: the playwright knows the next day what he has achieved and how much his work is worth, while an Italian playwright has to wait for ten to fifteen *very spread out* premières, and his life goes on like that. Moreover, the audience's view is almost always contradictory.[76]

We know from the interview with Catapano, also in 1904, that when asked why she hasn't written a play until now Serao confesses it is perhaps because she is afraid of the Italian public's criticism.[77] Returning to Serao's essay on Italian theatre, she goes on to mention the most important dramatists currently writing in Italy, citing "Giuseppe

Giacosa; Roberto Bracco; Marco Praga; Girolamo Rovetta; Gabriele D'Annunzio; Giannino Antona Traversi and three or four less well-known ones," before lamenting the fact that the government currently offers no financial subvention whatsoever, despite Novelli's efforts to persuade the government to fund state theatres. She then describes the *Compagnie di prosa* – the various itinerant theatre companies – and the nomadic lifestyle of Italian actors, expressing sympathy in particular with women performers:

> There are many very good ones, who are also very beautiful, young, and full of talent, as well as some gallant actors [but] who do not have their own theatre where they can stay for more than a month: they go from town to town, from theatre to theatre, changing region or theatre up to eight times a year. They are never hired for more than two months; on average, they stay for 40 days and sometimes only give 15 performances in this town or that theatre.[78]

In describing Italian spectators, Serao writes that they "expect to see the most famous actors in the most celebrated comedies or dramas (e.g., Virginia Reiter in *Zazà* and *Madame Sans-Gêne*; Tina di Lorenzo in *Pamela Nubile* and *Francillon*)," but that what Italian audiences love the most is a play by Alexandre Dumas *fils*, or, "to please the young women, Ohnet's *Le Maître de forges*, or, to give the lead female actor a break, Scribe's *Bataille de dames*!"[79] In reinforcing her already divisive discourse on national perceptions of actors, she then concludes that whereas Paris makes kings and queens of its actors, Italy "applauds them, fills them with flowers and presents, reviews them with enthusiasm, but certainly does not crown them."[80]

In her second instalment, she suggests that the success of Gerolamo Rovetta's *Romanticismo* (1901), which made more than 100,000 francs, was the result of the patriotic feeling that he stirs in the spectator, which she defends. Comparing Roberto Bracco's *Maternità* (1903) and Brieux's play of the same name, she then prevaricates, taking an unexpected (given the author's public position against feminism), strikingly outspoken and feminist stance on legislation concerning motherhood in Italy, which, she believes

> should break free from conventional norms of the man's name, honour and responsibility, and guarantee women who have children respect and the means to look after what is theirs, that is to say, the child.[81]

Indeed, contrary to popular belief concerning Serao's "anti-feminism," writing in 1906 in a published letter to the journalist Olga Ossani (1857–1933), she stated: "I profoundly respect feminism [...] I am also a feminist, I dare say, in my own way."[82] Returning to her essay, Serao evaluates

Bracco's recent comedy adapted for the French stage, *Il frutto acerbo* (Unripe Fruit, 1904), as "light-hearted, erotic, and rather Boccaccian, but rich with psychological and physiological observations." She then finishes her comments on Bracco – whom she describes as a feminist – by saying that it is thanks to his plays that Italian theatre is beginning to establish itself abroad.[83]

Following a critique of Marco Praga's *L'ondina* (1903) in which she questions whether his ending, which "ought to be a sad revelation of brutal reality for spectators," but which instead "takes on the character of an almost idyllic episode surrounded by a vaporous atmosphere of touching sentimentality," she appears to criticise D'Annunzio by claiming that, with the exception of his *La figlia de Iorio* (The Daughter of Iorio, 1904) it would appear that "triumphing as a playwright is not the way forward for our sparkling poet," a view that is shared, it would seem, by the retired actor Giacinta Pezzana.[84] In a letter addressed to Sibilla Aleramo, Pezzana criticises the opening night of D'Annunzio's *La nave* (1908) at the Teatro dell'Argentina in Rome: "How deceitful D'Annunzio is! He announces tragedies [...] and then tricks you so well that you are watching choreographed dancing and hear singing; but where is the tragedy? Well!"[85]

Serao lauds Duse for animating D'Annunzio's works "with her supreme art and talent in so many scenes," before criticising the "lack of action" and "poor theatricality" of his works that have prevented him from enjoying the limelight as a playwright.[86] In a striking attack, she then (strangely) appears to accuse D'Annunzio of "stealing" the theme of *La figlia de Iorio* from Francesco-Paolo Michetti's (1851–1929) painting of the same name, to which she attributes the play's attraction and seduction which "do not feature in any other D'Annunzian play."[87] Moreover, she attributes the success of the play to "the revelation of D'Annunzio's theatrical Art, Eleonora Duse, the Only, the Unique being who can interpret his art," before going on to proclaim the play's success an "accident, a fortuitous event, a beautiful and poetic episode due to several favourable circumstances."[88] In what is undoubtedly a stridently opinionated and critical piece of writing, Serao concludes her essay by making a general remark about the Italian national character and auguring in the unification of Italian *society*, in order that Italian theatre may prosper.[89] The differences between Italian audiences across the peninsula that Serao is at pains to draw attention to are nevertheless called into question when viewed in the light of intriguing comments Duse reportedly made on the stereotypical differences between spectators of southern and northern Europe during an interview with Georg Brandes (1842–1927). Upon Brandes enquiring as to whether Ibsen's plays find favour among the Italians, Duse said:

> Of course [Ibsen] finds favour [...] But it must be admitted that, here and there, to things you northern people take seriously, we in Rome

attach a tinge of the comical. You ask for an example? You perhaps remember in *Rosmersholm* where Rosmer and Rebekka, at the close of the second act, say good night to each other. Quite unconsciously, as it seems, they are passionately in love with each other. As they part, Rosmer says: "Good night." Rebekka: "Are you going upstairs so early this evening, too?" Rosmer: "This evening, as usual." Rebekka: "Good night, and sleep well." After those words the whole house burst out laughing. This coolness seemed so comical to the Romans that I did not dare reproduce the piece again. There you have the difference between the northern and the southern temperament.[90]

From Page to Stage and Screen

The novel *Dopo il perdono* was largely well-received in France and Britain, though less well so in Italy.[91] Writing in the British periodical *The Athenæum* in 1906, the journalist Guido Biagi (1855–1925) describes Serao as "the Italian George Sand," and refers to the "strong qualities always inherent in the romantic work of this powerful writer."[92] The French woman writer and critic Jean Dornis, which was the pseudonym for Élena Goldschmidt-Franchetti (also known as Mme Guillaume Beer), in her *Le Roman Italien contemporain* (The Contemporary Italian Novel, 1907) also associates Serao with George Sand, albeit after having criticised the ending of the novel, in which the former lovers are destined to live out their lives together "unhappily."[93] According to an anonymous Rome correspondent of *The Morning Post*, it was the theatre actor Madame Réjane who asked Serao to adapt her novel for the French stage.[94]

Après le pardon was by no means the first stage adaptation of a Seraian novel or *novella*; her short story *La dama dall'abito nero e dal ramo di corallo rosso* (The Woman in the Black Dress with a Red Coral Branch) had been adapted as a monologue and performed in Rome and Paris in 1904 by "the great actress Irma Marazzi-Diligenti"[95] (though sources differ on this, with Lelièvre's *Le Théâtre dramatique Italien en France, 1855–1940* (1959) suggesting the monologue was adapted from Serao's "Lo sconosciuto" (The Unknown) from her collection *Fior di passione*).[96] In the same year, her novel *Suor Giovanna della Croce* (1890) was adapted with Gaston Jollivet for the stage, but traces of its performances are scarce.[97] Subsequent Seraian *novelle* to be adapted for the stage include the aforementioned *O Giovannino, o la morte*, adapted with Ernesto Murolo, and *I cavallucci di legno di Matilde Serao* (Wooden Epitaphs by Matilde Serao), which is based on her short story *Un intervento* and adapted with Antoine Léry, first performed on 11 December 1923 by the *Compagnia* Palmarini.[98] Nevertheless, in her interview with Catapano for *Il Secolo XX*, Serao informs readers that she is finally writing a play in four acts with four characters, with rapid action and without too much analysis. She continues: "Even with the usual *they*, *she*, and *he*, I can say that it will not be one of the usual variations on the threesome of adultery."[99] According to writer Camillo Antona Traversi (1857–1934) in his *Ricordi parigini*, at the first reading of the play where he and Réjane were present, it was very well received and Réjane was the first to say how much she was delighted by it.[100] Prior to its premiere on 19 November 1907, *Le Figaro* of 16 November 1907 reprinted excerpts from Dornis's book by way of preparing the reader for Serao's theatre début. However, describing Serao as a "fecund novelist," an "admirable woman," and a "natural flower of the Mediterranean," as well as referring to her "great spontaneity along with an innate lively emotion," the publication curiously omitted Dornis's critique of the novel *Après le pardon*, preferring instead to highlight Serao's originality and skill as a novelist.[101]

A significant feature of the novel that is absent from the play is, of course, the omniscient narrator's descriptions, couched in what Pia Leonore Bertucci has described as Serao's "language of passion."[102] In what could be described, rather, as a "language of affect" – one that is rooted in rational critique – Serao's narrator draws attention in particular to the female guests' responses to an *Aria di chiesa* by Alessandro Stradella (1644–82), sung at the wedding of the anti-hero, Marco Fiore, and Elena/Maria's foil, Vittoria Colonna:

> With the deference of an artist and perhaps with sincere feeling, the famous singer lent such a painful and tortured emphasis as never before to Stradella's lament and cry. And the listeners were taken aback and compelled [...] above all, some women went pale with emotion; and their eyes veiled over with tears [...] And again, all the pierced ears, all the secretly transfixed souls [...] in that society so rich [...] among those exquisitely dressed women covered in jewellery [...] felt the power of that melody.[103]

Serao simultaneously depicts faithfully a typical high-society wedding while providing the (woman) reader with access to the psyche of imagined women spectators' responses to the *aria*. Moreover, she educates middle-class (women) readers on how to critique and evaluate a performance of a moving musical composition, drawing her readers in – positioning them as both voyeurs and vicarious participants through her depiction of an experience all very familiar to her women readers. Her example of audience responses to the performance both offers a "slice of life" and a glossary of useful terms for her (women) readers to adopt when expressing delight at listening to, or watching, a live music performance: "What a singer Varisco is!"; "Divine, divine!"; "He makes such an overwhelming impression on me"; "Stradella's aria is so beautiful!"[104]

The play ran for 12 nights in Paris and was never revived there. Nonetheless, according to a (female?) reviewer writing as "ED. S" in the *Journal des débats politiques et littéraires* on the opening night, certain scenes received emphatic applause, and Mme Réjane was praised highly for her nuanced and expressive performance.[105] Similarly, Réjane is complimented by an (almost definitely) female reviewer in *La Française: Journal de progrès féminin* (The French Woman: Journal of Women's Progress), yet the play itself received a lukewarm reception: the first two acts were "slow-moving" and the dialogues and monologues were "monotonous" (in a faithful reworking of the novel, Act II takes place in Venice, though in the Italian version of the play this is cut and instead the act takes place in Rome).[106] Writing for *Les Annales politiques et littéraires* on 24 November 1907, the writer and journalist Yvonne Sarcey (pseudonym for Madeleine Brisson, 1869–1950) published an interview with Serao on the occasion of the performances of *Après le pardon*, which Sarcey mentions twice in order to publicise Serao's French début as a playwright, by bringing to readers' attention the current run of performances. Sarcey expresses her pleasure in meeting Serao, referring to her as "the admirable author of *After the Pardon*," "this astonishing novelist," her "larger-than-life character," and her "powerful imagination," before concluding she is "solid, happy, and adorably good-natured."[107] During the interview, intriguingly, Sarcey mentions that Serao refers to the characters in her play as her "children," citing her joy in reworking her novel for the French stage: "I am going to see my children, all my children from *After the Pardon*, come to life at Mme Réjane's theatre," describing her "pleasure" and "emotion."[108] The image evoked here of Serao's characters personified as her children who Serao necessarily mothers, nurtures, and brings to life through her work is particularly striking, and offers valuable insight into the way in which Serao viewed herself as a writer.

Serao's connections and networks in France broke down in the lead-up to World War I due to the aforementioned apparently Germanophile stance of her *Il Giorno*. On Italy's entry into World War I in 1915, the French filmmaker Germaine Albert-Dulac (1882–1942) interviewed Serao for *La Renaissance politique, littéraire et artistique*. Despite (unfairly) depicting Serao as a traitor and enemy of France, Albert-Dulac nevertheless describes her "dark and very intelligent eyes" and characterises her as a "thinking being," as well as a "powerful force," before telling her: "we love your work; we love you; we celebrate you."[109] We also know from Adolfo Franci's *Italiani e forestieri* (1930) that another well-known French woman writer known mononymously as Colette (1873–1954), had wanted to meet Serao one summer when they were staying in the same hotel in Saint-Moritz, but Serao refused on the basis that, though she very much admired the writer, she did not care for her "*avant guarde*" lifestyle (Colette was bisexual).[110]

In April 1919, as previously mentioned, the Roman film company La Gladiator Film released a cinematic version of *Dopo il perdono* in Milan directed by Ugo De Simone, with Helena Makowska (1893–1964) and Guido Trento (1892–1957) in the lead roles. Serao's own newspaper, *Il Mattino*, rather tongue-in-cheekily and self-consciously published a review of the film in January 1920 following its Neapolitan screening at the Cinema Vittoria:

> There were numerous spectators yesterday evening at the Cinema Vittoria for the première of the extraordinary film *Dopo il perdono* by our great writer Matilde Serao. Helena Makowska is an incomparable interpreter and the *mise-en-scène* is stately and grandiose, all contributing to its great success.[111]

The film was released in Portugal in December 1921.

Conclusion

It is impossible to know what was passing through the minds of the hundreds of women spectators in France who attended one of the 12 performances of *Après le Pardon* in 1907. Likewise, we will never understand completely how women spectators responded in Australia, the UK, and elsewhere to watching Bertini on the silent screen, or to Eleonora Duse's international stage and screen performance(s), and to Adelina Patti, the "Nightingale," on her world tours. And yet, we know that many devoured Serao's novels in translation, marvelled at Duse's novel acting style, were beguiled by Bertini's elegance and overstated, alluring posturing, and delighted by Patti's vocal prowess. Middle-class women's appreciation of "foreign" plays, stories, and films was enhanced by their awareness of these prolific Italian women as avid theatre-goers, performers, and cinema-goers themselves: women writers and performers like Serao, Duse, Bertini, and Patti, challenged their women spectators (and readers) as intermediaries, initiating them, as "Symbolic Mothers" into cultural fields, as individual agents, consumers, and critical respondents supporting and guiding them on how to reflect deeply and critically on themes of love, sex, relationships, adultery, and betrayal, shame, guilt and marriage playing out before them on stage and screen. In this way, women writers and performers were self-consciously inviting readers and spectators to participate in, and adopt, their stars' critical and affective stances as spectators. Women playing the role of the Fallen Woman/Magdalene figure – like Madame Réjane in Paris, Emma Gramatica in Naples, and Helena Makowska in De Simone's film – addressed on a deep level, and for the duration of rehearsals and performances, the themes of romantic love's "shelf life," of betrayal, and forgiveness.

Women spectators who felt oppressed by social mores, the patriarchal order, and enforced domesticity, pitied, admired, and covertly identified with the Fallen Women on page, stage, and screen, as she by proxy gave them a voice, an outlet; in turn, Fallen Women characters sublimated spectators' feelings and spoke for them, on behalf of them, much more than politicians, statesmen, and the clergy by whom they were not at all represented.

Consequently, this may have aroused in them new feelings in relation to their erotic and sexual selves. In publishing her own spectating processes and practices, both critical and emotive, for a predominantly female readership (by drawing attention to *le spettatrici* in the theatre auditorium: *who* was in attendance; *how* they were dressed; how *enthusiastically* and seriously they watched and listened, in her *Mosconi* and elsewhere), Serao acted as an intermediary and surrogate, thus drawing her readers into the theatrical or cinematic event, as if they were present. Moreover, as a Neapolitan woman from an earlier generation to that of the first recognised female film director of Italy, Elvira Notari (1875–1946), it is possible to suppose that Serao may have paved the way – however unconsciously or consciously – for Notari to realise her own artistic talents as a director.

Notes

1 Julie K. Allen, "Divas Down Under: The Circulation of Asta Nielsen's and Francesca Bertini's films in Australasian Cinemas in the 1910s," *Studies in Australasian Cinema* 11:2 (2017), 59–76 (72).
2 Christopher Duggan, *A Concise History of Italy*, 2nd edition (Cambridge: Cambridge University Press, 2014), p. 177.
3 Susan Glenn, *Female Spectacle: The Theatrical Roots of Modern Feminism* (Cambridge: Cambridge University Press, 2000), p. 3.
4 Silvana Patriarca, *Italian Vices: Nation and Character from the Risorgimento to the Republic* (Cambridge: Cambridge University Press, 2010), pp. 2–3.
5 The analysis in this chapter is based on the coverage of Italian divas' transnational receptions. Data have been drawn from digitised databases, including: the British Library's Nineteenth Century UK Periodicals and its British Newspaper Archive; the National Library of Australia's Trove Digitised Newspapers; American Periodicals; the HathiTrust Digital Library; the Bibliothèque Nationale de France's Gallica Digital Library; Women: Transnational Networks, and British Theatre, Music and Literature: High and Popular Culture from Nineteenth Century Collections Online; and the North American Women's Letters and Diaries database. Access to Nineteenth Century Collections Online was facilitated by two Visiting Fellowships at the University of Oxford during 2019 (at St. Catherine's College, and at Harris Manchester College), as well as by the University of Strathclyde.
6 Allen, "Divas Down Under," p. 64.
7 John Rosselli, *Singers of Italian Opera: The History of a Profession* (Cambridge: Cambridge University Press, 1992), p. 116.
8 Hilary Poiriss, "She Came, She Sang … She Conquered? Adelina Patti in New York," in *European Musicians in New York City, 1840–1900*, ed. by John Graziano (Rochester, NY: University of Rochester Press, 2006), pp. 218–34 (p. 221).
9 Ouida, "The New Woman," *The North American Review* 158:450 (May 1894), 610–19 (614).
10 Author unknown, "A Woman's Memories of Old Vienna," in *The Living Age*, 25 September 1920, pp. 790–96 (p. 794).

11 Author unknown, "Adelina Patti," *Life*, 17 February 1910, p. 276.
12 Charles K. Harris, *The Last Farewell* (1903). See the Duke University Libraries Digital Collections https://library.duke.edu/digitalcollections/hasm_a3755 [accessed 20 March 2020].
13 Olga Signorelli, *Eleonora Duse* (Rome: Angelo Signorelli, 1938), p. 287.
14 Paul Fryer, "Duse Recorded," in *Eleonora Duse and Cenere (Ashes): Centennial Essays*, ed. by Maria Pia Pagani and Paul Fryer (Jefferson, North Carolina: McFarland, 2017), pp. 72–89 (p. 78).
15 Letter from Eleonora Duse to the director of *Le Gaulois* published on 29 January 1902, cited in Mirella Schino, *Il teatro di Eleonora Duse* (Bologna: Il Mulino, 1992), pp. 244–7 (p. 246).
16 Gemma Ferruggia, *La nostra vera Duse* (Milan: Sonzogno, 1924), p. 66.
17 A., "Eleonora Duse," *Il corriere dei teatri: periodico artistico teatrale*, 22 (10 June 1899), p. 1.
18 Author unknown, "Globe Theatre," *The Woman's Home Journal*, 14 (8 April 1893), p. 12.
19 The play was premiered at the Teatro Carignano in Turin on 14 January 1884 with Duse in the lead role of Santuzza.
20 Mel Gussow, "Books of the Times: The Actress who Became the Original 'Doozy'," in *New York Times*, 22 August 2003 www.nytimes.com/2003/08/22/books/books-of-the-times-the-actress-who-became-the-original-doozy.html [accessed 2 May 2018]. On Le Gallienne's biography of Duse, see: Eva Le Gallienne, *The Mystic in the Theatre: Eleonora Duse* (New York: Farrar, Straus & Giroux, 1966).
21 Mary Ann Smart, "Verdi Sings Erminia Frezzolini," *Verdi Forum* 24:1 (1997), 13–22 (20).
22 Joseph Farrell, "Eleonora Duse nei paesi anglosassoni," in *Voci e anime, corpi e scritture: atti del convegno internazionale su Eleonora Duse*, ed. by Maria Ida Biggi and Paolo Puppa (Rome: Bulzoni, 2009), pp. 163–75 (p. 174).
23 See: Melissa Bradshaw *Amy Lowell, Diva Poet* (Farnham and Burlington: Ashgate, 2011), pp. 131–52.
24 Author unknown, "Eleonora Duse in London," *New York Times*, 8 May 1894, p. 4.
25 Theda Bara, "The Curse on the Moving-Picture Actress: Describing the Conflict in Her Artistic Experiences of the Moving-Picture Art," *Forum*, 62 (July 1919), 83–94 (93–4). My italics.
26 George William Frederic Lees, "The Art of Eleonora Duse," *The Lady's Realm*, 3 (November 1897–April 1898), 41–6 (45).
27 Sub Rosa, "On My Bookshelf," in *The Gentlewoman and Modern Life*, 1804 (24 January 1925), p. 119.
28 Author unknown, "Eleonora Duse," in *The Gentlewoman and Modern Life*, 1184 (15 March 1913), p. 51.
29 Helen Zimmern, "Eleonora Duse," *Fortnightly Review* 67:402 (June 1900), 980–93 (984–5).
30 *Ibid.*, pp. 984–5.
31 Alice Rohe, "Only In America," in *The Independent*, 11 April 1925, p. 405.
32 Fryer, "Duse Recorded," p. 84.
33 Rohe, "Only In America," p. 405.
34 Maria Pia Pagani, "An Actress-Manager for the Italian Film Industry in the 1910s," *Nineteenth Century Theatre and Film* 45:1 (2018), 81–95 (83).

35 *Ibid.*, p. 86.
36 Bertini Films produced, among others, the following titles: *La lussuria/Luxury* (1919); *La piovra/The Octopus* (1919); *La Contessa Sara/Countess Sara* (1919); *Mariute* (1918).
37 Patricia Bianchi, "L'attrazione fatale dell'«arte muta», dal libro al teatro fino al cinema," in *Visibili, invisibili. Matilde Serao e le donne nell'Italia post-unitaria*, ed. by Gabriella Liberati, Giuseppe Scalera, and Donatella Trotta (Rome: Centro Nazionale di Ricerca, 2016), pp. 149–64 (p. 153). The film was produced by Caesar Film and released on 28 October 1915 in Rome, with subsequent releases in Finland (1 May 1916), Sweden (18 December 1916), Denmark (12 February 1917), Japan (10 June 1918), Brazil, and Russia.
38 Monica Dall'Asta, "Francesca Bertini," in *Women Film Pioneers Project*, ed. by Jane Gaines, Radha Vatsal, and Monica Dall'Asta (New York, NY: Columbia University Libraries, 2018) https://wfpp.columbia.edu/pioneer/francesca-bertini/ [accessed 27 March 2019].
39 Allen, "Divas Down Under," p. 62.
40 *Ibid.*, p. 70.
41 Advertisement, "Francesca Bertini," *Mudgee Guardian and North-Western Representative*, 7 June 1915, p. 20. The film was possibly Negroni's *L'amazzone mascherata* (1914), which was released in America as *The Woman Who Dared* in 1915.
42 Advertisement, "Bombay Amusements," *The Times of India*, 10 December 1917, p. 11.
43 Advertisement, *The Scotsman*, 29 September 1919, p. 1.
44 Advertisement, "In the Halls," in *The Shanghai Times*, 24 December 1915, p. 7. The film was released in America in March 1915 under the title *The Woman Who Dared.*
45 Giorgio Bertellini, "Italian Americans' Transnational Film Culture in 1920s New York City," in *Making Italian America: Consumer Culture and the Production of Ethnic Identities*, ed. by Simone Cinotto (New York: Fordham University Press, 2014), pp. 84–98 (p. 84).
46 Advertisement, "Coming to the Theaters," in *The Washington Post*, 22 April 1915, p. 16.
47 See: *Matilde Serao: International Profile, Reception, and Networks*, ed. by Gabriella Romani, Ursula Fanning, and Katharine Mitchell (Paris: Classiques Garnier, 2022).
48 Matilde Serao, "Preface," *Dopo il perdono* [1904] (Milan: Fratelli Treves, 1920), pp. vii–xi; (pp. xi–x).
49 Marie-Gracieuse Martin-Gistucci, *L'Œuvre romanesque de Matilde Serao* (Grenoble: Presse universitaires de Grenoble, 1973), p. 264, ftn. 4. The conference, titled "Beatrice," was held in connection with the celebration of the sexcentenary of Dante's muse Beatrice on the status and culture of women in Italy, and was hosted by the Naples Philological Society in 1895.
50 *Ibid.*, p. 525.
51 Mario Sandri, "Gli uomini del giorno: Matilde Serao," *Modernissima* 37 (Milan: Casa editrice italiana, 1920), p. 25. The play in three acts premiered at the Teatro Nazionale in Rome on 13 November 1912 and was staged by the *Compagnia* Magnetti. According to Sandri, it toured the entire peninsula "in a marvellous and victorious tour" (p. 25). Serao's long story and Murolo's adaptation formed the basis of the screenplay to the film directed by

Luigi Chiarini, *Via delle cinque lune* (1942), with the setting transferred from Naples to Rome.

52 Writing in *La Revue hebdomadaire*, Henry Bordeaux criticises "Decourcelle's adaptation," which he says is poor, suggesting Decourcelle should have titled "his" play *After Love*. See: Henry Bordeaux, "La Vie au théâtre," in *La Revue hebdomadaire*, 30 November 1907, p. 614. An unknown author with the pseudonym "ED. S," writing in the *Journal des débats politiques et littéraires*, takes a similar view in suggesting Decourcelle should have titled "his" play *Before the Pardon*. See: ED. S., "Théâtres," in *Journal des débats politiques et littéraires*, 21 November 1907, p. 2.

53 Author unknown, "Eduardo De Filippo: In quel palco al Teatro Fiorentini," interview with Lucio Villari in *La Repubblica*, 21 February 1977, pp. 10–11.

54 Sandri, "Gli uomini del giorno," p. 28, though Sandri states that at the time of writing Serao had not seen it, nor had she given her opinion on it. See, also: Gaetano Fusco, "'Ah, poeti, romanzatori, drammaturghi, fratelli miei...': Matilde Serao e il cinema," in *Immagine n. 2: Note di storie del cinema*, ed. by Silvio Alovisio and Michele Canosa (Cattedrale: Rome, 2010), pp. 91–109 (p. 103). The film was released on 1 April 1919.

55 Jean Dornis, *Le Roman Italien contemporain* (Paris: Ollendorf, 1907), p. 159.

56 Matilde Serao, *Fantasia* [1883], ed. by Alfredina D'Ascenzo (Bologna: Millennium, 2006), p. 61.

57 Matilde Serao, *Cuore infermo* [1881] (Rome: Luccarini, 1988), pp. 49–50.

58 Serao, *Cuore infermo*, p. 101. The popular novelists referred to are Pierre Alexis Ponson du Terrail (1829–1871) and Xavier de Montépin (1823–1902). They would undoubtedly have been at the forefront of Flaubert's mind when he created his character Emma Bovary, who read romantic French novels voraciously.

59 Matilde Serao, *Fantasia*, trans. by Henry Harland and Paul Sylvester, 4th edition (London, 1891), pp. 73–5. (Paul Sylvester was the pseudonym of the English woman of German origin, Pauline Schletter.)

60 Martin-Gistucci, *L'Œuvre romanesque*, p. 456.

61 *Ibid.*, p. 525. Letter dated 20 October 1884.

62 Eucardio Momigliano, "La Serao in Francia," *Nuova Antologia*, 467 (May–August 1956), 76–80 (76).

63 Martin-Gistucci, *L'Œuvre romanesque*, p. 458.

64 The following additional novels were translated by Hérelle: *All'erta sentinella!* (1899); *La Ballerina* (1899); *Suor Giovanna della Croce* (1901); *Fantasia* (1901); *Storia di due anime* (1904); *Evviva la vita!* (1909).

65 Momigliano, "La Serao in Francia," p. 78.

66 Cited in Renée Lelièvre, *Le Théâtre dramatique Italien en France, 1855–1940* (Paris: Armand, 1956), p. 100; p. 292, ftn. 37.

67 Martin-Gistucci, *L'Œuvre romanesque*, p. 462, ftn. 13. Letter to Georges Hérelle, 2 November 1895.

68 Henry Bordeaux, "La Vie au théâtre," in *La Revue hebdomadaire*, 30 November 1907, p. 611.

69 Martin-Gistucci, *L'Œuvre romanesque*, p. 462, ftn. 13. Letter to Primoli, 11 June 1898.

70 Francesca Bertini, *Il resto non conta* (Pisa: Giardini, 1969), p. 138.

71 *Ibid.*, p. 458.

72 Martin-Gistucci, *L'Œuvre romanesque*, pp. 458–62.
73 Sandri, "Gli uomini del giorno," p. 24.
74 X., "Chronique théâtrale: Madame Matilde Serao," in *Le Temps*, 29 August 1904, p. 1.
75 Matilde Serao, "L'Année théâtrale Italienne," trans. by "L.G.," in *Le Temps*, 29 August 1904, p. 1.
76 *Ibid.* Italics my emphasis. Serao was not the only Italian woman writer of the first half of the twentieth century to pilot her début play on Parisian audiences before bringing it back to Italy: Sibilla Aleramo staged her *Endymion* at Les Ouvriers theatre for a run of performances beginning on 9 March 1923. By all accounts it was well received there, but not in Italy.
77 Martin-Gistucci, *L'Œuvre romanesque*, p. 525.
78 Serao, "L'Année théâtrale Italienne," p. 1.
79 *Ibid.*
80 *Ibid.*
81 *Ibid.*
82 See: Antonia Arslan, "Una voce dal *Ventre di Napoli* nella "galassia sommersa" del suo tempo," in *Visibili, invisibili: Matilde Serao e le donne nell'Italia post-unitaria*, ed. by Gabriella Liberati, Giuseppe Scalera, and Donatella Trotta (Rome: Centro Nazionale di Ricerca, 2016), pp. 49–60 (p. 44), letter published in *Il Giorno*, 6 September 1906.
83 Serao, "L'Année théâtrale Italienne," 5 September 1904, p. 1.
84 *Ibid.*
85 Letter to Sibilla Aleramo, 14 January 1908, housed at the Biblioteca Livia Simone, La Scala, Milan.
86 *Ibid.*, p. 1.
87 *Ibid.*
88 *Ibid.*
89 Serao, "L'Année théâtrale Italienne," p. 2. My italics.
90 Georg Brandes, "Eleonora Duse'," *The Living Age*, 15 October 1926, pp. 165–70 (p. 168).
91 Renato Landi refers to Serao's novel as "a novel that is not worth very much" in his review for *Apollon* no. 9 (Rome, September 1919). Cited in Vittorio Martinelli, *Il cinema muto italiano: i film del dopoguerra, 1919* (Turin: Nuova Eri, 1992), p. 86.
92 Guido Biagi, "Italian Literature," *The Athenæum*, 6 October 1906, pp. 395–7 (p. 396).
93 Dornis, *Le Roman Italien contemporain*, p. 187; p. 182. Yet another reference to Serao as the "Italian George Sand" appears in an article in the American women's journal *The Home-Maker*. See: Luizi Conforti, "The Italian George Sand. (Matilde Serao)," *The Home-Maker* 5:4 (1891), 132–4.
94 Author unknown, *The Morning Post*, 6 February 1907, p. 8.
95 Serao is quoted here in the aforementioned interview with Catapano, cited in Martin-Gistucci, *L'Œuvre romanesque*, p. 525.
96 Lelièvre, *Le Théâtre dramatique Italien en France, 1855–1940*, p. 305.
97 Martin-Gistucci suggests all traces of this ever having been performed are lost (*L'Œuvre romanesque*, p. 528), though there is an article in the *Journal des débats* in Gallica by the Swiss critic Maurice Muret, in which he writes: "We are reminded of her touching play *Sœur Jeanne de la Croix*," 22 July 1921, p. 3, though the term "récit" in French is admittedly ambiguous.

98 Martin-Gistucci, *L'Œuvre romanesque*, p. 528.
99 *Ibid.*, p. 525.
100 Camillo Antona Traversi, *Riccordi parigini* (Ancona: La Lucerna, 1919), p. 178.
101 Jean Dornis, "Matilde Serao," *Le Figaro*, 16 November 1907, p. 2.
102 Bertucci is referring specifically to the depiction of female relationships in Serao's *œuvres*. See: Pia Leonore Bertucci, "Da lei, tutto: Female Relationships in the Narratives of Matilde Serao," (unpublished doctoral thesis, University of Chapel Hill, 2008), pp. 21–57.
103 Matilde Serao, *Dopo il perdono* (Rome: La Nuova Antologia, 1905), p. 90.
104 *Ibid.*, p. 92.
105 ED. S., "Théâtres," p. 2.
106 Interim, "Le Théâtre," in *La Française: Journal de progrès féminin*, 1 December 1907, p. 3.
107 Yvonne Sarcey, "Les Lettres de la cousine: Matilde Serao," in *Les Annales politiques et littéraires*, 24 November 1907, pp. 499–500.
108 *Ibid.*
109 Germaine Albert-Dulac, "Une Conversation avec Mme Matilde Serao," in *La Renaissance politique, littéraire et artistique*, 6 February 1915, pp. 13–14 (p. 13).
110 Adolfo Franci, *Italiani e forestieri* (Milan: Ceschina, 1930), p. 89.
111 Gibus (Matilde Serao), "Mosconi," in *Il Mattino*, 21–22 January 1920, p. 2.

Conclusion

In shifting recent focus in feminist silent film history away from reclaiming lost female film pioneers towards an emphasis on rediscovering lost women spectators, this book has sought to uncover a vibrant and successful Italian female culture industry existing at the turn of the twentieth century – one which was both national and international, and which extended to the French- and English-speaking worlds.[1] It was a transnational female culture industry through which an "affective alliance"[2] of middle-class women spectators learned about sex, love, and relationships via the theatre auditorium and silent screen (perhaps) far more than via the written word. The civil and social freedoms that came with being an internationally renowned female performer in the public eye were in stark contrast to the everyday lives of middle-class women in Italy until 1919, when the *maritalis auctoritas* (which made a wife financially dependent on her husband) was finally abolished. Changes to women's legal and social subordination to men were in no small measure effected thanks to women's "stepping up" during World War I into roles previously occupied by men as workers outside the domestic sphere. Yet had it not been for two generations of women performers and writers in the public eye prior to 1914, who travelled the world as talented, independent professionals, taking ownership of their careers as directors and managers of *Compagnie* (and in Serao's case, her own daily newspaper), the war years may not have been taken on with the same degree of inner confidence by women whose husbands, fathers, and sons were fighting on the front line. Discussing the stereotypical cultural differences between Italian and "Anglo-Saxon" women prior to World War I, an article in the British *Ladies' Home Journal* (somewhat condescendingly) boasts about the women travellers to Italy and the "single woman," who

> [...] carried with her – besides Baedeker and camera – a fine ideal, which she handed out generously – freedom of sex and emancipation. The freedom with which thc British and American woman tramps the globe, spends money, enjoys without stint and without having to render account to anyone, was a source of wonder and envy to her Italian sisters. It was fascinating, dangerous and contagious.[3]

DOI: 10.4324/9780429293511-8

The freedom with which the talented Italian women performers and writers discussed in this book "tramped the globe", clearly overlooked by this author, was a source of national pride and promise for their women spectators and fans, who would one day also venture out beyond the confines of their home. As early as 1976, František Cerný published an article on women tragic actors in European theatre at the end of the nineteenth and beginning of the twentieth century, in which he imagined how women spectators might have responded to them:

> In this period, women dreamed of a happier life. They saw in female actors and their plays a hope for a better future, and tragic female actors reinforced these dreams more or less intensely; [...] they expressed and reinforced spectators' hopes to go on living. A very characteristic key moment among female actors around 1900 is the technique of directing their pensive gaze towards the distance, towards the future which, perhaps, will offer more favourable conditions for the development of human existence.[4]

The performers' and writers' nurturing and supportive "public" friendships with one another (Serao-Duse; Aleramo-Pezzana; Serao-Bertini; Duse-Aleramo) also had positive repercussions and reverberations for spectators and readers, who were indirectly and unconsciously(?) encouraged to seek out similar bonds of affection and affirmation in their everyday lives. Evidence of Mary Ann Doane's and Elisabeth Bronfen's desiring feminine gazes are laid bare in Bertini's admiration of the "great" Tina di Lorenzo, "a highly intelligent and deeply elegant female actor who had moved and fascinated [her],"[5] and the positive feedback loop among women spectators, writers, and performers is demonstrated in her memoir in which she confesses that Serao's "novels had inhabited [her] Neapolitan years with dreams" before they even met.[6] As we saw in Chapter 4, another woman actor who spoke highly of Serao's (in this case, screenplay) writing was Maria Carni, who, playing the role of Elena di Soubise in *La mia vita per la tua* (My Life for Yours), eulogised Serao's ability to write a film:

> [Wi]th this screenplay Matilde Serao has not only shown herself once more to be the greatest modern writer but has also revealed some absolutely wonderful theatrical elements and, most importantly, has been able to make film like no other writer thus far.[7]

The multipolar female gazes at the stage and screen in late nineteenth-century Italy and beyond were far removed from the masculine stereotypes circulating in the collective imagination. Excerpts from life-writings, columns in journals for women and in newspapers, and realist fiction provided in this book all exemplify plainly a nascent spectatorship-in-the-making among middle-class women that was at once epistemophilic, critical, discerning, visceral, and emboldening. The many paradoxes of the Fallen Woman/Magdalene figure on stage and screen referred to here – for example, that she was at once strong (in her beliefs and character) and "weak" (if she had a physical or mental health condition), that she was "marked" for her apparent transgressions, yet sympathetic in the eyes of her creators and spectators – were at once internalised and dismissed by spectators, who saw in her first and foremost the performer singing, speaking, and articulating her role.

Examples of the ways in which both spectators and performers distanced themselves from the mythical, masculine-constructed, tired Fallen Women *trope* is revealed in Duse's rejection of it by the 1920s, when she argued that Dumas *fils*'s "Fallen Women" and their "just punishment" was a thing of the past.[8] Similarly, a teacher and spectator from Venafro (in the province of Isernia between Naples and Rome) named Concetta Cipolla (1885–1915) signed her love letters addressed to the poet and writer Angelo Maria Tirabassi (1879–1933) "Violetta" after Verdi's *La traviata* with conscious irony.[9] As we saw in Chapter 3, further evidence for a preference among women spectators and performers for strong female characters is revealed in Duse's confession at the end of her career to Francesca Bertini that the character she had preferred performing the most was Ibsen's Nora in *A Doll's House*, who took the decision to free herself from a patriarchal and oppressive domestic life.[10] Actual women readers (and, by association, spectators) show an outright snub of the *cliché* of the woman reader/Fallen Woman *à la* Madame Bovary devouring romantic novels: Silvia Ferro (mentioned in Chapter 3), writing a letter to her friend Luisa in 1907 which she copies in her diary, counsels her to read with caution

> [t]hose violent and exaggerated scenes that magnify and intoxicate [and that] are so poisonous that little by little they infiltrate our hearts and minds and very often lead to destruction. Read [the book?] carefully, calmly, reflecting well from a moral point of view. Try to benefit from the good examples of characters in the book and try to improve yourself and correct those small defects that we all suffer from.[11]

Divas and writers blazed a trail for women, providing their spectators and readers with fleeting but vital moments of identification and escapism from the monotony of their daily lives, inviting women spectators to play with fictional worlds and imagined selves. And it is more than possible that the "lost" women spectators recovered in this book might have pinned on women performers and writers the hope that they, too, might one day live more freely and independently.

Notes

1 See: https://wfpp.columbia.edu/ [accessed 27 July 2019].
2 Lawrence Grossberg, *Dancing In Spite of Myself: Essays on Popular Culture* (Durham: Duke University Press, 1997), pp. 29–63 (p. 44).
3 Marie Van Vorst, "The Italian Woman's Drive for Freedom," in *The Ladies' Home Journal*, January 1921, p. 25; p. 44. I am grateful to Rachael Alexander for bringing this article to my attention.
4 František Cerný, "Les tragédiennes comme un phénomène caractéristique du théâtre européen à la fin du XIXeme et au commencement du XXeme siècle," in *The Role of the Actor in the Theatrical Reform of the Late 19*th *and Early 20*th *Centuries*, ed. by Milan Lukeš (Prague: University of Prague Karlova, 1976), pp. 23–36 (p. 33). The observation is echoed by Angela Dalle Vacche, who says that

> "Duse's [...] open-ended acting style recalled Italian women's habit of assuming expressions of religious absorption. The so-called 'mystical look,' with eyes raised to the sky and hands brought together in prayer, was how most women posed for a photographic portrait. This Catholic cliché was adopted by innumerable aunts and mothers in the family album [...]."

See: Angela Dalle Vacche, *Diva: Defiance and Passion in Early Italian Cinema* (Austin: University of Texas Press, 2008), pp. 4–5.
5 Francesca Bertini, *Il resto non conta* (Pisa: Giardini, 1969), p. 97. Italics my own.
6 *Ibid.*, p. 97.
7 Author unknown, "Maria Carmi parla del 'soggetto' che Matilde Serao ha scritto ed ella ha interpretato per la MONOPOL FILM di Roma," in *La vita cinematografica*, 34–35, 15–22 September 1914, pp. 41–2.
8 Maria Di Rienzo, "Eleonora Duse", in *Who's Who in Gay & Lesbian History: From Antiquity to World War II*, ed. by Robert F. Aldrich and Gary Wotherspoon (London: Routledge, 2001), p. 138–9 (p. 138).
9 Irene Palombo, "'La mia delizia e la mia croce': Echi della *Traviata* nelle lettere al poeta Angelo M. Tirabassi," in *Scrivere d'amore: Lettere di uomini e donne tra Cinque e Novecento*, ed. by Manola Ida Venzo (Rome: Viella, 2015), pp. 409–32 (p. 412).
10 Bertini, *Il resto non conta*, p. 106.
11 Entry dated 21 June 1907, diary of Silvia Ferro held at the Archivio dei diari, Pieve Santo Stefano.

Appendix

Women's Opera, Theatre, and Silent Film Cited in Order of Reference*

Novelist *(n)* Playwright *(p)* Composer *(c)* Librettist *(l)* Screenwriter *(s)* Director *(d)* Translator *(t)*	*Title* play *(p)* opera *(o)* film *(f)*	Date and place of first publication/ performance/ screening in Italy/diva in the starring role	*Plot* *(plot and characterisation may vary according to form. The summary and character names refer to the version cited in column three)*
Euripides (Ancient Greece, *p*); Alexandre Soumet (1831, *p*); Felice Romani (*l*); Vincenzo Bellini (*c*)	*Medea* (Greek myth); *Norma, ou l'infanticide* (*p*); *Norma* (*o*)	26 December 1831, Teatro alla Scala, Milan (*o*)/ **Giuditta Pasta**	The action takes place in Gaul under the Roman occupation. A high Druid priestess, who broke her chastity vows by having had two children by the Roman proconsul, discovers that her lover is cheating on her with her friend. When he refuses to give up his new lover, Norma publicly confesses her betrayal to her people and is sentenced to death by burning; she is joined on the pyre by her lover.
Giovanni Verga (1880 *n*, *p*); Pietro Mascagni (*c*); Guido Menasci (*l*); Giovanni Targioni-Tozzetti (*l*)	*Cavalleria rusticana*	14 January 1884, Teatro Carignano, Turin (*p*)/ **Eleonora Duse**; 17 May 1890, Rome, Teatro Costanzi (*o*)/**Gemma Bellincioni**	Set in a late nineteenth-century Sicilian village. A soldier, Turiddù, returns from military service to discover that his fiancée, Lola, has married the local carter, Alfio. Taking revenge, he seduces Santuzza, who is in love with Turiddù and becomes pregnant. Overcome by jealousy, Lola begins an adulterous affair with Turiddù. Feeling betrayed, dishonoured, and abandoned, Santuzza tells Alfio of his wife's betrayal. Alfio challenges Turiddù to a duel, and he accepts, though not before asking his mother to look after Santuzza in the event of his death. Alfio kills Turiddù, and his mother and Santuzza are left distraught.

Novelist *(n)* **Playwright** *(p)* **Composer** *(c)* **Librettist** *(l)* **Screenwriter** *(s)* **Director** *(d)* **Translator** *(t)*	*Title* play *(p)* opera *(o)* film *(f)*	**Date and place of first publication/ performance/ screening in Italy/diva in the starring role**	*Plot* *(plot and characterisation may vary according to form. The summary and character names refer to the version cited in column three)*
Mario Caserini (*d*); Emiliano Bonetti and G. Monleone (*s*)	*Ma l'amor mio non muore*	October 1913, Turin (*f*)/**Lyda Borelli**	Elsa, the daughter of a Colonel who kills himself because he is unjustly accused of treason for stealing military plans, escapes to the Riviera, where she becomes a successful singer and pianist under the pseudonym Diana Cadouleur. She meets and falls in love with Prince Maximilian, heir to the Grand Duke, who is unaware of her true identity. On a boat trip on Lake Locarno, they meet Moise Stahr, whom Elsa had previously rejected, and who, recognising her, retaliates by spreading the news of her relationship with the prince. The Grand Duke orders the prince home. After he goes to look for Elsa, upon discovering her real identity, he learns she has taken poison.
Henrik Ibsen (1879, *p*) Luigi Capuana (*t*)	*Et dukkehjem/ Casa di bambola*	15 February 1889, Teatro Gerbino, Turin (*p*)/**Emilia Aliprandi Pieri**	A middle-class wife, Nora, forges her father's signature in order to obtain a loan to cover the cost of travel to Italy to cure her sick lawyer husband. When he learns of his wife's fraud sometime later, he is outraged and concerned for his own social reputation. Upon recognising that her husband sees her as nothing more than a "doll," she decides to walk out of their marriage, leaving behind her three children.

Novelist *(n)* **Playwright** *(p)* **Composer** *(c)* **Librettist** *(l)* **Screenwriter** *(s)* **Director** *(d)* **Translator** *(t)*	*Title* play *(p)* opera *(o)* film *(f)*	**Date and place of first publication/ performance/ screening in Italy/diva in the starring role**	*Plot* *(plot and characterisation may vary according to form. The summary and character names refer to the version cited in column three)*
Nino Oxilia (*d*); Alberto Fassini (*s*)	*Rapsodia satanica/ Satanic Rhapsody*	July 1917 (*f*)/**Lyda Borelli**	Based on the Faustian tale. An upper-class elderly woman, Alba d'Oltrevita, makes a pact with the devil, Mephistopheles, to regain her youth in exchange for agreeing not to fall in love. She is courted by two brothers, one of whom she prepares to marry, while the other shoots himself and dies. Mephistopheles returns to restore Alba's old age for not complying with their agreement.
Antoine François Prévost d'Exiles (1731, *n*); Giacomo Puccini (*c*)	*Histoire du chevalier des Grieux et de Manon Lescaut/ Manon Lescaut*	1 February 1893, Teatro Regio, Turin (*o*)/**Cesira Ferrani**	Set in the second half of the eighteenth century. An upper-class student, Des Grieux, falls in love with Manon, whose father is sending her to a convent. The couple escape when they learn of a plot to abduct her, but Des Grieux cannot afford Manon's taste for luxury, and she leaves him to become Geronte's mistress in Paris. However, she is bored by Geronte, who is elderly, and thinks of Des Grieux. He returns to her, but it is too late, and Manon is arrested and imprisoned for prostitution. She is deported to New Orleans, but Des Grieux manages to board her ship. Once there, the lovers make their way across the desert to seek refuge in a British settlement, but Manon is exhausted and cannot go on. She dies of thirst and Des Grieux of exhaustion.

Novelist *(n)* **Playwright** *(p)* **Composer** *(c)* **Librettist** *(l)* **Screenwriter** *(s)* **Director** *(d)* **Translator** *(t)*	*Title* play *(p)* opera *(o)* film *(f)*	**Date and place of first publication/ performance/ screening in Italy/diva in the starring role**	*Plot* *(plot and characterisation may vary according to form. The summary and character names refer to the version cited in column three)*
Victorien Sardou (1887, *p*); Giacomo Puccini (*o*); **Francesca Bertini** and Alfredo De Antoni (*d*)	*La Tosca*/ *Tosca*	14 January 1900, Teatro Costanzi, Rome (*o*)/ **Hariclea Darclée**; 1918 (*f*) / **Francesca Bertini**	Set in Rome in 1800 during the Battle of Marengo. Floria Tosca – a celebrated singer – reveals the Roman consul's hiding place in exchange for an end to her revolutionary lover's torture. The Chief of Police, Scarpia, bargains with Tosca: providing she will consent to sex with him, he will free her lover. Tosca is repelled but nonetheless agrees, although not before persuading Scarpia to instruct his men to arrange a mock execution and to write a safe-conduct out of Rome for herself and her lover. While he is writing the safe-conduct, she stabs him to death with a knife. Believing that she and her lover are "safe," she witnesses the "mock" execution of her lover, but it is real, and so she jumps from the top of the Castel Sant'Angelo to her death.
Pierre Loti (1887, *n*); John Luther Long (1898, *n*); Giacomo Puccini (*c*)	*Madame Chrysanthème*/ *Madam Butterfly*/ *Madama Butterfly*	17 February 1904, Teatro alla Scala, Milan (*o*)/ **Rosina Storchio**; revised version 28 May 1904, Brescia (*o*)/ **Solomiya Krushelnytska**	Set in contemporary times in Nagasaki. A 15-year-old girl, Cio-Cio-San, falls in love with an American soldier and renounces her faith to marry him. He leaves Japan for America, and meanwhile, she has a son. Her husband returns three years later with his "real" American wife and announces he has come to take away their son. Consequently, Madam Butterfly commits ritual suicide.

Novelist *(n)* **Playwright** *(p)* **Composer** *(c)* **Librettist** *(l)* **Screenwriter** *(s)* **Director** *(d)* **Translator** *(t)*	*Title* play *(p)* opera *(o)* film *(f)*	**Date and place of first publication/ performance/ screening in Italy/diva in the starring role**	*Plot (plot and characterisation may vary according to form. The summary and character names refer to the version cited in column three)*
Giacomo Puccini (*c*); Giuseppe Adami, Alfred Maria Willner, and Heinrich Reichert (*l*)	*La rondine/ The Swallow*	27 March 1917, Grand Théâtre de Monte Carlo (*o*)/**Gilda Dalla Rizza**	Set in Paris in the mid-nineteenth century. A high-class courtesan, Magda, is nostalgic for her days as a working girl when she spent happy evenings dancing, and decides to disguise herself and spend an evening at her old haunt. She meets Ruggero there, and they plan a new life together, but she secretly worries she is deceiving him. They move to the French Riviera, and Ruggero is excited about marrying Magda and having a family, but Magda can deceive him no longer, and regretfully returns to her old life as a courtesan, leaving Ruggero devastated.
Giacomo Puccini (*c*); Giovacchino Forzano (*l*)	*Suor Angelica*, one-act opera, part of *Il trittico*	14 December 1918, Metropolitan Opera, New York (*o*)/**Geraldine Farrar**	Set in the late sixteenth century. Suor Angelica is in a convent out of punishment: seven years previously her noble family sent her there for having a child out of wedlock. Her aunt visits her, and orders that she sign a document renouncing her claim to her inheritance because her sister is to be married. Suor Angelica refuses, saying she cannot forget the memory of her illegitimate son. Her aunt informs her that her son died two years ago of a fever, and Suor Angelica collapses, devastated. She makes poison and commits suicide.

Novelist *(n)* **Playwright** *(p)* **Composer** *(c)* **Librettist** *(l)* **Screenwriter** *(s)* **Director** *(d)* **Translator** *(t)*	*Title* play *(p)* opera *(o)* film *(f)*	**Date and place of first publication/ performance/ screening in Italy/diva in the starring role**	*Plot* *(plot and characterisation may vary according to form. The summary and character names refer to the version cited in column three)*
Carlo Gozzi (1762, *p*); Friedrich Schiller (1802, *p*); Giacomo Puccini and Franco Alfano (*c*); Giuseppe Adami and Renato Simoni (*l*)	*Turandot*	25 April 1926, Teatro alla Scala, Milan (*o*)/**Rosa Raisa**	In legendary times in Peking, a beautiful princess, who is avenging her ancestor who was raped and murdered, agrees to marry only on the condition that her suitor correctly answers three enigmas, otherwise he is beheaded. Upon seeing her, Prince Calaf immediately falls in love and summons her to answer her riddles, which he does so correctly. Seeing her in distress, he takes pity and challenges *her* to an enigma: to reveal his name before dawn, and if she does, he will die. A slave girl, Liù, who is in love with Calaf, is tortured by the princess's guards in order to reveal Calaf's name. She takes a knife and commits suicide in order to conceal his name. The prince then reveals his name, and Turandot, apparently feeling moved by Liù's gesture, yields, and agrees to marry him.
Salvatore Di Giacomo (*p*); **Francesca Bertini**/ Gustavo Serena (*d*)	*Assunta Spina*	27 March 1909, Teatro Nuovo, Naples (*p*)/ **Adelina Magnetti;** 28 October 1915 (*f*)/**Francesca Bertini**	Set in Naples in contemporary times. Assunta, a laundry worker, is engaged to a violent butcher, Michele, and is courted by Raffaele. At a feast in nearby Posillipo, she accepts his offer to dance when Michele ignores her. Blinded by rage, he slashes her face and is subsequently arrested. Assunta claims at the court trial that Michele would never wound her, but the jury does not believe her, and Michele is sentenced to two years in prison for assault. The court Vice-Chancellor, Federigo, offers to help Assunta, but only if she becomes his mistress. Michele is released early from prison, and finding Assunta and Federigo together, Michele kills Federigo. When the police arrive, Assunta takes the blame for Michele's crime and is sent to prison.

Novelist *(n)* Playwright *(p)* Composer *(c)* Librettist *(l)* Screenwriter *(s)* Director *(d)* Translator *(t)*	*Title* play *(p)* opera *(o)* film *(f)*	Date and place of first publication/ performance/ screening in Italy/diva in the starring role	*Plot* *(plot and characterisation may vary according to form. The summary and character names refer to the version cited in column three)*
Grazia Deledda (1904, *n*); Eleonora Duse and Febo Mari (*d*)	*Cenere/ Ashes*	1916 (*f*)/**Eleonora Duse**	Set in contemporary times in rural Sardinia. Rosalia, who has an illegitimate child and is abandoned by the child's father, is unable to provide for her son, Anania. She entrusts Anania to his wealthy father, who has since married, leaving Anania with an amulet as a token of remembrance. Years pass by, and Anania, now fully-grown, is about to marry his childhood sweetheart, and so goes in search of his mother to invite her to his wedding and to live with them when they are married. Rosalia recognises him from the amulet he is carrying, and Anania is dismayed to discover his mother is poor. She suggests he sends her the amulet wrapped in a white cloth if his betrothed accepts her, and in a coloured cloth if she does not. Rosalia waits for the answer in suspense, and when she receives the amulet wrapped in a coloured cloth, unable to bear the feeling of abandonment once again, she takes her own life.
Victor Hugo (1835, *p*); Amilcare Ponchielli (*c*); Arrigo Boito (*l*)	*Angelo, Tyran de Padoue/ La Gioconda*	8 April 1876, Teatro alla Scala, Milan (*o*)/**Maddalena Mariani Masi**	Set in seventeenth-century Venice. Gioconda is in love with Enzo, who loves Laura, who is married. Barnaba, the villain, is in love with Gioconda. When Laura saves Gioconda's mother's life, Gioconda decides to facilitate Enzo and Laura's elopement. Having done so, rather than suffer Barnaba's advances, she commits suicide on learning that Barnaba has murdered her mother.

Novelist *(n)* **Playwright** *(p)* **Composer** *(c)* **Librettist** *(l)* **Screenwriter** *(s)* **Director** *(d)* **Translator** *(t)*	*Title* play *(p)* opera *(o)* film *(f)*	**Date and place of first publication/ performance/ screening in Italy/diva in the starring role**	*Plot (plot and characterisation may vary according to form. The summary and character names refer to the version cited in column three)*
Giuseppe Verdi (*c*); Antonio Ghislanzoni (*l*); François Auguste (*Painter*); Ferdinand Mariette (*Egytologist*)	*Aida*	24 December 1871, Khedivial Opera House, Cairo (*o*)/ **Teresa Stolz**	Set in ancient Egypt. The Egyptians have captured and enslaved Ethiopian princess, Aida. An Egyptian military commander, Radamès, struggles with his secret love for Aida and his loyalty to the King of Egypt. The king's daughter, Amneris, is in love with Radamès, but he does not return her feelings. Amneris tricks Aida into believing Radamès is dead in order to ascertain whether or not Aida is her rival. She is enraged to discover Aida's love for Radamès. Having won the battle against the Ethiopians, Radamès is told by the King of Egypt he can have anything he wants and asks that the Ethiopian slaves be spared their lives. The King of Egypt grants his wish and tells Radamès he will become his successor and marry Amneris. Aida and her father remain as hostages to ensure that the Ethiopians do not avenge their defeat. Radamès then reveals military plans to Aida and her father, not realising their true identities, and is arrested as a traitor and condemned to death, much to Amneris's distress. Aida has hidden in the dark vault in which Radamès has been condemned to death and dies in Radamès's arms.
Prosper Mérimée (1845, *n*); Georges Bizet (1875, *c*); Henri Meihac, Ludovic Halévy (*l*); Antonio De Lauzières (*t*); Gerolamo Lo Savio (*d*)	*Carmen*	15 October 1879, Teatro Bellini, Naples (*o*)/**Celestine Galli-Marié**; 1909 (*f*)/**Vittoria Lepanto**	Set in the early nineteenth century in Seville, a cigarette factory worker, Carmen, flirts with a soldier, Don José, whose mother wants him to return home and marry the chaste Micaëla. Carmen is arrested for attacking a co-worker with a knife. Left alone with Don José, she beguiles him with a song and dance. Agreeing to free her hands, Don José is pushed to the ground and Carmen runs away leaving Don José to be arrested for dereliction of duty.

Novelist *(n)* Playwright *(p)* Composer *(c)* Librettist *(l)* Screenwriter *(s)* Director *(d)* Translator *(t)*	*Title* play *(p)* opera *(o)* film *(f)*	Date and place of first publication/ performance/ screening in Italy/diva in the starring role	*Plot* *(plot and characterisation may vary according to form. The summary and character names refer to the version cited in column three)*
			Two months pass and Carmen learns of Don José's release at Lillas Pastia's Inn, where the toreador, Escamillo, has made an entrance and has set his sights on Carmen, who brushes him aside. Carmen performs a seductive dance for Don José and invites him to escape with her. At first, he refuses, but he attacks a superior officer who wants to arrest Carmen, and so joins her and the smugglers. Months pass and Carmen has become bored with José and reads her cards, foretelling their deaths. Escamillo arrives and José expresses anger at the bullfighter when he declares his infatuation with Carmen. Micaëla arrives to tell José that his mother is dying, and he agrees to depart, vowing to Carmen he will return. At the bullfight, Carmen and Escamillo are in love, but Carmen agrees to speak to José, who pleads with her to return to him. She refuses, returning the ring he gave her, and he stabs her to death. He confesses to killing Carmen and is sent to jail.
Antonio Lozzi (*c*; *l*); **Amelia Rosselli** (1924, *p*)	*Emma Liona*	25 May 1895, Teatro La Fenice, Venice (*o*)/**Erina Borlinetto**	Based on the life of Lady Emma Hamilton (1765–1815), and set in 1799 in Naples. Emma Liona, wife of the Ambassador of England in Naples, is jealous of her lover Romei's new conquest, the young virgin, Carmela, daughter of a revolutionary king who is imprisoned. Romei threatens Emma if she does anything to harm Carmela. During a solo dance for the court, Emma tries to seduce Romei, but he only thinks of the pious Carmela. The king's military officer, Fra Diavolo, is jealous of Emma's love for Romei, who Emma taunts, which makes him

Novelist *(n)* **Playwright** *(p)* **Composer** *(c)* **Librettist** *(l)* **Screenwriter** *(s)* **Director** *(d)* **Translator** *(t)*	*Title* play *(p)* opera *(o)* film *(f)*	**Date and place of first publication/ performance/ screening in Italy/diva in the starring role**	*Plot* *(plot and characterisation may vary according to form. The summary and character names refer to the version cited in column three)*
			furious and he refuses her arm. Emma orders him to leave the party. Carmela is informed by Lady Hamilton that Romei is a traitor and has been imprisoned. Carmela pleads with her to save her father the king. Lady Hamilton says if Carmela agrees to marry Fra Diavolo, her father will be saved. Carmela initially refuses, but suffering upon seeing that her father is being taken to be killed, she agrees to do so. Emma summons Romei from prison and tells him she still loves him. Romei reminds her that she cursed him publicly, for which Emma apologises. Romei asks her what happened to Carmela; Emma is offended and tries to persuade him to renew their previous love affair. Romei demands to know where he can find Carmela. Emma tells him Carmela has married Fra Diavolo, and Romei strangles Emma to death.
Victor Hugo (1831, *p*); Amilcare Ponchielli (*c*); Enrico Golisciani and Antonio Ghislanzoni (*l*)	*Marion Delorme*	17 March 1885, Teatro alla Scala, Milan (*o*)/**Romilda Pantaleoni**	Set in 1638, a Parisian courtesan, Marion, has gone to live in the countryside with her lover, Didier, from whom she is concealing her true identity, going by the name of Maria. A former "protector," the Marquis of Saverny, learns of his previous mistress's elopement and cannot believe she actually ran away for love. He goes to see her, and Didier notices the friendly relationship between Maria and the stranger. Didier challenges his rival to a duel, but a new edict sentences to death anyone taking part in one. A guard offers to release Didier from prison providing Marion agrees to be his; she reluctantly accepts, but Didier insults her, having learned of her true identity. He forgives her before he dies, and Marion is left alone.

Novelist *(n)* **Playwright** *(p)* **Composer** *(c)* **Librettist** *(l)* **Screenwriter** *(s)* **Director** *(d)* **Translator** *(t)*	*Title* play *(p)* opera *(o)* film *(f)*	**Date and place of first publication/ performance/ screening in Italy/diva in the starring role**	*Plot* *(plot and characterisation may vary according to form. The summary and character names refer to the version cited in column three)*
Alexandre Dumas *fils* with Pyotr Korvib-Krukovsky (1876, *p*); Alfredo Catalani (*c*); Antonio Ghislanzoni (*l*)	*Les Danicheff/ Edmea*	27 February 1886, Teatro alla Scala, Milan (*o*)/ **Virginia Ferni-Germano**	The action takes place in sixteenth-century Bohemia. Edmea and Oberto swear eternal love to one another before he departs on a long journey. Oberto's father, the Count, who disapproves of his son's love for Edmea, decides by virtue of his authority that Edmea will be married to Ulmo, who is in love with her. Ulmo asks her to be his wife as a sister, but she refuses. Forced to sign the nuptial act, Edmea throws herself in the river, into which Ulmo also disappears to save her. Escaping death, Edmea has lost her reason and believes she is the fairy of the River Elbe in search of a king, who once loved her. Ulmo (posing as Edmea's brother) and Edmea, arrive at a tavern and are invited to the home of Baron Waldeck. His guests include the Count and Oberto, who is suffering Edmea's loss. Oberto immediately recognises Edmea's voice, and upon seeing Oberto, she regains her reason. Oberto and Edmea escape and Ulmo is left in despair having saved Edmea only to lose her to his rival. Oberto takes Edmea back to his home, unaware of Edmea's marriage to Ulmo. Near Oberto's mother's tomb, Edmea reveals her marriage and the two plot to flee when Ulmo arrives looking very pale. Ulmo announces he will kill himself to eliminate any obstacle between them; all he asks for is a kiss on his forehead from Edmea, whose virginity, he assures Ulmo, is intact. The Count arrives informing his son of the dissolution of the wedding, and Edmea grants Ulmo's last wish.

Novelist *(n)* **Playwright** *(p)* **Composer** *(c)* **Librettist** *(l)* **Screenwriter** *(s)* **Director** *(d)* **Translator** *(t)*	*Title* play *(p)* opera *(o)* film *(f)*	**Date and place of first publication/ performance/ screening in Italy/diva in the starring role**	*Plot* *(plot and characterisation may vary according to form. The summary and character names refer to the version cited in column three)*
Walter Scott (1819, *n*); Gaetano Donizetti (*c*); Salvadore Cammarano (*l*)	*The Bride of Lammermoor/ Lucia di Lammermoor*	26 September 1835, Teatro San Carlo, Naples (*o*)/ **Fanny Tacchinardi Persiani**	Set in a castle in the early eighteenth century in Scotland. Lucia and Edgardo have been meeting in secret when a guard notices Edgardo's intrusion and informs Enrico, Lucia's brother. Enrico is determined to end the relationship given his hatred for Edgardo's family. Lucia tells her maid that she has had an apparition: the ghost of a girl killed next to a fountain at the entrance to the park beside the castle. Her maid tells Lucia it is a warning and she must renounce her love for Edgardo, who arrives and tells Lucia he must leave for France for political reasons; they swear a vow of marriage and exchange rings. Enrico has arranged for Lucia to marry Arturo and has forged a letter seemingly proving that Edgardo has forgotten her and taken a new lover. Enrico arranges for Lucia's tutor to persuade her to give up Edgardo for the good of the family. Reluctantly, Lucia signs the marriage contract, at which point Edgardo appears and curses her, demanding that they return their rings. Enrico challenges Edgardo to a duel, and he accepts upon hearing that Lucia is already enjoying her bridal bed. In reality, she has gone mad and murdered her bridegroom, Arturo, and killed herself. When Edgardo is informed, he commits suicide, hoping to be reunited with Lucia in heaven.

Novelist *(n)* **Playwright** *(p)* **Composer** *(c)* **Librettist** *(l)* **Screenwriter** *(s)* **Director** *(d)* **Translator** *(t)*	*Title* play *(p)* opera *(o)* film *(f)*	**Date and place of first publication/ performance/ screening in Italy/diva in the starring role**	*Plot (plot and characterisation may vary according to form. The summary and character names refer to the version cited in column three)*
Henri Murger (1851, *n*); Ruggero Leoncavallo (*c*); King Vidor (1926, *d*)	*Scènes de la vie de bohème*/ *La Bohème*	6 May 1897, Teatro La Fenice, Venice (*o*)/**Rosina Storchio**	Set in Paris in 1838. A group of bohemian students, artists, and working girls enjoy a meal at a café where they cannot pay the bill. Barbemuche, Musette's lover and protector, pays the bill, but soon leaves her, refusing to pay her debts any longer. Musette becomes Marcello's lover but soon leaves him as he cannot provide for her. Mimì has allowed herself to be carried off by Count Paul but soon leaves him, motivated by her love for Rodolfo. However, he, along with Marcello, forces both women to leave their apartment. Mimì later returns to Rodolfo and dies of tuberculosis.
Pietro Mascagni (*c*); Luigi Illica (*l*)	*Iris*	22 November 1898, Teatro Costanzi, Rome (*o*)/ **Hariclea Darclée**	Set in Japan in legendary times. A young lord in search of adventures plans to kidnap Iris, the young and innocent daughter of a blind old man. Disguised as a child of the sun, Osaka conquers Iris's heart during a puppet show. Kyoto, Osaka's assistant, leaves money and a note implying Iris has abandoned her father, and Samurai carry her to Kyoto's geisha house. Osaka tries to seduce Iris but is bored by her simplicity and innocence. Osaka tells Kyoto to get rid of Iris, and thinking he can make some money out of her Kyoto exposes her on a balcony to the crowds. Her father, having assumed that Iris went to the geisha house of her own accord, arrives and curses her, flinging mud in her face. Overwhelmed by her father's incomprehensible actions, and before the repenting Osaka returns, Iris throws herself into a shaft leading to a sewer. The next morning, she revives, but quickly becomes delirious and imagines she hears voices of the three men – Osaka, Kyoto and her father – each mocking her, before dying.

Novelist *(n)* **Playwright** *(p)* **Composer** *(c)* **Librettist** *(l)* **Screenwriter** *(s)* **Director** *(d)* **Translator** *(t)*	*Title* play *(p)* opera *(o)* film *(f)*	**Date and place of first publication/ performance/ screening in Italy/diva in the starring role**	*Plot* *(plot and characterisation may vary according to form. The summary and character names refer to the version cited in column three)*
Alexandre Dumas *fils* (1848, *n*; 1852, *p*); Giuseppe Verdi (*c*); Francesco Maria Piave (*l*)	*La Dame aux camélias*/ *La traviata*	6 March 1853, Teatro La Fenice, Venice (*o*)/ **Fanny Salvini-Donatelli**	Set in Paris and its vicinity in the early nineteenth century. Violetta Valéry, a famed courtesan, is throwing a party to celebrate her recovery from illness. She is introduced to the bourgeois Alfredo Germont, and they fall in love and decide to move to the countryside together. Violetta abandons her former lifestyle and financially supports their relationship for three months. Upon learning this from the maid, Alfredo goes to Paris to settle matters. While he is away, his father, Giorgio Germont, visits Violetta, and demands that she break off her relationship with his son for the sake of his family since her relationship with his son is "threatening" his daughter's engagement. In distress, she makes the honourable sacrifice by agreeing to leave Alfredo; Giorgio is touched by Violetta's nobility. Violetta writes a farewell letter to Alfredo and reluctantly returns to her life of debauchery in Paris, becoming involved with a baron. At a party, Alfredo humiliates Violetta, throwing his gambling winnings at her feet after he has forced her to admit that she is in love with the baron. Later, as Violetta lies dying of tuberculosis, she receives a letter from Alfredo's father telling her that he has been informed of her noble sacrifice and is on his way to her to ask for her forgiveness. Violetta dies in Alfredo's arms.

Novelist *(n)* **Playwright** *(p)* **Composer** *(c)* **Librettist** *(l)* **Screenwriter** *(s)* **Director** *(d)* **Translator** *(t)*	*Title* play *(p)* opera *(o)* film *(f)*	**Date and place of first publication/ performance/ screening in Italy/diva in the starring role**	*Plot* *(plot and characterisation may vary according to form. The summary and character names refer to the version cited in column three)*
Gabriel Dupont (*c*); Henri Caïn (*l*); Amintore Galli (*translator*)	*La cabrera*	16 May 1904, Teatro Lirico, Milan (*o*)/ **Gemma Bellincioni**	A village-tale set near San Sebastián in Spain in the 1890s. A goat herd, Amalia, causes her son's death in order to win her lover.
Wilhelmine von Hillern (1883, *n*); Alfredo Catalani (*c*); Luigi Illica (*l*)	*Die Geyer-Wally/ La Wally*	20 January 1892, Teatro alla Scala, Milan (*o*)/**Hariclea Darclée**	Set in the Austrian Tyrol in 1800, Wally's rich landowner father tells her daughter she must marry his friend, Gellner. She refuses, since she is in love with her father's enemy, Hagenbach, and so her father banishes her. She goes off to live in the mountains and returns a year later when her father has died to claim her inheritance. At a party, she is wrongly led to believe by Gellner that Hagenbach is betrothed to Afra, whom Wally insults. To avenge the insult, Hagenbach accepts a challenge to win a kiss from Wally. When Wally realises she has been the victim of a cynical bet, she promises to marry Gellner if he will kill Hagenbach. Gellner hurls him into a ravine, and Wally, feeling remorse, rushes to save him and returns him to Afra, to whom Wally leaves all her wealth. Wally returns to her refuge in the mountains and is eventually joined by Hagenbach, who confesses his love. The lovers are reconciled and Hagenbach goes to search for a path back down the mountain but is hit by an avalanche, and Wally hurls herself to her death.

Novelist *(n)* **Playwright** *(p)* **Composer** *(c)* **Librettist** *(l)* **Screenwriter** *(s)* **Director** *(d)* **Translator** *(t)*	*Title* play *(p)* opera *(o)* film *(f)*	**Date and place of first publication/ performance/ screening in Italy/diva in the starring role**	*Plot* *(plot and characterisation may vary according to form. The summary and character names refer to the version cited in column three)*
Pietro Mascagni (*c*); Paul Bérel (*l*)	*Amica*	13 May 1905, Teatro Costanzi, Rome (*o*)/ **Amalia Karola**	Set in the Piedmontese Alps around 1900. A farm owner is celebrating his adopted niece Amica's imminent marriage to his stepson, Giorgio. Giorgio is jealous of his brother, Renaldo, whose charm has won over Amica's heart. Upon learning of his niece's love for Renaldo, Amica's uncle refuses to allow them to marry, so Renaldo and Amica escape together during a storm, and Giorgio sets out to find them and kill his rival. Upon discovering that his rival is, in fact, his brother, he is shocked and devastated and falls unconscious. Taking his brother's side, Renaldo holds Amica responsible for his brother's suffering despite the fact she protests her innocence and says she had never encouraged Giorgio's love. Renaldo tells her their love is now impossible and escapes into the mountains, leaving Amica alone. She decides to follow him but falls into the ravine watched by the two dismayed brothers.
Eugène Scribe and Ernest Legouvé (1849, *p*); Francesco Cilea (*c*); Arturo Colautti (*l*)	*Adrienne Lecouvreur*/ *Adriana Lecouvreur*	6 November 1902, Teatro Lirico, Milan (*o*)/**Angelica Pandolfini**	Set in Paris in 1730. Adriana, a famous actor, is adored by many, but she is in love with Maurizio, the Count of Saxony. Adriana gives him some violets to put in his buttonhole; however, Maurizio has another admirer, the Princesse de Bouillon. Upon seeing the violets in his buttonhole, she asks how he came by them. Maurizio presents them to her, but despite being grateful for her help at court, he admits he no longer loves her. Although she guesses he has a lover, he won't reveal her name. Adriana arrives and Maurizio tells her his meeting with the princess was political and they must arrange her escape. Adriana believes him, but

Novelist *(n)* Playwright *(p)* Composer *(c)* Librettist *(l)* Screenwriter *(s)* Director *(d)* Translator *(t)*	*Title* play *(p)* opera *(o)* film *(f)*	Date and place of first publication/ performance/ screening in Italy/diva in the starring role	*Plot* *(plot and characterisation may vary according to form. The summary and character names refer to the version cited in column three)*
			when she meets the princess, they are both immediately suspicious of one another. The princess eventually discovers that her rival is, in fact, Adriana, and resolves to poison her. Upon receiving a box with the faded violets and a note that she believes is from Maurizio, Adriana kisses the violets, at which point Maurizio arrives and reveals he did not send the violets. Adriana has been poisoned to death by the princess.
Umberto Giordano (*c*); Henri Caïn, Edouard Adenis and Lorenzo Stecchetti (*l*)	*Marcella*	9 November 1907, Teatro Lirico, Milan (*o*)/**Gemma Bellincioni**	The action takes place in Paris in 1910. Giorgio is a prince in disguise who presents himself as an artist and poet. He meets Marcella in a restaurant, and she tells him she is alone and poor. They fall for one another and move to the countryside, where they have been living for three months when Drasco arrives to ask Giorgio to return to his people, who need him. Marcella listens, unseen, to their conversation and discovers Giorgio's true identity. In distress, she resolves to leave him. Giorgio wants Marcella to follow him, but Marcella knows she cannot be the wife of a prince. She is abandoned and falls to the ground in despair.
Pietro Mascagni (1911, *c*); Luigi Illica (*l*)	*Isabeau/ Lady Godiva*	20 January 1912, Teatro La Fenice, Venice (*o*)/**Maria Llacer Casali**	Based on the thirteenth-century English legend of Lady Godiva. King Raimondo holds a tournament to find a husband for his beautiful and chaste daughter, Isabeau, but she refuses all noble suitors. As a punishment, the king orders her to ride naked through the city, but her people respect her and demand from him an edict condemning to blindness anyone who dares look at

Novelist *(n)* **Playwright** *(p)* **Composer** *(c)* **Librettist** *(l)* **Screenwriter** *(s)* **Director** *(d)* **Translator** *(t)*	*Title* play *(p)* opera *(o)* film *(f)*	**Date and place of first publication/ performance/ screening in Italy/diva in the starring role**	*Plot* *(plot and characterisation may vary according to form. The summary and character names refer to the version cited in column three)*
			her. A falconer, Folco, who is unaware of the edict, stares at Isabeau during her ride and is arrested. Isabeau visits him in prison and falls in love. She begs her father to pardon him, but her people rise up against Folco and kill him. Isabeau throws herself over his body and dies with him.
Carlo Merli (*c*); Pietro Rossi (*l*)	*Melisenda*	9 February 1913, Teatro La Fenice, Venice (*o*)/**Ines Cesari**	*Not known*
Giovanni Verga (1880 *n*; *p*)	*La lupa*	26 January 1896, Teatro Gerbino, Turin/ (*p*)**Eleonora Duse**	Set in contemporary times in rural Sicily. A sensual and seductive farm worker, Gnà Pina, falls in love with a man returned from military service, Nanni, who is in love with her chaste daughter, Maricchia. Pina offers him her daughter in marriage and her house as an extra dowry, reserving a corner in the kitchen where she sleeps. Her daughter refuses, but Pina threatens to kill her if she fails to comply with her wishes. The daughter eventually falls in love with her husband, who also succumbs to her mother, Pina's, sexual power. Tormented by Pina, Nanni kills her with an axe.
Victorien Sardou (1882, *p*); Umberto Giordano (*o*); Giuseppe de Liguoro, Gustavo Serena and **Francesca Bertini** (*d*)	*Fédora/Fedora*	4 October 1883, Teatro Valle, Rome (*p*)/ **Eleonora Duse**; 17 November 1898, Teatro Lirico, Milan (*o*)/**Gemma Bellincioni**; December 1916 (*f*)/**Francesca Bertini**	A widowed Russian princess sets out to avenge her deceased lover's assassination on the eve of their marriage but becomes the victim of her vow when she falls in love again. She meets the suspected assassin, Count Ipanoff, in Paris, only to learn that her *fiancé* had betrayed her with Ipanoff's wife. Meanwhile, she has written to the authorities in Russia naming the Count's brother as one of the assassins. They spend days in a delirium of love only

Novelist *(n)* **Playwright** *(p)* **Composer** *(c)* **Librettist** *(l)* **Screenwriter** *(s)* **Director** *(d)* **Translator** *(t)*	*Title* play *(p)* opera *(o)* film *(f)*	**Date and place of first publication/ performance/ screening in Italy/diva in the starring role**	*Plot* *(plot and characterisation may vary according to form. The summary and character names refer to the version cited in column three)*
			to learn that the Count's brother has died in prison and their heartbroken mother has also died. Fedora confesses her part in their deaths to the Count, who consequently disavows her. Feeling distraught, Fedora drinks poison and dies in the Count's arms.
Alexandre Dumas *fils* (1873, *p*); Gero Zambuto, Giovanni Pastrone (*d*)	*La moglie di Claudio*	August 1873, Genoa (*p*)/ **Adelaide Tessero**; 1918 (*f*)/**Pina Menichelli**	Claudio is married to Cesarina, a frivolous and unfaithful woman with whom all tenderness has long ceased, also because of the death of their only son. While his wife moves from betrayal to betrayal spending her days idly, Claudio dedicates himself to the development of sophisticated weapons, developing the design of a new cannon. He is in love with the virtuous Jew, Rebecca, but cannot abandon himself to his feelings because of his religious faith, which prevents him from divorcing. Having seduced one of her husband's young collaborators, Cesarina is blackmailed by a spy who forces her to steal her husband's plans for the new weapon to be able to sell them to foreign powers. Claudio sees her stealing his plans and, exasperated and worried about the consequences of the leak of news about the cannon, he kills her.
Henri Meilac and Ludovic Halévy (1869, *p*); **Francesca Bertini** and Gustavo Serena (*d*)	*Frou-Frou/ Frou*	3 July 1882, Arena Nazionale, Florence (*p*)/ **Eleonora Duse**; 1918 (*f*)/**Francesca Bertini**	A bored, aristocratic wife and mother has an affair, elopes, but is forgiven when her husband kills her lover; she dies in her husband's arms.

Novelist *(n)* **Playwright** *(p)* **Composer** *(c)* **Librettist** *(l)* **Screenwriter** *(s)* **Director** *(d)* **Translator** *(t)*	*Title* play *(p)* opera *(o)* film *(f)*	**Date and place of first publication/ performance/ screening in Italy/diva in the starring role**	*Plot* *(plot and characterisation may vary according to form. The summary and character names refer to the version cited in column three)*
Gabriele D'Annunzio (*p*); Riccardo Zandonai (1914, *o*)	*Francesca da Rimini*	9 December 1901, Teatro Costanzi, Rome (*p*)/ **Eleonora Duse**	Based on Canto IV of Dante's *Inferno* and dedicated to Duse, who was D'Annunzio's lover, the play is told from the perspective of Francesca, who falls in love with her brother-in-law-to-be, Paolo. His other brother, Malatestino, attempts to rape Francesca, who finds refuge in Paolo's arms. The lovers are caught *in flagrante* and are murdered.
Matilde Serao (*n*, 1888; *p*; *s*); Ernesto Murolo (*p*); Gino Rossetti (*d*)	*O Giovannino, o la morte!*	13 November 1912, Teatro Nazionale, Rome (*p*)/ **Adelina Magnetti**; 1915 (*f*)/**Pina Cicogna**	Set in Naples in contemporary times. The orphaned Chiarina lives with her stepmother, Donna Gabriella, who runs a pawn shop, and who refuses to allow Chiarina to marry her *fiancé*, Giovannino. He asks Donna Gabriella to approve their marriage, and she agrees, much to Chiarina's surprise. During Giovannino's weekly visits, Donna Gabriella and Giovannino develop a flirtatious relationship. Upon returning from church one day, she sees her stepmother and Giovannino kissing. Feeling distraught, she throws herself from the balcony and dies.
Gabriele D'Annunzio (*p*)	*La figlia di Iorio*	2 March 1904, Teatro Lirico, Milan (*p*)/**Irma Gramatica**	Set in primitive rural Abruzzo, Mila di Codra is estranged by her father, Jorio. She falls in love with a young shepherd, Aligi, who is promised to another woman in an arranged marriage, but he loves Mila. He prepares to go to Rome to seek an annulment, but before he does so his father tries to rape Mila, and Aligi tries to kill his father to protect Mila. Aligi is condemned to death and given poison to drink before his execution, but Mila takes the blame for having "bewitched" Aligi. She is taken away to be burned to death, while Aligi, now under the influence of the poison, curses her. Mila dies at the stake.

Novelist *(n)* **Playwright** *(p)* **Composer** *(c)* **Librettist** *(l)* **Screenwriter** *(s)* **Director** *(d)* **Translator** *(t)*	*Title* play *(p)* opera *(o)* film *(f)*	**Date and place of first publication/ performance/ screening in Italy/diva in the starring role**	*Plot* *(plot and characterisation may vary according to form. The summary and character names refer to the version cited in column three)*
Victorien Sardou (1870, *p*); Gustavo Serena (*d*)	*Fernande/ Fernanda*	20 March 1874, Teatro Mercadante, Naples (*p*)/ **Teresa Leigheb**; 1917 (*f*)/**Francesca Bertini**	Set in Paris. Clotilde, the mistress of the Marquis des Arcis, suspects her lover has been deceiving her with Fernande, whom she follows home. Upon seeing that Fernande lives in a gambling house and is the lover of its keeper, Roqueville, Clotilde resolves to "rescue" Fernande and her mother, who are placed in an apartment in Clotilde's house. The Marquis visits Clotilde, who tricks him into believing that she wants to end their affair to test the strength of his love, but much to Clotilde's dismay the Marquis seems relieved: he confesses that he is, in fact, in love with a young woman he sees at the theatre (Fernande). Clotilde sets out to take revenge on the Marquis by introducing him to Fernande, whose background the Marquis is unaware of, though Fernande is under the impression he knows it. After their wedding, Clotilde plots to present the Marquis with a letter of confession from Fernande, but Clotilde is foiled by her cousin Pommerol, who intercepts the letter and locks her in her room leaving Fernande and the Marquis to go on their honeymoon. Upon their return, Clotilde denounces Fernande to the Marquis. Clotilde's vengeance seems complete, only Pommerol appears with the letter proving that Fernande was unaware of her husband's ignorance of her chequered past. Pommerol persuades the Marquis to forgive his wife given that Roqueville has been killed in a duel and the Marquis is very much in love. The Marquis agrees, leaving Clotilde feeling mortified.

Novelist *(n)* **Playwright** *(p)* **Composer** *(c)* **Librettist** *(l)* **Screenwriter** *(s)* **Director** *(d)* **Translator** *(t)*	*Title* play *(p)* opera *(o)* film *(f)*	**Date and place of first publication/ performance/ screening in Italy/diva in the starring role**	*Plot* *(plot and characterisation may vary according to form. The summary and character names refer to the version cited in column three)*
Victorien Sardou (1881, *p*); Giuseppe De Liguoro and **Francesca Bertini** (*d*)	*Odette*	4 October 1881, Teatro Valle, Rome (*p*) /**Eleonora Duse**; 1916 (*f*)/ **Francesca Bertini**	The first act is set 15 years in the past in Paris. Odette's husband, Lord Henry Trevene, is away on business in England, and his wife returns home from the opera with Prince Troubitzkoy, with whom she is having an affair. She receives a note informing her that her husband is returning home sooner than expected. He arrives as the prince is leaving, and Odette begs her husband not to kill her. He orders her to leave and she is forbidden to say goodbye to their little daughter, Eva. 15 years later in Nice, Eva has been taught to believe her mother is dead, and Lord Shandon is seeking her hand in marriage. However, his mother won't allow the marriage to go ahead unless Odette, now living a life of a high-class courtesan, renounces her title. Odette consents on the condition that she can see her child. Following their encounter, Odette commits suicide.
Jan Neruda (*p*)	*Francesca di Rimini*	1860, Prague (*p*)/Unknown	Inspired by Dante's *Inferno* Canto IV and set in Renaissance Italy, Francesca is married for political reasons to a disfigured nobleman. Forbidden to fulfil her true feelings for her brother-in-law, Paolo, she pays for her adultery with her life.
Felice Cavallotti (*p*)	*Lea*	7 January 1889, Teatro Manzoni, Milan (*p*)/**Italia Vitaliani**	Set in contemporary times. Riccardo kidnaps Lea in order to marry her, and they spend their honeymoon in a remote village to hide from Lea's parents, who oppose the marriage. Lea's mother sets a trap: she pretends to be on her deathbed and calls for her daughter. Upon her arrival, Lea is taken to a convent. Riccardo searches for Lea in

Novelist *(n)* Playwright *(p)* Composer *(c)* Librettist *(l)* Screenwriter *(s)* Director *(d)* Translator *(t)*	*Title* play *(p)* opera *(o)* film *(f)*	Date and place of first publication/ performance/ screening in Italy/diva in the starring role	*Plot* *(plot and characterisation may vary according to form. The summary and character names refer to the version cited in column three)*
			vain for eight months, but upon receiving her death certificate he marries Ida and has a son. Seven years pass, and on Riccardo's name day Lea arrives having escaped from the convent and seeks to reclaim her rightful status as Riccardo's wife. But his son pleads with Lea to imagine how her mother would feel if she were abandoned by her child. Riccardo professes his love for Lea, who, recognising that she cannot break up his new family, takes her own life.
Matilde Serao (*s*); Emilio Ghione (*d*)	*La mia vita per la tua!*	5 December 1914, Rome (*f*)/ **Maria Carmi**	Count Granville expects a handsome inheritance from his uncle, but this goes instead to his cousins, the Dukes of Roger Ferry because the uncle is disgusted by Granville's reckless behaviour. However, the Dukes die in a car crash on their way home from a summer ball, and their fortune passes to their children, while Granville reluctantly accepts an annual income of 20 thousand lire. He swears vengeance, telling his lover, Elena De Soubise, that she will help him to get revenge. His niece, Arletta, is a 15-year-old student at a school in the surrounding hills of Rome. She is struck by loneliness and fear and has only one confidante: Clara Formont, a music teacher, who advises her to abandon the world and give herself to God, which she does, leaving her fortune to her brothers. Gastone, one of her brothers, lives a bohemian life in Paris among artists and models. He is introduced to a mysterious Polish woman who seduces him at a dance party, and whom he falls for. She invites him back to her villa for the

Novelist *(n)* Playwright *(p)* Composer *(c)* Librettist *(l)* Screenwriter *(s)* Director *(d)* Translator *(t)*	*Title* play *(p)* opera *(o)* film *(f)*	Date and place of first publication/ performance/ screening in Italy/diva in the starring role	*Plot* *(plot and characterisation may vary according to form. The summary and character names refer to the version cited in column three)*
			night, but then abandons him the following day, leaving Gastone distraught. He enlists as a volunteer in the foreign legion and dies on African soil. His brother, Andrea, is the first secretary of the French Embassy in Rome and is involved with the Marquise of Viel Castel, Elena De Soubise, who has been sent by Granville to seduce him, but who returns his love. When Granville announces that the general steward has learned of Granville's plan, he tells Elena that she must leave. But she would rather die, and so she stabs herself with the same dagger intended for Andrea with a note: "My life for yours!"
Matilde Serao (1890, *n/s*); Alberto Carlo Lolli (*d*)	*Addio, amore!*	7 September 1916 (*f*)/**Mary Bayma-Riva**	Set in Naples in 1880. Two sisters, Anna and Laura, who belong to a noble family, are orphaned and taken in by a noble guardian, Cesare Dias. The youngest of the two sisters, Anna, falls in love with Cesare and declares her love threatening suicide. Surprised, but attracted by her youthful charm, Cesare marries her. Following a short period of serenity, the relationship is disrupted by Laura's envy and jealousy, and Laura and Cesare begin an affair. When Anna learns of the betrayal, she takes her own life, while her husband dies in a duel with his wife's lover.

Novelist *(n)* **Playwright** *(p)* **Composer** *(c)* **Librettist** *(l)* **Screenwriter** *(s)* **Director** *(d)* **Translator** *(t)*	*Title* play *(p)* opera *(o)* film *(f)*	**Date and place of first publication/ performance/ screening in Italy/diva in the starring role**	*Plot* *(plot and characterisation may vary according to form. The summary and character names refer to the version cited in column three)*
Matilde Serao (1893, *n/s*); Ubaldo Maria Del Colle (*d*)	*Castigo*	1917 (*f*)/**Mary Bayma Riva**	The sequel to *Addio, amore!* (Farewell, Love!), Anna's ghost returns embodied in the Englishwoman, Hermione, who, according to Laura, looks identical to Anna. Racked with guilt from his wife's suicide, Cesare Dias wishes to fight a duel with Anna's lover, Luigi, who has fled to Germany. Upon his return to Italy, he meets Hermione in Florence and falls in love. Meanwhile, Laura, who feels no guilt from Anna's death, has managed to persuade Cesare to marry her, though he still loves Anna. Cesare receives news from Luigi that he is in Rome, and so goes there to fight him in a duel. Cesare sees Hermione, who he thinks is Anna, as does Laura, who sees Hermione at the opera. Luigi is badly injured in the duel. At a garden party in Naples, Luigi confesses to Hermione that he is in love with her. Assuming Hermione is Anna's ghost, Laura asks for her forgiveness before Hermione leaves on a yacht bound for Gibraltar. In another duel, Luigi kills Cesare, who dies believing in Anna's innocence (e.g., that Luigi was not her lover). Luigi travels the seas in search of Hermione, who has drowned.
Matilde Serao (*s*), Giulio Antamoro (*d*)	*Il doppio volto*/ The Double Head	May 1918 (*f*)/ **Helen Arnold**	*Not known*
Matilde Serao (1908, *n/s*); Ubaldo Maria Del Colle (*d*)	*Temi il leone*/ Beware the Lion	March 1919 (*f*)/ **Maria Jacobini**	Teresa Gargiulo's dead mother has left Teresa a Saint Teresa pendant inscribed with the words "*temi il leone*" (beware the lion). The lion refers to the coat of arms of a powerful Neapolitan family named Vargas. Teresa's mother had been victimised by Francesco Vargas, and now, Teresa is poised to be Giorgio Vargas's

Novelist *(n)* Playwright *(p)* Composer *(c)* Librettist *(l)* Screenwriter *(s)* Director *(d)* Translator *(t)*	*Title* play *(p)* opera *(o)* film *(f)*	**Date and place of first publication/ performance/ screening in Italy/diva in the starring role**	*Plot* *(plot and characterisation may vary according to form. The summary and character names refer to the version cited in column three)*
			victim. Giorgio tries to seize Teresa's fortune by employing an assassin, but the murder attempt is thwarted when the bullet bounces off the Saint Teresa pendant. Undeterred, and intent on robbing Teresa of her fortune, Giorgio sets about seducing her with the promise of security and noble stature. Tragically, Teresa replicates her mother's fate by dying in childbirth.
Pierre Berton and Jules Simon (1898, *p*); Ruggero Leoncavallo (*c*) Ernesto-Maria Pasquali (*d*);	*Zazà*	10 November 1900, Teatro Lirico, Milan (*o*)/**Rosina Storchio;** 1909 (*f*)/**Lydia De Roberti**	Set in contemporary times in France. Zazà, whose mother is an ex-artist and alcoholic, is rescued by Cascart, who is in love with Zazà. He manages to find her work as a *soubrette* in a café in Saint-Etienne, and she begins an affair with Milio, whom she loves. After three months, Milio tells Zazà that he has to go to America. Cascart arrives and tells Zazà that he saw Milio in the company of another woman in Paris. Zazà goes to Paris to discover (unbeknownst to Milio) that he has a wife and child. Devastated, she returns to Saint-Étienne and tells Cascart she wishes to work again now that her love story is over. She tells Milio she knows everything and makes him wrongly believe that she has told his wife about them. Milio's reaction is violent: he insults Zazà and declares his love for his wife. Upon discovering that Milio's love for his wife and child trumps his love for her, she is abandoned, heartbroken.

Novelist *(n)* **Playwright** *(p)* **Composer** *(c)* **Librettist** *(l)* **Screenwriter** *(s)* **Director** *(d)* **Translator** *(t)*	*Title* play *(p)* opera *(o)* film *(f)*	**Date and place of first publication/ performance/ screening in Italy/diva in the starring role**	*Plot* *(plot and characterisation may vary according to form. The summary and character names refer to the version cited in column three)*
Roberto Bracco (*p*); Ugo De Simone (*d*)	*Maternità*	February 1903, Teatro Manzoni, Milan (*p*)/**Tina Di Lorenzo;** October 1917 (*f*)/**Italia Almirante-Manzini**	Claudia di Montefranco has been unable to conceive for the first ten years of her marriage, having longed for a child. Upon discovering she is pregnant, she retires to the countryside to await the arrival of the baby in peace as motherhood becomes the sole aim of her life. Disaster strikes when her husband arrives with news from her doctor, who says her child cannot be born except at the expense of her life, and that an immediate operation is necessary. She cannot bear to sacrifice her child and induces an attack that ends in her and her child's death.
Roberto Bracco (*p*)	*Il frutto acerbo*	April 1904, Teatro Sannazaro, Naples (*p*)/ **Virginia Reiter**	*Not known*
Marco Praga (*p*); A. Albertoni (*d*)	*L'ondina*	24 April 1903, Teatro Regio, Turin (*p*)/**Tina Di Lorenzo;** August 1917 (*f*)/ **Bianca Virginia Camagni**	*Not known*

**Plays, operas, and films referred to in this book that do not feature Fallen Women or* femmes fatales *as their central characters are omitted from this table.*

Bibliography

A., "Eleonora Duse," *Il corriere dei teatri: Periodico artistico teatrale*, 22, 10 June 1899

"A Woman's Memories of Old Vienna," *The Living Age*, 25 September 1920

Abbate, Carolyn, *Unsung Voices: Opera and Musical Narrative in the Nineteenth Century* (Princeton, NJ: Princeton University Press, 1991)

———, "Opera, or the Envoicing of Women," in *Musicology and Difference: Gender and Sexuality in Music Scholarship*, ed. by Ruth A. Solie (Berkeley, University of California Press, 1993), pp. 225–58

Adami, Giacomo, ed., *Giacomo Puccini epistolario* (Milan: Mondadori, 1982)

"Adelina Patti," *Life*, 17 February 1910

Albert-Dulac, Germaine, "Une Conversation avec Mme Matilde Serao," *La Renaissance politique, littéraire et artistique*, 6 February 1915

Aleramo, Sibilla, *Dal mio diario (1940–1944)* (Rome: Tumminelli, 1945)

———, *Un amore insolito: Diario, 1940–1944* (Milan: Feltrinelli, 1979)

———, *A Woman*, trans. by Rosalind Delmar (Berkley and Los Angeles: University of California Press, 1980)

———, *Una donna* [1906] (Milan: Feltrinelli, 2020)

Allen, Julie K., "Divas Down Under: The Circulation of Asta Nielsen's and Francesca Bertini's films in Australasian Cinemas in the 1910s," *Studies in Australasian Cinema* 11:2 (2017), 59–76

Allen, Virginia M., *The Femme Fatale: Erotic Icon* (Troy, NY: Whitston Publishing Company, 1983)

Allum, Percy, "Catholicism," in *The Cambridge Companion to Modern Italian Culture*, ed. by Zygmunt G. Barański and Rebecca West (Cambridge: Cambridge University Press, 2004, 2nd edn.), pp. 97–112

Alovisio, Silvio, "La spettatrice muta: Il pubblico cinematografico femminile nell'Italia del primo Novecento," in *Non solo dive: Pioniere del cinema italiano*, ed. by Monica Dall'Asta (Bologna: Cineteca di Bologna, 2008), pp. 269–88

Anderson, Linda, *Autobiography*, 2nd edn. (London: Routledge, 2010)

Ang, Ien, *Watching Dallas: Soap Opera and the Melodramatic Imagination* (London: Methuen, 1985)

Anita, *La donna*, 10 May 1872

Annunziata, Gina, "Matilde Serao e il cinematografo," in *Non solo dive: Pioniere del cinema italiano*, ed. by Monica Dall'Asta (Bologna: Cineteca di Bologna, 2008), pp. 249–55

Arslan, Antonia, *Dame, droga e galline: Romanzo popolare e romanzo di consumo tra '800 e '900* (Padova: Cleup, 1977)

———, "Una voce dal *Ventre di Napoli* nella "galassia sommersa" del suo tempo," in *Visibili, invisibili: Matilde Serao e le donne nell'Italia post-unitaria*, ed. by Gabriella Liberati, Giuseppe Scalera, and Donatella Trotta (Rome: Centro Nazionale di Ricerca, 2016), pp. 49–60

Ashbrook, William, "The Nineteenth Century: Italy," in *The Oxford History of Opera*, ed. by Roger Parker (Oxford: Oxford University Press, 1994), pp. 114–37

Baccini, Ida, "Pietro Mascagni," *Cordelia*, 27 November 1892

Baioni, Massimo, ed., *Patria mia. Scritture private nell'Italia unita* (Bologna: Il Mulino, 2011)

Balbo, Cesare, *Delle speranze d'Italia* (Florence: Le Monnier, 1844)

Banes, Sally, *Dancing Women: Female Bodies on Stage* (London: Routledge, 1998)

Banti Alberto Mario and Paul Ginsborg, "Introduzione," in *Storia d'Italia. Annali 22. Il Risorgimento*, ed. by Alberto Mario Banti and Paul Ginsborg (Turin: Einaudi, 2007), pp. xxiii–iv

Bara, Theda, "The Curse on the Moving-Picture Actress: Describing the Conflict in Her Artistic Experiences of the Moving-Picture Art," *Forum*, July 1919, 83–94 (93–4)

Barthes, Roland, "The Death of the Author," in *Image, Music, Text* [1968] (New York: Hill and Wang, 1977)

Bauman, Rebecca H., "Melodrama and Italian Culture," *Italian Studies* 70:3 (2015), 416–20

Bayman, Louis, *The Operatic and the Everyday in Post-War Italian Film Melodrama* (Edinburgh: Edinburgh University Press, 2014)

Beales, Derek and Eugenio F. Biagini, *The Risorgimento and the Unification of Italy* (Harlow: Longman, 2002)

Beccari, Gualberta Alaide, "Giacinta Pezzana-Gualtieri," *La donna*, 10 May 1873

———, "Giannina Milli," *La donna*, 30 October 1876

———, "La donna e l'Arte," *La donna*, 30 November 1878

———, "Una proposta," in *La donna*, 25 November 1880

Belsey, Catherine, *Critical Practice* (London: Routledge, 1980)

Bennett, Susan, *Theatre Audiences: A Theory of Production and Reception* (London: Routledge, 1997)

Berger, John, *Ways of Seeing* (London: Harmondsworth, 1972)

Bernardini, Aldo, *Cinema muto italiano*, Vol. 2 (Rome and Bari: Laterza, 1980)

Bertellini, Giorgio, "Introduction: Traveling Lightness," in *Italian Silent Cinema: A Reader*, ed. by Giorgio Bertellini (New Barnet: John Libbey Publishing, 2013)

———, "Italian Americans' Transnational Film Culture in 1920s New York City," in *Making Italian America: Consumer Culture and the Production of Ethnic Identities* ed. by Simone Cinotto (New York: Fordham University Press, 2014), pp. 84–98

Bertini, Francesca, *Il resto non conta* (Pisa: Giardini, 1969)

Bertoni Jovine, Dina, "Funzione emancipatrice della scuola e contributo della donna all'attività educativa," in *L'emancipazione femminile in Italia: Un secolo di discussioni 1861–1961* ed. by Comitato di associazioni femminili per la parità di retribuzione (Florence: La Nuova Italia, 1963), pp. 223–75

———, *Storia dell'educazione popolare in Italia*, (Bari: Laterza, 1965)

Bertucci, Pia Leonore, "Da lei, tutto: Female Relationships in the Narratives of Matilde Serao," (unpublished doctoral thesis, University of Chapel Hill, 2008)

Biagi, Guido, "Italian Literature," *The Athenæum*, 6 October 1906, pp. 395–97

Bianchi, Patricia, "L'attrazione fatale dell'«arte muta», dal libro al teatro fino al cinema", in *Visibili, invisibili. Matilde Serao e le donne nell'Italia post-unitaria*, ed. by Gabriella Liberati, Giuseppe Scalera, and Donatella Trotta (Rome: Centro Nazionale di Ricerca, 2016), pp. 149–64

Billson, Marcus, "The Memoir: New Perspectives on a Forgotten Genre," *Genre* 10 (1977), 259–82

Bolton, Lucy, "Beautiful Penitent Whore: The Desecrated Celebrity of Mary Magdalene," *Celebrity Studies* 11:1 (2020), 25–42

"Bombay Amusements," *The Times of India*, 10 December 1917

Bontempi, Francesco, *La donna e la legislazione italiana: Raccolta delle disposizioni contenute nei codici relative alla donna* (Turin: Tipografia del giornale Il Conte Cavour, 1871)

Bordeaux, Henry, "La Vie au théâtre" *La Revue hebdomadaire*, 30 November 1907

Bradshaw, Melissa, *Amy Lowell, Diva Poet* (Farnham and Burlington: Ashgate, 2011)

Brandes, Georg, "Eleonora Duse," *The Living Age*, 15 October 1926, pp. 165–70

Bronfen, Elisabeth, "Women Seeing Women Seeing Women," in *Women Seeing Women: A Pictorial History of Women's Photography from Julia Margaret Cameron to Annie Leibovitz*, ed. by Lothar Schirmer (London: Haus, 2002), pp. 9–34

———, "*Femme Fatale*: Negotiations of Tragic Desire," *New Literary History*, 35:1 (2004), 103–16

Brooks, Peter, "Melodrama, Body, Revolution," in *Melodrama: Stage, Picture, Screen*, ed. by Jacky Bratton, Jim Cook, and Christine Gledhill (London: British Film Institute, 1994), pp. 11–24

Bruni, Oreste, *Le nostre donne. Considerazioni d'un direttore di scuole femminili* (Florence: G. Barbèra, 1886)

Bruno, Giuliana, *Streetwalking on a Ruined Map: Cultural Theory and the City Films of Elvira Notari* (Princeton: Princeton University Press, 1993)

Buss, Helen M., "Memoirs," in *Encyclopaedia of Life Writing: Autobiographical and Biographical Forms*, Vol. 2, ed. by Margaretta Jolly (London and Chicago: Fitzroy Dearborn, 2001) pp. 595–6

Buttafuoco, Anna, *Questioni di cittadinanza: Donne e diritti sociali dell'Italia liberale* (Siena: Protagon Editori Toscani, 1995)

Caesar, Ann Hallamore, Gabriella Romani, and Jennifer Burns, eds., *The Printed Media in Fin-de-siècle Italy: Publishers, Writers, and Readers* (Oxford: Legenda, 2011)

———, "Writing by Women in Post-Unification Literary Culture: The Case for De-segregation," in *Women and Gender in Post-Unification Italy: Between Public and Private Spheres*, ed. by Katharine Mitchell and Helena Sanson (Oxford: Peter Lang, 2013), pp. 225–44

Campana, Alessandra, *Opera and Modern Spectatorship in Late Nineteenth-Century Italy* (Cambridge: Cambridge University Press, 2013)

Caneppele, Paolo, "Research on Local Moviegoing: Trends and Future Perspectives," in *Italian Silent Cinema: A Reader*, ed. by Giorgio Bertellini (New Barnet: John Libbey Publishing, 2013), pp. 305–14

"Can the Camera Immortalise the Melancholy Mask of Eleonora Duse?," *Current Opinion*, 1 July 1917

Carlson, Marvin, "Theatre Audiences and the Reading of Performance," in *Interpreting the Theatrical Past: Essays in the Historiography of Performance*, ed. by Thomas Postlewait and Bruce A. McConachie (Iowa City: University of Iowa Press, 1989), pp. 82–98

Cavarero, Adriana, *Tu che mi guardi, tu che mi racconti: Filosofia della narrazione* (Milan: Feltrinelli, 1997)

———, *A più voci. Filosofia dell'espressione vocale* (Milan: Feltrinelli, 2003)

Cecconi, Annamaria, "Le emozioni della spettatrice d'opera," *Nuova Civiltà delle Macchine* 1–2 (1998), 164–71

———, "Il genere del pubblico: questioni per una storia della ricezione femminile nelle arti della scena" in *Nuove frontiere per la storia di genere*, ed. by Laura Guidi and Maria Rosaria Pelizzari (Salerno: University of Salerno Press, 2013), pp. 181–213

Cerný, František, "Les tragédiennes comme un phénomène caractéristique du théâtre européen à la fin du XIXeme et au commencement du XXeme siècle," in *The Role of the Actor in the Theatrical Reform of the Late 19th and Early 20th Centuries*, ed. by Milan Lukeš (Prague: University of Prague Karlova, 1976), pp. 23–36

Champagne, John, *Italian Masculinity as Queer Melodrama: Caravaggio, Puccini, Contemporary Cinema* (Basingstoke: Palgrave Macmillan, 2015)

Chiappini, Simonetta, "La voce della martire. Dagli «evirati cantori» all'eroina romantica," in *Storia d'Italia*, Annali 22: Il Risorgimento, ed. by Alberto Mario Banti and Paul Ginsborg (Turin: Einaudi, 2007), pp. 289–328

Chiminello, Adele, *La donna*, 30 January 1877

Cinotti, Leonia, *La donna*, 31 May 1868

Clark, Martin, *Modern Italy 1871–1982* (London and New York: Longman, 1984)

Clément, Catherine, *L'opéra, ou la défaite des femmes* (Paris: Éditions Grasset & Fasquelle, 1979)

———, *Opera, Or, The Undoing of Women*, trans. by Betsy Wing, first published 1988 (London: Tauris, 1997)

Colombi, La Marchesa, "Colore del tempo," *Vita intima*, 4 November 1890

———, "Colore del tempo," *Vita intima*, 30 December 1890

———, *Prima Morire* [1881] (Rome: Lucarini, 1988)

———, "Teste Alate," in *Serate d'inverno* [1879] (Ferrara: Luciana Tufani Editrice, 1997)

———, *Un matrimonio in provincia* [1885] (Novara: Interlinea, 1999)

———, *A Small-Town Marriage*, trans. by Paula Spurlin Paige (Evanston, IL: Northwestern University Press, 2001)

Colombo, Fausto, *La cultura sottile. Media e industria culturale in Italia dall' Ottocento agli anni Novanta* (Milan: Bompiani, 1999)

Colombo Ascari, Rosalia, "Feminism and Socialism in Anna Kuliscioff's Writings," in *Mothers of Invention: Women, Italian Fascism, and Culture*, ed. by Robin Pickering-Iazzi (Minneapolis, MN and London: University of Minnesota Press, 1995), pp. 1–25

Cometto, Maria Teresa, *La Marchesa Colombi. La prima giornalista del Corriere della Sera* (Turin: B. L. U., 1996)

"Coming to the Theaters" in *The Washington Post*, 22 April 1915

Conforti, Luizi, "The Italian George Sand. (Matilde Serao)," *The Home-Maker*, 5:4 (1891)

Corabi, Gilda, "Scrittrici dell'Ottocento," in *Atlante della letteratura italiana* III, ed. by Domenico Scarpa (Turin: Einaudi, 2012), pp. 162–76

Cosslett, Tess, Celia Lury, and Penny Summerfield, eds., *Feminism and Autobiography: Texts, Theories, Methods* (London: Routledge, 2000)

Cottam, Rachel, "Diaries and Journals: General Survey," in *Encyclopedia of Life Writing: Autobiography and Biographical Forms*, ed. by Margaretta Jolly (London and Chicago: Fitzroy Dearborn Publishers, 2001), pp. 267–68

Covato, Camilla, "Educate ad educare: ruolo materno e itinerari formativi," in *L'educazione delle donne: Scuole e modelli di vita femminile nell'Italia dell' Ottocento*, ed. by Simonetta Soldani (Milan: Franco Angeli, 1991), pp. 131–47

"Cronaca femminile," *La donna*, 30 November 1881

D'Annunzio, Gabriele, *Il fuoco* [1898] (Milan: Mondadori, 1967)

D'Ascenzo, Alfredina, "Introduzione", *Fantasia* by Matilde Serao [1883] ed. by Alfredina D'Ascenzo (Bologna: Millennium, 2006)

Dall'Asta, Monica, "L'altra metà del cinema muto italiano," in *Non solo dive: Pioniere del cinema italiano*, ed. by Monica Dall'Asta (Bologna: Cineteca di Bologna, 2008), pp. 9–16

———, "Francesca Bertini," in *Women Film Pioneers Project*, ed. by Jane Gaines, Radha Vatsal, and Monica Dall'Asta (New York, NY: Columbia University Libraries, 2018) https://wfpp.columbia.edu/pioneer/francesca-bertini/ [accessed 27 March 2019]

Dalle Vacche, Angela, *Diva: Defiance and Passion in Early Italian Cinema* (Austin: University of Texas Press, 2008)

Davis, Tracy C., *Actresses as Working Women: Their Social Identity in Victorian Culture* (London: Routledge, 1991)

De Filippo, Eduardo (1977), "Eduardo De Filippo: In quel palco al Teatro Fiorentini," Interview with Lucio Villari, *La Repubblica*, 21 February 1977

De Francisci, Enza, *A 'New' Woman in Verga and Pirandello: From Page to Stage* (Oxford: Legenda, 2018)

De Giorgio, Michela, *Le italiane dall'Unità ad oggi: Modelli culturali e comportamenti sociali* (Rome: Laterza, 1992)

De Gubernatis, Angelo, *Dizionario biografico degli scrittori italiani* (Florence: Le Monnier, 1879)

De Man, Paul, "Autobiography as De-Facement," *Modern Languages Notes*, 94 (1979), 919–30

De Nunzio Schilardi, Wanda, *L'Invenzione del reale: Studi su Matilde Serao* (Bari: Palomar, 2004)

De Staël-Holstein, Germaine, *Corinne, ou l'Italie* (Paris: Garnier frères, 1869)

Di Belgiojoso, Cristina, "Della presente condizione delle donne e del loro avvenire," *Nuova Antologia* 1 (1866), 96–113

Di Rienzo, Maria, "Eleonora Duse", in *Who's Who in Gay & Lesbian History: From Antiquity to World War II*, ed. by Robert F. Aldrich and Gary Wotherspoon (London: Routledge, 2001), p. 138–9

Diaz, Silvia, "The Attractions of the 'Cinema Attractions' to Female Spectatorship," (unpublished doctoral thesis, Lehigh University, 2004)

Dijkstra, Bram, *Idols of Perversity: Fantasies of Feminine Evil in fin-de-siècle Culture* (Oxford: Oxford University Press, 1986)

Doane, Mary Ann, "Film and the Masquerade: Theorizing the Female Spectator," *Screen* 23:3–4, 1982, 74–87

———, *The Desire to Desire: The Woman's Film of the 1940s* (Bloomington: Indiana University Press, 1987)

———, *Femmes Fatales: Feminism, Film Theory, Psychoanalysis* (London: Routledge, 1991)

Dolan, Jill, *The Feminist Spectator as Critic* (Ann Arbor: UMI Research Press, 1988)

Donato Ventura, Luigi, *Memoirs and Artistic Studies of Adelaide Ristori*, trans. by Giorgio Mantellini (London: Doubleday, Page & Co., 1907)

Dornis, Jean, *Le Roman Italien contemporain* (Paris: Ollendorf, 1907)

———, "Matilde Serao," *Le Figaro*, 16 November 1907

Downing, Lisa, *Desiring the Dead: Necrophilia and Nineteenth-Century French Literature* (Oxford: Legenda, 2003)

Duffett, Mark, *Understanding Fandom: An Introduction to the Study of Media Fan Culture* (London: Bloomsbury, 2013)

Duggan, Christopher, *A Concise History of Italy* (2nd edn.) (Cambridge: Cambridge University Press, 2014)

Dyer, Richard, *Stars* (London: British Film Institute, 1979)

Eco, Umberto, *Storia della bellezza* (Milan: Bompiani, 2007)

ED. S, "Théâtres" in *Journal des débats politiques et littéraires*, 21 November 1907

"Eleonora Duse in London," *New York Times*, 8 May 1894

"Eleonora Duse," *The Gentlewoman and Modern Life*, 15 March 1913

Emilia, *Le parole nascoste* (Milan: Rossellina Archinto, 1987)

Evans, Richard, *The Feminists: Women's Emancipation Movements in Europe, America and Australasia 1840–1920* (London: Barnes and Noble, 1977)

Ewen, Stuart, *Captains of Consciousness: Advertising and the Social Roots of Consumer Culture* (New York: McGraw-Hill Books, 1976)

Fanning, Ursula, "Maternal Prescriptions and Descriptions in Post-Unification Italy," in *Women and Gender in Post-Unification Italy: Between Public and Private Spheres*, ed. by Katharine Mitchell and Helena Sanson (Oxford: Peter Lang, 2013), pp. 13–37

Farinelli, Giuseppe, *Storia del giornalismo italiano: Dalle origini ai nostri giorni* (Turin: UTET, 1997)

Farrell, Joseph, "Eleonora Duse nei paesi anglosassoni," in *Voci e anime, corpi e scritture: Atti del Convegno internazionale su Eleonora Duse*, ed. by Maria Ida Biggi and Paolo Puppa (Rome: Bulzoni, 2009), pp. 163–75

Ferrari Da Lodi, Carlotta, "Di alcuni Luoghi insigni del Nabucco di Verdi," *La donna*, 10 August 1872

Ferruggia, Gemma, *La nostra vera Duse* (Milan: Sonzogno, 1924)

Flaubert, Gustave, *Madam Bovary*, trans. by Geoffrey Wall (London: Penguin, 1995)

Flora, "Da Firenze. La lettura di Tommaso Salvini al Circolo Filologico," *La donna*, 30 November 1881

"Francesca Bertini," *Mudgee Guardian and North-Western Representative*, 7 June 1915

Franchini, Silvia, and Simonetta Soldani, eds., *Donne e giornalismo. Percorsi e presenze di storia di genere* (Milan: Franco Angeli, 2004)

Franci, Adolfo, *Italiani e forestieri* (Milan: Ceschina, 1930)

Freshwater, Helen, *Theatre & Audience* (Basingstoke: Palgrave MacMillan, 2009)

Fryer, Paul, "Duse Recorded," in *Eleonora Duse and* Cenere (Ashes): *Centennial Essays*, ed. by Maria Pia Pagani and Paul Fryer (Jefferson, NC: McFarland, 2017), pp. 72–89

Fusco, Gaetano, '"Ah, poeti, romanzatori, drammaturghi, fratelli miei…": Matilde Serao e il cinema', in *Immagine n. 2: Note di storie del cinema*, ed. by Silvio Alovisio and Michele Canosa (Cattedrale: Rome, 2010), pp. 91–109
G. G, "Teatri di artisti (Frammento di lettera)," in *Cordelia*, 26 February 1893
Gaetani-Tamburini, Emanuele, "Linda Monti-Brunner: la sua carriera, i suoi trionfi, le sue interpretazioni," *Cronaca dei Teatri*, 15 December 1905
Gibson, Mary, *Prostitution and the State in Italy, 1860–1915* (New Brunswick and London: Rutgers University Press, 1986)
Gibus del *Mattino* (Matilde Serao), "Api, Mosconi, e Vespe," *Il Mattino*, 22–23 March 1892
———, *Saper vivere: Norme di buona creanza* (Naples: Tocco, 1900)
Gigi, Il dottor (Neera?), "L'arte di vivere," *Vita intima*, 17 June 1890
Gilbert, Sandra M., and Susan Gubar, *The Madwoman in the Attic: The Woman Writer and the Nineteenth-Century Literary Imagination* (New Haven: Yale University Press, 2000)
Girard, René, *Deceit, Desire and the Novel: Self and Other in Literary Structure*, trans. by Yvonne Freccero (Baltimore, MD: Johns Hopkins Press, 1965)
Gledhill, Christine, *Home is Where the Heart Is: Studies in Melodrama and the Woman's Film* (London: British Film Institute, 1987)
Glenn, Susan, *Female Spectacle: The Theatrical Roots of Modern Feminism* (Cambridge: Cambridge University Press, 2000)
Gombrich, Ernst, *Art and Illusion: A Study in the Psychology of Pictorial Representation* (New York: Pantheon Books, 1960)
Gramsci, Antonio, *Letteratura e vita nazionale* (Turin: Einaudi, 1950)
———, *Selections from Cultural Writings*, ed. by David Forgacs and Geoffrey Nowell-Smith (London: Lawrence & Wishart, 1985)
Gregg, Melissa and Gregory J. Seigworth, "An Inventory of Shimmers," in *The Affect Theory Reader*, ed. by Melissa Gregg and Gregory J. Seigworth (Durham and London: Duke University Press, 2010), pp. 1–25
Grossberg, Lawrence, "Another Boring Day in Paradise: Rock and Roll and the Empowerment of Everyday Life (1984)," and "Postmodernity and Affect: All Dressed Up with No Place to Go (1988)", in *Dancing In Spite of Myself: Essays on Popular Culture* (Durham: Duke University Press, 1997), pp. 29–63; pp. 145–65
Gundle, Stephen, *Bellissima: Feminine Beauty and the Idea of Italy* (New Haven and London: Yale University Press, 2007)
———, "Stars and Stardom in the Study of Italian Cinema," *Italian Studies* 63:2 (2008), 261–26
———, *Fame Amid the Ruins: Italian Film Stardom in the Age of Neorealism* (New York: Berghahn Books, 2019)
———, "The Five Faces of the Femme Fatale," in *Italian Cinema from the Silent Screen to the Digital Image*, ed. by Joseph Luzzi (London: Bloomsbury, 2020), pp. 123–40
Gussow, Mel, "Books of the Times: The Actress who Became the Original 'Doozy'," *New York Times*, 22 August 2003 www.nytimes.com/2003/08/22/books/books-of-the-times-the-actress-who-became-the-original-doozy.html [accessed 2 May 2021]
Habermas, Jürgen, *The Structural Transformation of the Public Sphere: An Enquiry into a Category of Bourgeois Society*, trans. Thomas Burger, with the assistance of Frederick Lawrence, 9th ed. [1969] (Cambridge: Polity, 2006)

Hallamore Caesar, Ann, "Women Readers and the Novel in Nineteenth-Century Italy," *Italian Studies* 56:1 (2001), 80–97

———, "Crossing the Public/Private Divide: The *Salotto* and the Theatre in Late-Nineteenth-Century Italy," in *Theatre, Opera, and Performance in Italy from the Fifteenth Century to the Present: Essays in Honour of Richard Andrews*, ed. by Brian Richardson, Simon Gilson, and Catherine Keen (Leeds: Maney, 2004), pp. 216–29

———, "Writing by Women in Post-Unification Literary Culture: The Case for De-segregation," in *Women and Gender in Post-Unification Italy: Between Public and Private Spheres*, ed. by Katharine Mitchell and Helena Sanson (Oxford: Peter Lang, 2013), pp. 225–44

Hansen, Miriam, *Babel and Babylon: Spectatorship in American Silent Film* (Cambridge, MA and London: Harvard University Press, 1991)

Hanson, Helen, and Catherine O'Rawe, eds., *The Femme Fatale: Images, Histories, Contexts* (Basingstoke and New York: Palgrave Macmillan, 2010)

Harris, Charles K., *The Last Farewell* (1903) Historic American Sheet Music https://library.duke.edu/digitalcollections/hasm_a3755 [accessed 20 March 2020]

Hartman, Saidiya, *Wayward Lives, Beautiful Experiments: Intimate Histories of Social Upheaval* (New York: W.W. Norton & Company, 2019)

Haskins, Mary, *Mary Magdalen: Myth and Metaphor* (London: Harper Collins, 1993)

Hayward, Susan, *Cinema Studies: The Key Concepts*, 3rd edn. (London and New York: Routledge, 2006)

Hipkins, Danielle and Katharine Mitchell, "*Le traviate*: Suffering Heroines and the Italian State Between the 19th and 21st Centuries," in *Prostitution and Sex Work in Global Visual Media: New Takes on Fallen Women*, ed. by Danielle Hipkins and Kate Taylor (London and Basingstoke: Palgrave Macmillan, 2017), pp. 195–297

Hoberman, Ruth, "Biography: General Survey," in *Encyclopaedia of Life Writing: Autobiographical and Biographical Forms*, Vol. 1, ed. by Margaretta Jolly (London and Chicago: Fitzroy Dearborn, 2001), pp. 109–12

Interim, "Le Théâtre," *La Française: Journal de progrès féminin*, 1 December 1907

"In the Halls," in *The Shanghai Times*, 24 December 1915

Irace, Erminia and Adolfo Scotto Di Luzio, "Le istuzioni culturali del regno d'Italia (1861–1945)," in *Atlante della letteratura italiana* III, ed. by Domenico Scarpa (Turin: Einaudi, 2012). pp. 438–47

Jameson, Fredric, "Reification and Utopia in Mass Culture," *Social Text* 1 (1979), 130–48

Jandelli, Cristina, *Le dive italiane del cinema muto* (Palermo: L'Epos, 2006)

———, "La Marion di Vivanti e Bertini, dalla pagina allo schermo e ritorno," in *Cinema e scritture femminili: Letterate italiane fra la pagina e lo schermo*, ed. by Lucia Cardone and Sara Filippelli (Rome: Trerefusi, 2011), pp. 19–30

Jolly, Margherita, "Editor's Note: Aims, Scope, and Selection of Entries," in *Encyclopaedia of Life Writing: Autobiographical and Biographical Forms*, Vol. 1, ed. by Margaretta Jolly (London and Chicago: Fitzroy Dearborn, 2001), pp. ix–x

Jones, Verina, "Journalism, 1750–1850," in *A History of Women's Writing in Italy*, ed. by Letizzia Panizza and Sharon Wood (Cambridge: Cambridge University Press, 2000), pp. 120–34

Kerber, Linda K., "Female Worlds, Woman's Place: The Rhetoric of Women's History," *The Journal of American History* 75:1 (1988), 9–39

Kosofsky Sedgwick, Eve, *Between Men: English Literature and Male Homosocial Desire* (New York: Columbia University Press, 1985)

Kroha, Lucienne, *The Woman Writer in Late-Nineteenth-Century Italy: Gender and the Formation of Literary Identity* (Lewiston, NY: E. Mellen Press, 1992)

Laglaize, J. B., "Nel mondo della musica: La prima rappresentazione della *Lucia di Lammermoor* al Teatro San Carlo in Napoli," *Cordelia*, 4 March 1894

Lamerichs, Nicolle, *Productive Fandom: Intermediality and Affective Reception in Fan Cultures* (Amsterdam: Amsterdam University Press, 2018)

Le Gallienne, Eva, *The Mystic in the Theatre: Eleonora Duse* (New York: Farrar, Straus & Giroux, 1966)

Ledger, Sally, *The New Woman: Fiction and Feminism at the* fin-de-siècle (Manchester: Manchester University Press, 1997)

Lees, George William Frederic, "The Art of Eleonora Duse," *The Lady's Realm*, 3, (November 1897–April 1898), pp. 41–46

Lelièvre, Renée, *Le Théâtre dramatique Italien en France, 1855–1940* (Paris: Armand, 1956)

Leonardi, Susan J., and Rebecca A. Pope, *The Diva's Mouth: Body, Voice, Prima Donna Politics* (New Brunswick, NJ: Rutgers University Press, 1996)

Liszt, Franz, "Lettres d'un bachelier ès musique," in Jean Chantavoine, *Franz Liszt: Pages Romantiques* (Paris: F. Alcan, 1912), pp. 147–240

Lotti, Denis, ed., *Emilio Ghione, memorie e confessioni. Scritti sul cinematografo (15 anni di arte muta)* (Rome: Associazione Italiana per la Ricerche di Storia del Cinema, 2011)

Louis, "La femme au theatre," *Le Méphisto: Journal artistique, littéraire, satirique*, 25 January 1882

Mack Smith, Denis, *Italy: A Modern History* (Ann Arbor: University of Michigan Press, 1969)

Magherini, Graziella, *La sindrome di Stendhal* (Florence: Ponte alle Grazie, 1989)

Mantegazza, Paolo, *Dizionario d'igiene per le famiglie* (Sesto S. Giovanni: Casa Editrice Madella, 1911)

Marazzini, Claudio, *La lingua italiana: profilo storico* (Bologna: Il Mulino, 1998)

Marchesini, Daniele, "L'analfabetismo femminile nell'Italia dell'Ottocento: caratteristiche e dinamiche," in *L'educazione delle donne: Scuole e modelli di vita femminile nell'Italia dell'Ottocento*, ed. by Simonetta Soldani (Milan: Franco Angeli, 1991, 2nd edn.), pp. 37–56

"Maria Carmi parla del 'soggetto' che Matilde Serao ha scritto ed ella ha interpretato per la MONOPOL FILM di Roma," in *La vita cinematografica*, 34–35, 15–22 September 1914

Mariani, Laura, *Il tempo delle attrici: Emancipazionismo e teatro in Italia fra Ottocento e Novecento* (Doria: Mongolfiera, 1991)

———, "Giacinta Plays Thérèse," trans. by John Dean and Bianca Mastrominico, in *The Open Page* 8 (2003), 84–91

———, ed., *L'attrice del cuore: Storia di Giacinta Pezzana attraverso le lettere* (Florence: Le lettere, 2005)

Martin-Gistucci, Marie-Gracieuse, *L'Œuvre romanesque de Matilde Serao* (Grenoble: Presse universitaires de Grenoble, 1973)

Martinelli, Vittorio, *Il cinema muto italiano: I film del dopoguerra, 1919* (Turin: Nuova Eri, 1992)

Mascari, Giuseppina, "'Donne all'opera.' La voce del pubblico femminile Milanese attraverso le pagine del *Corriere delle dame* (1804–1818)," in *Il genere del pubblico: Questioni per una storia della ricezione femminile nelle arti della scena*, ed. by Annamaria Cecconi in *Nuove frontiere per la storia di genere*, ed. by Laura Guidi and Maria Rosaria Pelizzari (Salerno: Università degli Studi di Salerno, 2013), pp. 199–206

"Matilde Serao e il cinematografo," in *Lo schermo*, 17, 11 December 1926

Mayne, Judith, *Cinema and Spectatorship* (London and New York: Routledge, 1993)

Mazza, "Ombre e riflessi," *Comoedia*, January, February, March issue 1909

McClary, Susan, *Feminine Endings: Music, Gender, & Sexuality* (Minneapolis: University of Minnesota Press, 1991)

McConachie, Bruce, *Engaging Audiences: A Cognitive Approach to Spectating in the Theatre* (Basingstoke: Palgrave Macmillan, 2008)

Medolesi, Claudio and Ferdinando Taviani, *Teatro e spettacolo nel primo Ottocento* (Rome: Laterza, 1991)

Meehan, Johanna, ed., *Feminists Read Habermas: Gendering the Subject of Discourse* (New York and London: Routledge, 1995)

Mill, John Stuart, *La servitù delle donne* (Milan: F. Legros, 1870)

Mitchell, Katharine, "'Sorelle in arte (e politica)': The 'Woman Question' and Female Solidarity at the *Fin de Siècle*," in *Women and Gender in Post-Unification Italy: Between Public and Private Spheres*, ed. by Katharine Mitchell and Helena Sanson (Oxford: Peter Lang, 2013), pp. 197–213

———, *Italian Women Writers: Gender and Everyday Life in Fiction and Journalism, 1870–1910* (Toronto: University of Toronto Press, 2014)

———, "Beauty Italian Style: Gendered Imaginings of, and Reponses to, Stage Divas in Early Post-Unification Literary Culture," in "The Diva in Modern Italian Culture," Special Issue, ed. by Katharine Mitchell and Clorinda Donato, *Italian Studies* 70:3 (August 2015), 330–46

Modleski, Tania *Loving With a Vengeance: Mass-Produced Fantasies for Women* (London: Methuen, 1982)

———, "Introduction," in *Studies in Entertainment: Critical Approaches to Mass Culture*, ed. by Tania Modleski (Bloomington and Indianapolis: Indiana University Press, 1986), pp. ix–xviii

———, "Hitchcock, Feminism and the Patriarchal Unconscious," in *Issues in Feminist Film Criticism*, ed. by Patricia Erens (Bloomington, IN: Indiana University Press, 1990), pp. 41–57 https://publish.iupress.indiana.edu/read/issues-in-feminist-film-criticism/section/f89f23a1-740a-4b81-bde5-92356d0a98c8 [accessed 20 May 2019]

Momigliano, Eucardio, "La Serao in Francia," *Nuova Antologia*, 467 (May–August 1956)

Morandini, Giuliana, *La voce che è in lei* (Milan: Bompiani, 1997)

Morelli, Salvatore, *La donna e la scienza, o la soluzione dell'umano problema* (Naples: Stab. tip. dell'Ancora, 1861)

Mori, Maria Teresa, "La moda del giorno," in *Giornali di donne in Toscana: Un catalogo, molte storie (1770–1945) II, 1900–1945*, ed. by Silvia Franchini, Monica Pacini, and Simonetta Soldani (Florence: Leo S. Olschki, 2007), pp. 384–9

Mulvey, Laura, "Visual Pleasure and Narrative Cinema," *Screen* 16:3 (October 1975), 6–18

———, *Fetishism and Curiosity* (Bloomington: Indiana University Press, 1996)

Muret, Maurice, *Journal des débats*, 22 July 1921

Neera, *Fotografie matrimoniali* (Catania: Giannotta, 1900)

———, "Il sorriso della Duse," *Il Marzocco*, 24 March 1901

———, *Una giovinezza del secolo XIX: Memorie* [1919] (Milan: Feltrinelli, 1980)

———, *Teresa*, trans. Martha King [1886] (Evanston: Northwestern University Press, 1998)

O'Rawe, Catherine, "The Italian Spectator and Her Critics," *The Italianist* 30 (2010), 272–89

Ortaggi Cammarosano, Simona, "Labouring Women in Northern and Central Italy in the Nineteenth Century," in *Society and Politics in the Age of the Risorgimento: Essays in Honour of Denis Mack Smith*, ed. by John A. Davis and Paul Ginsborg (Cambridge: Cambridge University Press, 1991), pp. 152–83

———, "Italian Women during the Great War," in *Evidence, History and the Great War: Historians and the Impact of 1914–18*, ed. by G. Braybon (Oxford: Berghahn, 2003), pp. 216–38

Otele, Olivette, *African Europeans: An Untold History* (London: C. Hurst & Co., 2020)

Ouida, "The New Woman," *The North American Review* 158:450 (May 1894), 610–19

Pagani, Maria Pia, "An Actress-Manager for the Italian Film Industry in the 1910s," *Nineteenth Century Theatre and Film* 45:1 (2018), 81–95

Paliotti, Vittorio, *Il Salone Margherita e la belle époque* (Rome: Benincasa, 1975)

Palombo, Irene, "'La mia delizia e la mia croce': Echi della *Traviata* nelle lettere al poeta Angelo M. Tirabassi", in *Scrivere d'amore: Lettere di uomini e donne tra Cinque e Novecento*, ed. by Manola Ida Venzo (Rome: Viella, 2015), pp. 409–32

Paolucci, Gabriella, "Amiche: Figure dell'amicizia femminile e femminismo," *Memoria* 32:2 (1991), 18–27

Pascal, Roy, *Design and Truth in Autobiography* (Cambridge: Harvard University Press, 1960)

Patmore, Coventry, *The Angel in the House*, 2nd edn. (London: John W. Parker and Son, West Strand, 1858)

Patriarca, Silvana, *Italian Vices: Nation and Character from the Risorgimento to the Republic* (Cambridge: Cambridge University Press, 2010)

Perrot, Michelle, ed., *A History of Private Life: From the Fires of Revolution to the Great War*, Vol. IV (Cambridge, MA: Belknap Press of Harvard University Press, 1990)

———, "Women, Power and History" in *Writing Women's History*, ed. by Michelle Perrot, trans. Felicia Pheasant (Oxford: Blackwell, 1992), pp. 160–74

Pisa, Beatrice, *Venticinque anni di emancipazionismo femminile in Italia: Gualberta Alaide Beccari e la rivista «La donna» (1868–1890)* (Rome: Elengraf, 1982)

Pisano, Laura, "Introduzione," in *Le donne del giornalismo: Da Eleonora Fonseca a Ilaria Alpi. Dizionario storico bio-bibliografico, secoli XVIII-XX*, ed. by Laura Pisano (Milan: Franco Angeli, 2004)

Pitassio, Francesco, "Famous Actors, Famous Actresses: Notes on Acting Style in Italian Silent Films" in *Italian Silent Cinema: A Reader*, ed. by Giorgio Bertellini (New Barnet, UK: John Libbey Publishing, 2013), pp. 255–62

Poiriss, Hilary, "She Came, She Sang … She Conquered? Adelina Patti in New York," in *European Musicians in New York City, 1840–1900*, ed. by John Graziano (Rochester, NY: University of Rochester Press, 2006), pp. 218–34

Pollock, Griselda, *Vision and Difference: Femininity, Feminism and Histories of Art* (London: Routledge, 1988)

Porter Abbott, Horace, *Diary Fiction: Writing as Action* (Ithaca and London: Cornell University Press, 1984)

Pozza, Giovanni, *Cronache teatrali di Giovanni Pozza (1886–1913)* (Vicenza: Neri Pozza, 1971)

Pullen, Kirsten, *Actresses and Whores: On Stage and in Society* (Cambridge: Cambridge University Press, 2005)

Radway, Janice, *Reading the Romance: Women, Patriarchy and Popular Literature* (London and Chapel Hill: University of North Carolina Press, 1984)

Raffaelli, Sergio, "On the Language in Silent Films in Italy," in *Italian Silent Cinema: A Reader*, ed. by Giorgio Bertellini (New Barnet, UK: John Libbey Publishing, 2013), pp. 247–53

Ragone, Giovanni, *Un secolo di libri. Storia dell'editoria in Italia dall'Unità al postmoderno* (Turin: Einaudi, 1999)

Ramsey-Portolano, Catherine, *Performing Bodies: Female Illness in Italian Literature and Cinema* (1860–1920) (Vancouver and Madison, NJ: Fairleigh Dickinson University Press, 2018)

———, *Nineteenth-Century Women Writers and the Woman Question: The Case of Neera* (New York: Routledge, 2021)

Rava, Luigi, *Per la "Dante Alighieri" (trenta anni di propaganda): Discorsi e ricordi, 1900–1931* (Rome: Società Nazionale Dante Alighieri, 1932)

Re, Lucia, "Passion and Sexual Difference: The Risorgimento and the Gendering of Writing in Nineteenth-Century Italian Culture," in *Making and Remaking Italy: The Cultivation of National Identity around the Risorgimento*, ed. by Albert Russell Ascoli and Krystyna von Henneberg (Oxford: Berg, 2001), pp. 155–200

———, "Eleonora Duse and Women: Performing Desire, Power and Knowledge," in "The Diva in Modern Italian Culture," ed. by Katharine Mitchell and Clorinda Donato, *Italian Studies* 70:3 (2015), 347–63

Ricaldone, Luisa, "Eighteenth-Century Literature," in *A History of Women's Writing in Italy*, ed. by Letizzia Panizza and Sharon Wood (Cambridge: Cambridge University Press, 2000), pp. 95–106

Robinson, Jane, *Bluestockings: The Remarkable Story of the First Women to Fight for an Education* (London: Viking, 2009)

Rohe, Alice, "Only In America," *The Independent*, 11 April 1925

Romani, Gabriella, "Women Writing Letters: Epistolary Practices in Nineteenth-Century Newspapers, Manuals and Fiction," in *Across Genres, Generations and Borders: Italian Women Writing Lives*, ed. by Susanna Scarparo and Rita Wilson (Newark: University of Delaware Press, 2004), pp. 24–37

———, Ursula Fanning and Katharine Mitchell, eds., *Matilde Serao: International Profile, Reception, and Networks* (Paris: Classiques Garnier, 2022)

Rosa, Sub, "On My Bookshelf," *The Gentlewoman and Modern Life*, 24 January 1925
Ross, Charlotte, *Eccentricity and Sameness. Discourses on Lesbianism and Desire Between Women in Italy, 1860s-1930s* (Oxford and New York: Peter Lang, 2015)
Rosselli, John, *The Opera Industry in Italy from Cimarosa to Verdi: The Role of the Impresario* (Cambridge: Cambridge University Press, 1984)
———, *Singers of Italian Opera: A History of a Profession* (Cambridge: Cambridge University Press, 1992)
Rutherford, Susan, "The Voice of Freedom: Images of the Prima Donna," in *The New Woman and Her Sisters: Feminism and Theatre, 1850–1914*, ed. by Vivienne Gardner and Susan Rutherford (New York and London: Harvester Wheatsheaf, 1992), pp. 95–113
———, *The Prima Donna and Opera, 1815–1930* (Cambridge: Cambridge University Press, 2006)
———, *Verdi, Opera, Women* (Cambridge: Cambridge University Press, 2013)
Salsini, Laura, "Private Lives, Public Letters: The Making of an Epistolary Heroine," *Italica* 88:4 (2011), 602–20
Salvini, Tommaso, *Ricordi, anedotti, impressioni* (Milan: Dumolard, 1895)
Sandri, Mario, "Gli uomini del giorno: Matilde Serao," *Modernissima* 37 (Milan: Casa editrice italiana, 1920)
Sanguanini, Bruno, *Il pubblico all'italiana: Formazione del pubblico e politiche culturali tra stato e teatro* (Rome: Franco Angeli, 1989)
Santovetti, Olivia, "The Cliché of the Romantic Female Reader and the Paradox of Novelistic Illusion: Federico De Roberto's *L'Illusione* (1891)," in *The Printed Media in Fin-de-siècle Italy: Publishers, Writers, and Readers*, ed. by Ann Hallamore Caesar and others (Oxford: Legenda, 2011), pp. 49–62
Sarcey, Yvonne, "Les Lettres de la Cousine: Matilde Serao," *Les Annales politiques et littéraires*, 24 November 1907
Sarcina, Angela, *La signora del Mattino con antologia dei* 'Mosconi' *di Matilde Serao* (Naples: La Conchiglia, 1995)
Schino, Mirella, *Il teatro di Eleonora Duse* (Bologna: Il Mulino, 1992)
Serao, Matilde, *Fantasia* [1883], trans. by Henry Harland and Paul Sylvester, 4th ed. (London: W. Heinemann, 1891)
———, Api, Mosconi e Vespe," *Il Mattino*, 23–24 March 1892
———, "Figure di donne: Quella che tace," *Il Giorno*, 28 March 1904
———, "L'année Théâtrale Italienne," trans. by "L.G.," *Le Temps*, 29 August 1904
———, "L'année Théâtrale Italienne," trans. by "L.G.," in *Le Temps*, 5 September 1904
———, "L'artista universale: Intervista di Matilde Serao con Sarah Bernhardt," *Il Giorno*, 21 December 1904
———, *Dopo il perdono* (Rome: La Nuova Antologia, 1905)
———, "Cinematografeide!," *Il Giorno*, 30 March 1906
———, "Essi non debbono aver ragione," *La moda del giorno* 1, 1 January 1911
———, *Il Giorno*, 2 March 1911
———, *Il Giorno*, 4 March 1913
———, *Il Giorno*, 6 November 1913
———, "Chi si commuoverà? Chi ammirerà?," *Il Giorno*, 29–30 April 1914
———, "In un teatro, tutti i teatri," *Il Giorno*, 9 January 1916

———, "Parla una spettatrice," *L'Arte muta. Rassegna di vita cinematografica*, 15 June 1916
———, *Current Opinion*, 1 July 1917
———, "Il grande avvenimento d'arte: *Tosca* al 'Maximum,'" *Il Giorno*, 14 April 1918
———, "Consiglio di Famiglia," *Cin*, 12 May 1918
———, *Addio, amore!* [1890] (Naples: Tommaso Villani, 1919)
———, "Mosconi", in *Il Mattino*, 21–22 January 1920
———, "Preface," in *Dopo il perdono* [1905] (Milan: Fratelli Treves, 1920), pp. vii–xi
———, *Ricordando Neera* (Milan: Fratelli Treves, 1920)
———, "Fantasma," *Il Giorno*, 8 September 1926
———, "Scuola normale femminile," *Il romanzo della fanciulla*, ed. F. Bruni [1885] (Naples: Liguori, 1985), pp. 146–85
———, *Cuore infermo* [1881] (Rome: Luccarini, 1988)
———, "La virtù di Checchina," in *La virtù delle donne* [1884] (Rome: Avagliano, 1999)
Setti, Dora, *La Duse com'era* (Milan: Pan, 1978)
———, *Emotional Arenas: Life, Love, and Death in 1870s Italy* (Oxford: Oxford University Press, 2020)
Sheehy, Helen, *Eleonora Duse: A Biography* (New York: Alfred A. Knopf, 2003)
Showalter, Elaine, *A Literature of Their Own: From Charlotte Brontë to Doris Lessing* (Princeton: Princeton University Press, 1977)
Sica, Anna and Alison Wilson, *The Murray Edwards College Duse Collection* (Milan: Mimesis, 2012)
Signorelli, Olga, *La Duse* (Rome: A. Signorelli, 1938)
———, *Eleonora Duse*, trans. by Isabel Quigly (London: Thames and Hudson, 1959)
Small, Christopher, "Performance as Ritual: Sketch for an Inquiry into the True Nature of a Symphonic Concert," in *Lost in Music: Culture, Style and the Musical Event*, ed. by Avron Levine White (London: Routledge & Kegan Paul, 1987), pp. 6–32
Smart, Mary Ann, "Verdi Sings Erminia Frezzolini", *Verdi Forum* 24:1 (1997), 13–22
Socrate, Francesca, "Commedia borghese e crisi di fine secolo," in *Scene di fine Ottocento: L'Italia fin de siècle a teatro*, ed. by Carlotta Sorba (Rome: Carocci, 2004), pp. 21–59
Soldani, Simonetta, "Premessa," in *L'educazione delle donne: Scuole e modelli di vita femminile nell'Italia dell'Ottocento*, ed. by Simonetta Soldani (Milan: Franco Angeli, 1991), pp. vii–xxi
Sorba, Carlotta, *Teatri: L'Italia del melodramma nell'età del Risorgimento* (Bologna: Il Mulino, 2001)
———, "Introduzione: Percorsi di ricerca fra teatro, cultura e società," in *Scene di fine Ottocento: L'Italia* fin de siècle *a teatro*, ed. by Carlotta Sorba (Rome: Carocci, 2004), pp. 9–20
———, "To Please the Public: Composers and Audiences in Nineteenth-Century Italy," *Journal of Interdisciplinary History* 36:4 (Spring 2006), 595–614
Spigolatrice, La, "Spigolando," in *La donna*, 20 August 1885
Stacey, Jackie, "Desperately Seeking Difference," *Screen* 28:1 (1987), 48–61
———, *Star Gazing: Hollywood Cinema and Female Spectatorship* (London and New York: Routledge, 1994)

Stead, Lisa, *Off to the Pictures: Cinemagoing, Women's Writing and Movie Culture in Interwar Britain* (Edinburgh: Edinburgh University Press, 2016)
Stendhal, *Rome, Naples and Florence*, trans. by Richard N. Coe (New York: John Calder, 1959)
Stokes, John, Michael R. Booth, Susan Bassnett, *Bernhardt, Terry, Duse: The Actress in Her Time* (Cambridge: Cambridge University Press, 1988)
Stott, Rebecca, *The Fabrication of the Late-Victorian Femme Fatale: The Kiss of Death* (Palgrave: Houndmills, Basingstoke, 1992)
Studlar, Gaylyn, *In the Realm of Pleasure: Von Sternberg, Dietrich, and the Masochistic Aesthetic* (New York: Columbia University Press, 1992)
"Teatri italiani," *La frusta teatrale*, 30 December 1862
Tellini, Gino, *Il romanzo italiano dell'Ottocento e Novecento* (Milan: Bruno Mondadori, 1998)
The Morning Post, 6 February 1907
The Scotsman, 29 September 1919
The Woman's Home Journal, 8 April 1893
Tommasèo, Niccolò and Bernardo Bellini, *Dizionario della lingua italiana* (Turin: UTET, 1879)
Tortella, Gabriel, "Patterns of Economic Retardation and Recovery in South-Western Europe in the Nineteenth and Twentieth Centuries," *Economic History Review* 47:1 (1994), 1–21
Tortora, Matilde, ed., *Matilde Serao a Eleonora Duse: Lettere* (Naples: Graus, 2004)
Traversi, Camillo Antona, *Ricordi parigini* (Ancona: La Lucerna, 1919)
Treveri Gennari, Daniela, Catherine O'Rawe, Danielle Hipkins, Silvia Dibeltulo, and Sarah Culhane, *Italian Cinema Audiences: Histories and Memories of Cinema-going in Post-war Italy* (London: Bloomsbury, 2020)
Ubersfeld, Anne, *Reading Theatre*, trans. by Frank Collins (Toronto: Toronto University Press, 2014)
"Un'intervista ad Adelaide Ristori," *Corriere della sera*, 17–18 January 1902
Valisa, Silvia, "Casa editrice Sonzogno. Mediazione culturali, circuiti del sapere ed innovazione tecnologica nell'Italia unificata (1861–1900)," in *The Printed Media in* Fin-de-siècle *Italy: Publishers, Writers, and Readers*, ed. by Ann Hallamore Caesar, Gabriella Romani and Jennifer Burns (London: Legenda, 2011), pp. 90–106
Van Vorst, Marie, "The Italian Woman's Drive for Freedom," *The Ladies' Home Journal*, January 1921
Verga, Giovanni, *Una peccatrice: Storia di una capinera; Eva; Tigre reale* (Milan: Mondadori, 1975)
———, "La serata della diva," in *Tutte le novelle* [1894] (Milan: Mondadori, 1979)
Veritas, *La rassegna degli interessi femminili*, 15 January 1887
Vertua Gentile, Anna, *Come devo comportarmi? Libro per tutti*, 2nd edn. (Milan: Ulrico Hoepli, 1897)
Vivanti, Annie, *Marion, artista di caffè-concerto* [1891] (Palermo: Sellerio, 2006)
Warner, Marina, *Alone of All Her Sex: The Myth and Cult of the Virgin Mary* (New York: Knopf, 1976)
Wagstaff, Christopher, "Cinema," in *Italian Cultural Studies: An Introduction*, ed. by David Forgacs and Robert Lumley (Oxford: OUP, 1996), pp. 216–32
Williams, Linda, "Melodrama Revised," in *Emotions: A Cultural Studies Reader*, ed. by Shari Daya (London and New York: Routledge, 2002), pp. 336–50

Wilson, Alexandra, *The Puccini Problem: Opera, Nationalism and Modernity* (Cambridge: Cambridge University Press, 2007)
Wood, Sharon, *Italian Women's Writing: 1860–1994* (London: Athlone Press, 1995)
X., "Chronique Théâtrale: Madame Matilde Serao," *Le Temps*, 29 August 1904
Zimmern, Helen, "Eleonora Duse," *Fortnightly Review* 67:402, June 1900

Databases and websites

Archivio Multimediale degli Attori Italiani (Florence: Florence University Press, 2012) http://amati.fupress.net/Main.uri
www.theguardian.com/stage/2020/feb/18/live-shows-get-your-heart-racing-scientists-prove-it [accessed 19 February 2020]
www.operabase.com [accessed 24 February 2020]
www.theguardian.com/music/musicblog/2014/feb/11/elitist-opera-cliches-alexandra-wilson [accessed 27 July 2019]
http://archiviostorico.teatrolafenice.it/ricerca.php [accessed 20 July 2020]
www.treccani.it/enciclopedia/gemma-ferruggia_(Dizionario-Biografico)/ [accessed 9 December 2020]
www.telegraph.co.uk/news/2019/08/07/disney-remake-home-alone/ [accessed 9 March 2020]
www.telegraph.co.uk/tv/2020/02/22/cast-hit-sitcom-friends-reuniting-anniversary-special [accessed 9 March 2020]
British Library's Nineteenth Century UK Periodicals and its British Newspaper Archive www.bl.uk/collection-guides/british-newspaper-archive
National Library of Australia's Trove Digitised Newspapers https://trove.nla.gov.au/newspaper/
American Periodicals https://about.proquest.com/products-services/aps.html
HathiTrust Digital Library www.hathitrust.org/
Bibliothèque Nationale de France Gallica Digital Library www.bnf.fr/en/gallica-bnf-digital-library
Women: Transnational Networks, and British Theatre, Music and Literature: High and Popular Culture from Nineteenth Century Collections Online www.gale.com/intl/primary-sources/nineteenth-century-collections-online
North American Women's Letters and Diaries database https://alexanderstreet.com/products/north-american-womens-letters-and-diaries
Duke University Libraries Digital Collections https://library.duke.edu/digitalcollections/hasm_a3755

Index

Note: Page numbers in *italics* refer to figures.